KT-199-315

King Arthur's Avalon

Also in Fontana

Citadels of Mystery   *L. S. de Camp and C. C. de Camp*
The Gothic Image   *Emile Male*
Stonehenge Decoded   *Gerald S. Hawkins*

GEOFFREY ASHE

King Arthur's Avalon

The Story of Glastonbury

Collins

FONTANA BOOKS

First published by Wm. Collins 1957
First issued in Fontana Books 1973
Second Impression August 1973
Third Impression May 1974

© Geoffrey Ashe 1957

Printed in Great Britain
Collins Clear-Type Press
London and Glasgow

A portion of Chapter Two is adapted from an
article published in *The Month* (April 1956)

We need not believe that the Glastonbury
legends are records of facts; but the existence
of those legends is a very great fact.

E. A. FREEMAN

CONDITIONS OF SALE:
This book is sold subject to the condition
that it shall not, by way of trade or otherwise,
be lent, re-sold, hired out or otherwise circulated
without the publisher's prior consent in any form of
binding or cover other than that in which it is
published and without a similar condition
including this condition being imposed
on the subsequent purchaser

CONTENTS

ILLUSTRATIONS

Preface to the Paperback Edition

Since *King Arthur's Avalon* was first published, in 1957, various things have happened which a reader should know and take into account. Also, this new edition gives me a welcome chance to add comments and afterthoughts.

I wrote under the spell of a conviction: that Glastonbury, England's New Jerusalem, is strong magic and not dead merely because its Abbey is ruined. That conviction has never deserted me. Whatever the nature of the magic, it is there and it will revive. The future is greater than the past. My aim was (and is) not antiquarian study for its own sake but the rebirth of Glastonbury with all it implies; and my motive in undertaking a book was partly to make the holy place better known, partly to define what it was and what it did imply.

In *King Arthur's Avalon* I was often groping. Later researches have carried me a long way further. If I were writing this book today I would do many things differently. Some statements would be modified, some perspectives would be altered. But I still think it is far more right than wrong as it stands. This preface is a supplement. It is not a recantation.

When I wrote, I was quite conscious of dissenting in sundry places from what was then official scholarship. I was also conscious of indulging in guesswork. As for the first point, official scholarship has altered so much that today I am largely unrepentant. There are few major issues where scholars can still claim to fault me with any confidence. As for my guesses, I am happier now with some than with others, but content to leave them till further study and debate sort them out. Even if they are utterly wrong I shall never regret having offered them. I have remarked elsewhere that there is a wrongness which can lead to rightness more effectively than rightness itself.

However, this book does contain several passages which later developments have already put in a fresh light, usually by supporting my suggestions. The most important are those on Arthur's grave; the Melwas legend; Cadbury-Camelot; and the Grail. The first three problems have been transformed by archaeology. I had the honour to be associated with all the archaeologists, and they described their work in a book published in 1968 under my editorship, *The Quest for Arthur's Britain*.

First, the grave. In *King Arthur's Avalon* (pages 181-3) I

urged that while the account given by the Glastonbury monks was fishy, the then-established dogma of a pure fraud was not wholly convincing. If the monks had concocted such a fraud, would they – could they – have done it quite like that? To my deep satisfaction Dr Ralegh Radford has since published a far weightier discussion tending the same way. He has shown that the monks' curious details, including the cross with Arthur's name on it, make perfect sense if the grave was authentic, whereas on the other hand they could hardly have known enough to invent it all.

In 1962-3 Dr Radford excavated the site. He proved that the story was true so far as it could still be checked, and that some prominent person was indeed buried there in the right period. Hence Arthur's grave may well have been genuine. It is a sad comment on academic attitudes that Professor R. F. Treharne's *The Glastonbury Legends*, published four years afterwards, simply parrots the 'fraud' theory and ignores Radford entirely; a tell-tale omission which is one of several reasons for treating that work with less than total respect.

A final note by the way: a reviewer complained that the inscription on the cross (pages 180, 182) is not the same in the text as in the illustration. The fact is that several slightly differing versions exist and I transcribed another.

Second, King Melwas of Somerset (pages 109-10). Here I was over-cautious. While the tale about the Queen may be mythical, there is now a case for Melwas's reality. In 1964-6 Philip Rahtz excavated the summit of the Tor and unearthed traces of a building of Arthurian date, plausibly the stronghold of a local sub-king such as Melwas would have been.

Third, Cadbury Castle (pages 13, 93, etc.), and its claim to be Camelot so far as anything can be – that is, the HQ of the historical Arthur. This raises the whole question of Arthur himself. I now realize that Chapter Three could have been strengthened. In particular, there is good reason to think that the Arthur entries in the *Annales Cambriae* (page 75) come from contemporary annals and therefore prove that he existed. But this is no place to air a vast topic which has been aired elsewhere. The matter of Cadbury is more specific.

In 1960 I made the first public proposal for a Cadbury excavation. When this took place during 1966-70 I was secretary of the excavation committee. May I here record my tribute to Leslie Alcock as a Director of genius and generosity, who, in a most exacting position, routed every critic and never put a foot wrong? The full description of the 'Camelot' dig, and its wide-ranging benefits to archaeology, must be left to him. But within the

8

strictly Arthurian field, he proved that this hill-fort was re-occupied and re-fortified on a huge scale during exactly the right period. The British leader who made Cadbury his citadel around A.D. 500 was at the very least an 'Arthur-type figure', a man who could have been Arthur. No archaeological trace of such a figure has been found anywhere else. Yes; quite probably Camelot.

This vindication of local folk-lore is impressive. Also it has affected our view of Arthur. In the light of the Cadbury military architecture he seems less like a Last-of-the-Romans, more like a Celt. He doubtless professed Christianity, he certainly defended the remnants of Roman culture, but he is more easily pictured as a reviver of the old Britain that stretches back into pre-Roman mists.

Finally, the Holy Grail. Some of Chapter Seven is frankly speculative and I regard it with mixed feelings. However, I have come across some further support for one or two of my specula-tions. Thus, the suggested esoteric link between the Grail and the Mary cult (pages 216ff) appears several times in the medita-ions of the visionary Anne Catherine Emmerich. I also find that my notion of 'scrying' or crystal-gazing as part of the Grail mystique (pages 211-12) has a basis in medieval magical practice. Hartlieb's *Book of All Forbidden Arts*, published in 1455, con-demns attempts to induce visions of angels by staring fixedly at the shining vessels of the Mass. The thing did happen.

With the legend of Joseph of Arimathea the question seems to remain open. Dr Valerie Lagorio has shown that whatever its origin may be, the legend has a Celtic flavour hinting at Welsh influences. Even Professor Treharne has conceded that it may derive from a Christian mission at Glastonbury which was indeed the first in Britain. But these cloudy topics are better left alone for the present.

Towards the end of *King Arthur's Avalon* my ignorance is to blame for two gaps.

I ought to have mentioned John Dee, the Tudor magician, Elizabeth I's astrologer-royal. It was Dee who dropped the first hints about a Zodiac, long before Mrs Maltwood (page 23). Also, his helper Kelley went to Glastonbury and brought back what he said was the Philosopher's Stone, with coded instructions for its use. The story of Dee's interest in Glastonbury and related themes would be worth putting together. I may add that my attitude to magic has altered somewhat and I regret the phrase applied on page 214 to Aleister Crowley (who claimed, by the way, to be Kelley re-incarnate).

The other omission is the Glastonbury Festival during the 1920s, run by Rutland Boughton and Laurence Housman, with backing from Bernard Shaw. Rutland Boughton's Arthurian music-dramas, and his attempt to make Glastonbury an English Bayreuth, were not lastingly successful but certainly ought to have been noted.

I must repeat, though, that I see rebirth as more important than history. In 1957 very few who concerned themselves with Glastonbury thought likewise. A slow change began in the following year, when the late Major Tudor Pole founded the Chalice Well Trust. This semi-religious body financed the Tor excavation. It has beautifully preserved Chalice Well, and issued a booklet telling more than is said in *King Arthur's Avalon*.

In 1963-4 the Festival was revived, briefly alas, as a civic venture. Among its supporters I would like to recall the late Rev. Sean McNamara. During his tragically short time as a priest in the town, St Mary's Church acquired the fine tapestry that hangs behind its altar, interweaving legend and history. His tenure coincided with a peak of organized Christian activity, one outcome being the restoration of the crypt under the Lady Chapel for interdenominational use.

But the real re-awakening – as I believe it to be, though it has not taken the shape I once expected – started with the discovery of Avalonian magic by junior seekers, so-called hippies or rather post-hippies, who were drifting into the district from the late 1960s onward. Books by John Michell influenced this new flowering. A more specific impulse came from the magazine *Gandalf's Garden*. In June 1971 a pop-mystical festival called the Glastonbury Fayre drew national publicity.

Since then the flow of junior pilgrims has been vigorous. At Easter 1972 about forty, who had settled in and around the enchanted area, formed themselves into a 'New Glastonbury Community'. Their Community has gradually taken root as part of the local scene. It publishes a magazine and maintains a centre in the town, quietly proclaiming a New Age that is to dawn in Glastonbury and spread without limit.

I do not know where this is going, but I do know, at last, that *King Arthur's Avalon* was not written in vain.

Geoffrey Ashe
November 1972

Chapter One

THE GLASS ISLAND

The Glastonbury landscape is weird. Yet the essence of its weirdness is hard to catch. A green quilted acreage of reclaimed marsh stretches away and away toward the low Somersetshire ranges, toward the caves of Cheddar and the willows of Sedgemoor. In the centre, visible at vast distances and at queer angles, a skewed cone five hundred feet in height shatters the skyline. This is Glastonbury Tor. Two satellites attend it, Chalice Hill and Wearyall Hill. Between them and over them the houses of Glastonbury cluster and climb. Long walls enclose the battered remnants of a gigantic ecclesiastical building.

Glastonbury's magic is polyhedral. It is a national shrine, standing for the creative reconciliation of races and provinces. Here, says the legend, they buried Arthur, the human symbol of British unity against the Saxon invaders. Here was the original haven of the Faith which made the country a single realm after the interval of Saxon division. Here the Britons and Saxons first learned to live at peace, and the vision of the United Kingdom was born. Here, in the Abbey's writing-room, the traditions of all the British Isles flowed together to engender a common consciousness. The great hymn *And did those feet in ancient time* has been justly called a second national anthem: how many people realise that in its opening stanza Blake alludes to a story told at Glastonbury?

Yet this same focal power has made the place a storm-centre of conflict. For Britain is eternally fated to be a world in herself yet also part of a larger world; and her strangely formative western shrine partakes of the same dualism, the same tension. Glastonbury has proved a testing ground for Christianity supplanting the legacy of Druidism, for the Roman order supplanting the Celtic, for the Church supplanting the cults. It is No Man's Land and all men's land; it is a Garden of the Hesperides and a Catholic sanctuary. There was a brief hour during the Middle Ages when poetic imagination wove all Glastonbury's threads into a single cord. Its Abbey rose to an apogee of honour. Pilgrims called it a second Rome. It wove so mighty a spell that nothing would do at the Reformation but total ruin. And still, through all that history of mysterious warfare and mysterious truce, the landscape endures. The enchantments of mist and sunset transform it from one day to another, and its final secret remains elusive.

Configuration is a part of that secret. Optically speaking, the landscape does not make sense. It is a monstrous refraction. The Tor, so obvious for so many miles, vanishes in the town and hides behind objects far too small to conceal it. Although a natural formation, it soars up in terraces like a Mexican pyramid from an inconsistent plain. A church tower which ought surely to be below displays itself on the summit, but without any church. If you climb up there yourself you see everything, yet absurdly enough you do not see the Abbey; Chalice Hill rears its shoulder in between. Oddest of all, the perspective is inside out. The small hills in the foreground contrive to look like big ones a long way off, while the remoter Mendips press in toward the heart of the panorama.

Jolted out of routine by such bizarre practical jokes, the mind responds by contributing more to the moment than its usual share. Subconsciously prompted, it interprets the landscape into something truly alien to common experience. The irrational scene loosens the grip of the Ordinary and gives scope to the Fantastic. Just by a matter of an inch, it jars open the magic casements.

2

Once upon a time Glastonbury was under the sea. But a stirring of geological forces pushed the Tor above the surface. For a while it looked out over empty water; then the sea-bed heaved itself up and became Somerset.

The new land went on rising. In the Neolithic era it was covered with a shrub forest, afterwards displaced by peat. From a high mark above its present elevation it sank again, and continued to sink, till its entry into history. When we first get a clear glimpse of the region, it lies near sea-level, covered with a brackish lagoon and interlacing rivers. Tides and floods keep the water from stagnation. Much of what seems like solid ground is morass, fringed by willows and yews, oaks and ash-trees. The Tor with its neighbourhood forms an island; Wearyall Hill is perhaps a separate island. Somewhere there are human beings.

For while this miniature Mediterranean was taking shape, different people were drifting across the country. Throughout a long stretch of years the inhabitants of Britain were dark little pre-Celts. Then, in the last millennium before Christ, the bigger Celts who had colonised Gaul found their way across, and strung themselves out from sea to sea. These particular Celts (others were to follow) lived on high ground and along the banks of rivers, keeping clear of the valleys and the forested hinterland. They did so because they had no ploughs worth mentioning. The best they could manage in the way of cultivation was to settle on light soil and scratch furrows in it. But they were not a negligible race. It was in the south-west, where they had regular communications with Brittany, that they excavated their strongest hill-forts and developed their fullest culture.

Not far from Glastonbury, on the side towards the English Channel, a Celtic fort called Cadbury Castle[1] stands on an isolated hill. It is roughly triangular, with four concentric earth ramparts. The outermost rampart rises forty-two feet, and between this and the second is a ditch twenty feet in depth. Two passageways through the quadruple earthwork open into an eighteen-acre enclosure. Roman coins have been discovered inside, suggesting occupation long after the passing of the original builders. Some say the Castle is Camelot; the village of Queen Camel, formerly plain Camel, is close by. A spring within the walls used to be known as Arthur's Well, and local lore added Cadbury to the list of magic hills where Arthur is thought to lie asleep. Archæologists in the district were once accosted by an anxious old man who asked them if they meant to dig up the King. With the Celts of the Castle the long Glastonbury enchantment began.

But closer to the Tor the same nation left a finer memento. In 1892 Arthur Bulleid, an antiquarian, used to stroll over a tract of peat a mile or so from the present town. Its reclamation was recent. A seventeenth-century map of the same area shows a patch of water five miles in circumference called Meare Pool, with several streams flowing into it. In that neighbourhood, Bulleid noticed, the maintenance of drainage ditches was an important operation. One day he

[1] See preface, p. 8.

13

started to puzzle about some hillocks or mounds which interrupted the level. These did not look natural. He asked the ditch-diggers if they ever found traces of human life, and they mentioned turning up bits of woodwork and pottery. Bulleid took a spade and unearthed two oaken beams and a dugout canoe.

The record of subsequent excavations, through many layers of flood-soil, reveals that in the third century B.C. some local Celts founded two 'lake villages' of a type known in Switzerland and elsewhere. Their aim was security. On the bed of the old lagoon, at Meare and Godney, they built up artificial islands. Godney was the more notable, and may fairly be counted as the original Glastonbury. It was added to at various dates; but in its last phase it covered an irregular polygon of three acres. Massive logs rested on the peat, cemented with clay and held in place by long piles. Anyone approaching dryshod had to walk along a hundred-foot causeway. Twelve feet short of the island it stopped; the water was deep enough to drown in; the visitor could only proceed if the sentries chose to lower a drawbridge. All round stood a formidable stockade of piles, and enemies who came in boats were met by a shower of red-hot pellets from slingers on a bank behind the stockade. Within the perimeter, connected by boardwalks, were sixty-five clay-floored wattle huts, mostly round, thatched, and ten or twenty feet in diameter.

Distinction, individuality—Glastonbury struck that note in its very inception.

The Lake Village was an outpost of what is classified as the La Tène Culture. Its inhabitants, of course, did not live as prisoners in their own fortress. They hollowed out serviceable canoes from oak trunks and paddled on to the calm lagoon. There they shot at the water-fowl of those days—including pelicans—with terra-cotta pellets discharged from slings. Or sometimes they fished, weighting their nets and lines with small sinkers made of lead, which they smelted out of Mendip ore. On accessible tracts of land they raised livestock (sheep, horses, pigs, cows, goats) and grew various kinds of grain, hauling it home along the causeway and pounding it in stone querns.

These people were adroit craftsmen, well provided with home-made articles. Bronze was the chief metal for household items, such as needles and bowls and mirrors and safety-pins. Knife-handles and combs were carved out of antler.

14

Iron was for tools: sickles, saws, axes, hammers, chisels. The men who handled the tools were excellent carpenters and knew the use of the lathe. They made looms and wash-tubs and eating utensils, ladders and spoked cartwheels, hinged doors and mortised beams. The village potters did superb work, but without the potter's wheel, very slowly and patiently.

It is the Lake Village's terra-cotta ware that teaches us to value its culture. Though not artists in the civilised sense, the Glastonbury craftsmen were great decorators, with a flair for giving beauty to common objects. They ornamented their bowls with flowing lines in graceful satisfying patterns. We never see a picture, but we do see a richly imaginative range of designs. The inspiration came from the south, from the Mediterranean; but the Somerset potters were more than copyists. Pots were not the only things decorated. Both sexes embellished themselves with bronze brooches and bangles, beads of glass and amber, and rings with jet in them. Such a tribe would never have lacked resources for hours of leisure. They played at dice, because the dice have been found, cubes cut out of antlers and numbered on their faces from one to six. There is also evidence of cock-fighting, a fashionable sport with the Celts in Gaul.

The Glastonbury area had easy communications by land and water, and a widespread though not voluminous trade, lubricated by a crude currency in the form of iron bars. Shale came to the village from Dorset, jet from Yorkshire, amber from the Baltic. The pottery designs and the bronze mirrors show southern influence. It is not utterly absurd to call the village a British Venice. Life must have been peaceful on the whole, but there are implements of war – iron spearheads and halberds, flint arrow-heads, and pellets showing the marks of fire (Cæsar describes hot pellets of the same sort whizzing among his troops in Gaul). At least one raid by supplanted predecessors left its trace for posterity. The objects disinterred by the excavators include little elongated skulls mounted as trophies, and human bones gnawed by dogs.

Even Cæsar might have learnt to respect Glastonbury. But he never came so far west. Cæsar's attack on Britain was one of his feebler enterprises. After a clumsy reconnaissance, he sailed over to Kent in the following year (54 B.C.), gained some rather fruitless victories north of the Thames, negotiated a face-saving treaty, and re-embarked. Nevertheless, change was in the air. Another invading Celtic nation was ramifying through Britain. The new occupants were the Belgæ, a technologically superior people. They used animal-drawn ploughs which turned the sod instead of scratching the surface, and these enabled them to cultivate virgin lands, pushing into the valleys and clearing the woods. Belgic pottery, though less pleasing to the eye than La Tène pottery, was shaped on the wheel. The Belgæ introduced coinage into Britain, imitating Greek models.

To a large extent they may have mixed peacefully with the sitting inhabitants. There are signs of assimilative trends over a long period. By the first century A.D. it is possible to piece together a single fairly definable British type. The average 'Briton,' it appears, was very slightly shorter than the present-day Englishman, with a head that projected at the back. He was fair, sturdy, and muscular. With a haircut and a shave and suitable clothes, he would not look outlandish in modern Harrogate or Hampstead. But the mingling of tribes which produce this reassuring person was certainly not entirely pacific. As late as the Christian era the Belgic vanguards often went armed. Raids and reprisals disturbed the west, and in one of these, possibly the last, Belgæ stormed the stockade of Godney Lake Village and smashed its terra-cotta for ever. Meare Village survived, but it ceased to create.

Unruffled by the æsthetic loss, much of Britain attained a loose political unity. This happened during the reign of the Emperor Tiberius. The first major British king was Cunobelin or Cymbeline: it is a slight shock to realise that he existed. Under his rule Britain developed a lively foreign trade. Her chief exports were agricultural, metallic, and human. British cattle and wheat went to feed the Gauls. British gold, silver, and iron attracted enough custom to justify energetic mining. Britons (contrary to a later sentiment) were frequently slaves, and they fetched fair prices in European markets. A continental demand grew up also for British hunting dogs. The Cunobelinic boom was not general. One setback was a slump in tin. Cornwall had formerly been the main source for the Mediterranean world. But the Romans had destroyed the fleet of the Gaulish nation which monopolised the carrying trade, and when Augustus opened up the tin mines of Spain, the Cornish industry sank into a lasting depression. Even during Cymbeline's reign it failed to recover.

On the whole, however, his kingdom flourished. The list of imports is very interesting indeed. The principal items named by contemporaries are bracelets, necklaces, amber, glassware, pottery, and wine. All are luxury goods. The Britain of those days was not dependent on overseas sources for any necessities whatever. Shakespeare's romantic picture has touches of truth. The island must have possessed a court and nobility with a certain pomp and moderately expensive tastes; while its economic position would have excused Cloten's boast to the Roman envoy –

> Britain is
> A world by itself, and we will nothing pay
> For wearing our own noses.

Yet this backwater realm could hardly hope to endure. Luckily or unluckily for itself, it lagged behind civilisation. London and Colchester existed, but even in the region under Cymbeline's direct rule there were no other towns, only hill-forts and fortified clearings. If a subject of the British King stood at the top of Dover Cliff on a clear day, he looked across at an empire beyond his ken: an empire that took its name from a City.

3

· When Cymbeline reigned, Glastonbury Tor still surmounted an island, with the River Brue lapping at its foot. The Britons are supposed to have called it Ynys-witrin, an epithet which is generally taken to mean the Isle of Glass. No one has positively explained it. Writers talk without much conviction about the blue-green colour of the water which flowed round the base, and about a plant used for making woad. The further we delve into this question of names, the more tiresome it appears. 'Glastonbury' itself is Anglo-Saxon – Glaestingaburg – and looks like a second rendering of the 'glass' motif. On the other hand, it may mean 'burh' (settlement) 'of the Glaestings' – whoever the Glaestings were. Medieval chroniclers give a legend accounting for it in terms of British folk-lore. Glasteing, a northern Celt, had a prize sow that escaped out of her sty and led him a chase across the Midlands. He nearly caught up with her at Wells, but she dodged him and trotted on through a watery and difficult tract (subsequently called the Sow's Way) till at last he found her at rest, suckling her piglets on an island under an apple-tree. Observing how fertile and secluded the island was, Glasteing brought his own family there, thus becoming the first person to colonise it. Hence the name, which the Anglo-Saxons must have adapted, rather than devised for themselves. 'Ynys-witrin' can be traced further back than 'Glaestinga-burg' – specifically, to a charter of A.D. 601 – but its true age is uncertain. An American philologist has tried to combine the theories by means of a complicated tale about a Briton named Glast who got the nickname Vitrinos because he painted his face with blue-green woad.

Glasteing's apple-tree introduces the topic of the much more interesting alternative name which the Isle received at some stage in its history and has never since lost: that is, Avalon. In Celtic lore Avalon was the rendezvous of the dead, a mysterious place where they passed over into another mode of existence. The antiquity of the name, as of its application to Glastonbury, is debatable; but the pagan Britons certainly had notions about such a place, whatever they called it. Ever since the Middle Ages men have main-tained, and men have denied, that the Isle of Glass was identified with Avalon from time immemorial. Avalon osten-sibly means 'apple-orchard,' and unprofitable assertions used to be made about the excellence of apples grown within the Tor's territory. Glasteing, of course, is represented as having coined the name from the tree where he found his wonderful pig. But some scholars, both in earlier and in later ages, have rejected apples entirely and conjured up the phantasm of Avalloc or Avallach, a Celtic demigod supposed to have officiated over the otherworld. Opinions differ as to whether he had a recognised address on the everyday map. However, one way or another, there is admittedly ground for arguing that the medieval identification of Glastonbury with Avalon was a mistake, a misconstruction of pagan Celtic belief.

Here the discussion of derivations may end. To the Britons, this island with the Tor on it was indubitably the Isle of Glass. It may also have been an Isle of the Dead. If it was the latter, then the Tor must have been sacred in pagan eyes, before any Christian built a church at the base or a chapel at the summit. We may now turn to consider this topic, dropping etymology with a sigh of relief.

The Britons held different opinions about the region of the departed. It is an over-simplification to reconstruct a univer-sal belief for them. They had none. Broadly speaking, two principal ideas prevailed. Either the soul passed into a sort of fairyland by way of a hill, or it migrated to an island. Water was thought to be an effective barrier against spirits; hence the popularity of the second belief. Islands of the dead could be, and were, geographically identified. Several were apparently Welsh; Rheged, for example, and Gresholm. The Britons' enchanted isles, caverns of sleeping heroes, and so forth, impressed even classical authors. Plutarch mentions them, and the sixth-century Procopius, doubtless on Breton authority, speaks of a country of shades beyond the Channel. At some stage of British culture (perhaps before, perhaps after, the conversion to Christianity, which long remained patchy and superficial) the myths tended to concentrate. A single Isle of Avalon emerged more and more clearly as the orthodox Afterworld. Quite likely the modern philologists are right, and Avalon was the realm of Avallach, a lord of the dead. To this island Arthur was carried off to be healed of his wounds. It was like the Fortunate Isles of the Greeks – a sunny, quiet, fruitful place, cut off from the frenzies of the world, untroubled by storms or plagues or wild beasts.

As to its location, there were two possible points of view. Avalon might be a Never-Never-Land in uncharted seas. Or it might be an identifiable spot. If the latter, however, the hill notion inevitably recurred. No earthly spot had the Avalonian characteristics. But the earthly Avalon could still be an island with an enchanted hill on it, leading to a happy domain occupied by the fairy prince Avallach.

Given this pattern of ideas, the Isle of Glass was exceptionally well qualified to be Avalon. Water encircled it, and a most remarkable hill rose from it. But no known author plainly equates Avalon with Glastonbury till the closing decade of the twelfth century, far removed from the last articulate pagan Britons. The voice that breaks the silence belongs to Giraldus Cambrensis, an observant commentator on current affairs. Writing of an attempt to find King Arthur's grave in the Abbey grounds, Giraldus explains that King Arthur was laid to rest in Avalon, and 'Avalon' was the old British name for Glastonbury. Giraldus has never heard of Avallach – he cites the 'apple' derivation – and he does not seem to be at all clear as to the larger role of Avalon in Celtic mythology. But he gives the Arthur story with care, saying that the King went to Glastonbury after receiving his last wounds because the Isle belonged to a kinswoman of his.

Giraldus wrote at a time when the Glastonbury monks

were anxious to stress their Arthurian inheritance. We have to acknowledge a propagandist motive behind the Avalon identification. The probable mental process, and the way in which the monks clinched their point, will emerge in due course. The immediate problem is whether they were merely inventing or guessing or inferring, or whether they had struck an actual tradition. It is my personal impression that they knew something; perhaps only a vague and unreliable rumour, but something. It is another question whether any vestige of what they knew has come down to us.

There is no reason why a British name and myth should not have survived. As late as the twelfth century, and later still, ancient Britain lived on in Wales and Brittany. When studying the literature of Giraldus's day, we can trace the veritable Celt in two contexts. Native Welsh manuscripts embalm relics of history and legend. Also, English and French romances of Arthur transmit British material at second or third or fourth hand. About the middle of the twelfth century, the literate classes of western Europe suddenly discovered pre-English Britain. Scholars visited Wales, resuscitated the somnolent Celtic lore, and composed British histories, or pseudo-histories. Welsh and Breton bards wandered by invitation among the French-speaking nobility propagating the saga of their own racial heroes. Out of the matter thus acquired, court poets and prose romancers constructed their artificial epics. The point, for the moment, is that the cycles of the Round Table and the Holy Grail do embody British tradition, but overlaid with stratum on stratum of medieval fashion and fantasy. It is only at this literary juncture that the Glastonbury lore really starts to develop. The problem is to decide how much of it existed in earlier times, and how this antique element can be disentangled from the forest of poetic elaboration.

As to the immediate question of Glastonbury's claim to be Avalon, the key document is not any Arthurian romance, but the *Life* of St Collen, a Welsh saint belonging to the darkest part of the Dark Ages. It tells how he went to Glastonbury and made his cell on the lower slope. One day he heard two peasants outside discussing Gwyn, King of the Fairies and Lord of Annwn, whose home they declared to be on that very hill. Collen put his head out and told them not to stand in awe of the fairies, who were certainly demons. They replied, shocked, that now he would have to meet Gwyn face to face. The saint withdrew into his cell. Soon afterwards a knock sounded on the door. 'Who is that?' said Collen. 'King Gwyn's messenger,' a voice replied. 'He bids you meet him on the top of the hill.' Collen declined the invitation. But the next day, and the next, the messenger returned, speaking in a menacing style. At last Collen agreed to go. He took some holy water and ascended the Tor. On the summit – or rather, in a magical place to which the summit gave access – he saw a beautiful castle, filled with retainers and musicians and exquisite maidens. King Gwyn sat in the midst on a golden chair. Greeting the hermit cordially, he offered him food; but Collen, wise in the ways of fairyland, hesitated about eating. Gwyn remarked: 'Have you ever seen men better dressed than these, in the red and blue liveries?' Collen answered: 'Their dress is good of its kind. But the red and the blue are the red of burning fire and the blue of cold.' While Gwyn pondered the implications of this retort, Collen suddenly tossed his holy water in every direction. The castle and all its occupants vanished, leaving the saint standing on the windy Tor with nothing in sight but clumps of grass.

While the manuscript containing St Collen's *Life* is a late one, the actual composition must be far earlier, and the tale clearly embodies a folk-belief in no way derived from literary sources. Gwyn is King of the Fairies and Lord of Annwn. Annwn appears to have been a kind of Hades, a marshalling-place of departed spirits related somehow to Avalon. Welsh tradition adds that Gwyn is the leader of the Wild Hunt, in which the souls of the dead are whisked out of their bodies and borne away through the thunderclouds. This Hunt occurs in folk-lore from Ireland to eastern Europe. Its personnel includes quite a number of real and fabulous heroes, Arthur among them. Its destination in any given version is the leader's abode. Thus Gwyn's presence goes far to establish a dim but venerable belief in the summoning of the dead to the Tor for passage to Annwn.

Celtic fairy mythology is often degenerate religion. When we encounter a vivid character or motif, it is legitimate to look for ancestral gods in the background. Some have held that Gwyn was originally a full-fledged otherworld deity scarcely distinguishable from Avallach. His full style is Gwyn ap Nudd, and his father in the old British pantheon was presumably Nodens, who ruled over the Severn and its estuary. Gwyn's appearances in other geographical contexts furnish details which help to suggest what happened at

Ynys-witrin. He is found among standing stones. He is found upon those 'fairy hills' which are anæmic descendants of the pagan ghost-hills. And at Pembrey, near Llanelly, he is found beside a pre-Christian cemetery.

That cemetery is crucial. Nobody knows where the Glastonbury Lake villagers buried their dead. Ynys-witrin, however, was the most convenient plot of dry land, and the natural place for them to use. Archæologists have not yet dug deep enough to prove that they used it; but the Prophecy of Melkin (to be examined later) implies that there actually was a medieval tradition about a pagan burial site. Granted this hypothesis – which has the merit of being verifiable, if anyone ever hits on the right place – we can form a picture of subsequent developments that is at least comfortably compatible with every known fact.

The Island with the hallowed graveyard acquired an otherwordly aura and came to be very widely regarded as an abode of Gwyn and a terminus of the Wild Hunt. Perhaps more, but at any rate this. The monks who arrived later could not dispel the supernatural atmosphere. Their home was surrounded by miles of marshland, and they could scarcely help observing the eerie effects of fog and will-o'-the-wisp. They built a chapel of St Michael on the Tor – the ruin of its successor is still there – and another by their own burial-place, doubly invoking the archangelic conqueror of the dark powers, and trying to impose a notion of suppression and transformation. In this attempt they were only imperfectly successful. Though few Welshmen came to the monastery, a learned series of Irish monks constituted a living repository of Celtic lore, and the Irishmen's whimsies refused to be restrained. By way of encouragement there were certain fables, Teutonic as well as Celtic, which represented the abode of the dead as encircled by a wall of glass. The Avalonian fancy grew, passed orally from generation to generation, and achieved respectability and recognition when the Celtic revival in the twelfth-century gave it value.

Reading the literature of that revival, we catch glimpses of the kind of day-dreaming that must have been going on through the Dark Ages. In the writings of the hagiographer Caradoc of Llancarfan we discover Melwas, King of the *Aestiva Regio* or Somerset, who kidnaps Guinevere and keeps her on Glastonbury Tor. When Melwas reappears shortly after in the Arthurian epics composed by Chrétien de Troyes, the place of the Queen's imprisonment is depicted as a haunt of shades. Elsewhere Chrétien speaks more specifically of the Isle de Voire or Glass Island in Melwas's dominions. It has extraordinary virtues: no storm ever strikes it, no thunder is ever heard; the weather is always temperate and there are no wild beasts. Here is Glastonbury invested with the attributes of the Fortunate Isles.

A second wraith who emerges from the twilight into romance is Evalake the Unknown, so called because no one knows where he was born or whence he came. He is Avallach transformed into a heathen prince, and he enters into a cryptic association with the legendary founders of Christian Glastonbury, who convert him to their religion. A vague comprehension of the Evalake myth begins to dawn in the thirteenth century, but the first romancers who mention him show no sign of grasping who he is. The theme reaches them in a disjointed condition. In part at least it has manifestly travelled a long way.

A Lake Villagers' burial ground on Ynys-witrin, with a resulting Ghosts' High Noon presided over by other-world deities, is enough to account for the few and fragmentary things that can safely be said about Glastonbury's Avalonian evolution. The hypothesis finds support, if feeble support, in medieval chronicle, and it will acquire further plausibility when we come to Arthur.

Imaginative writers have tried to portray Ynys-witrin as a pagan sanctuary of a far more extraordinary holiness than is here suggested. There is, for example, the theory of the Temple of the Stars. This was broached in the nineteen-thirties by a Mrs K. E. Maltwood,[1] at first anonymously. Afterwards she wrote under her own name and succeeded in interesting the Royal Astronomical Society of Canada. Her disciples allege that with large-scale maps and aerial photographs they can trace the outlines of huge symbolic figures in the Somerset lowland. These occupy a circle ten miles in diameter, with the Tor inside it. The shapes correspond roughly to patches of rising ground, and are delineated by streams and old roadways and the boundaries of ancient fields. Mrs Maltwood played absolutely fair with the public. She reproduced sections of the Ordnance Survey showing exactly how she constructed the figures. The accompanying text put forward astrological meanings for them, chiefly zodiacal, and related them to incidents in the cycle of the Holy Grail.

[1] See preface, p. 9.

The statement of the case is all perfectly accessible, such as it is, and every reader can draw his own conclusions. Some of the shapes are quite impressive – notably the Lion, which is out Somerton way – but others demand the eye of faith. In view of the enormous and improbable labour involved in forming earthworks more than a mile long, the evidence needs to be decisive; and it is certainly not that. Further archæological study, or aerial photography, may put it in a different light. Meanwhile we must content ourselves with the literary and traditional scraps. Certainly no iconoclasm has yet ruled out the belief that Glastonbury was either Avalon or Avalon under another name to at least a part of pre-Christian Britain. Topographical plausibility, the presence of Gwyn, the chapels of St Michael, the stories of Melwas and Evalake, all point the same way. It is really easier to believe than to disbelieve. And if you try the experiment of believing while in sight of the Tor, you will find that it is easier still.

4

The religion into which Glastonbury fitted, in whatever way it did fit, was a patchwork of cults harmonised and administered by a priestly caste. In the days when the Lake Village was flourishing, this caste dominated the Celtic tribes of Gaul and Ireland as well as Britain. The Gaulish organisation was the strictest and strongest, but Britain was the principal training centre, and, in general estimation, the fountain-head of doctrine. The priests were called druids. Doubtless the first thing to mention about them is that they did *not* build Stonehenge. Stonehenge was already ancient when the Celts arrived on Salisbury Plain. The druids' monuments are less obvious but perhaps equally notable.

'Druid' is a word of uncertain derivation. An alluring theory connects it with two root-syllables which would give it the meaning of 'One Who Knows.' In that case it would be, ultimately, much the same as 'wizard' and 'witch,' with distant relationships to other hierophantic titles such as 'Gnostic' and 'Brahmin.'

Etymologists now prefer a modified view. The druids, however, did profess to be a band of initiates. Their solidarity was intense. They were not a celibate order set apart from the world. Many had wives and children. But they monopolised education, and planned it so that its main function was the recruitment and development and glorification of their own caste. Any youth could secure exemption from military service by enrolling for the full course leading to druidical status. The inducement was powerful, but the course was intimidating. It lasted twenty years. Failure must have meant a wrecked life. The students gathered in remote fastnesses and consecrated groves. They received a tonsure, acquired the magic arts, learned the secret formulæ, and rose through the grades of initiation. Lectures expounded the druidical doctrines, such as metempsychosis, the transmigration of souls. The final tests included answering complicated riddles before a committee, and composing verses while under water. Success, however, was worth attaining. In Britain the druids wielded immense influence. In Gaul their hierarchy towered over the community. Its annual congress was the chief political fixture in the calendar. Every member could aspire to the position of Supreme Druid, with jurisdiction over the order and indirectly over society as a whole. It was a fine thing to be One Who Knew, especially since no layman could ask you to explain what your knowledge consisted of.

Some say the druids were profound teachers and philosophers. Others say they were humbugs. Their secretive and portentous manner did sometimes impress contemporaries. Several Greek and Latin authors describe them with a touch of respect. The doctrine of transmigration fascinated the Greeks, who thought it was the same that had been taught by their own arch-mystic Pythagoras. They speculated as to whether the druids had learnt from him. Pythagoras's disciples were not merely geometricians. They practised an esoteric cult of personal and social regeneration, which influenced Plato, and, through him, all subsequent European thought. Greeks familiar with Pythagorean ideas were struck, not only by the druids' teaching of metempsychosis, but by their stress on *esprit de corps* and initiation, and on the rightfulness of entrusting public affairs to initiates. But the givings and takings in the Pythagorean system can no longer be sorted out. It may not have been so very distinctive. The Master studied in Egypt, and one of his most grotesque and seemingly original theories has been found among the Burmese. He may have influenced the druids; on the other hand, the druids may conceivably have influenced him. According to one biographer, he attached great importance to a meeting with a mysterious traveller from the north parts.

It does not matter much. Some sort of interchange between the druids of Gaul and the Greek settlers in the west Mediterranean zone could have led to a certain assimilation of thought. But the nearer the Greeks and Romans came to the purer Druidism of Britain, the less sure they felt about the druids' claim to be thinkers. The supposed Secret Wisdom dissolved in problematical fogs. The concrete facts were pretentiousness and mumbo-jumbo and human sacrifice.

We can probably drop the notion that the Britons had a philosophical priesthood like the Brahmins of India. Their religion, as a fabric of ritual and belief, was not remarkable. Its remarkable feature was the priestly organisation itself, which gave it a peculiar ruthlessness and positive force.

The druids' universe was a maze, which laymen could never hope to thread without druidical help. There was no single God, or none openly proclaimed. The world was presented as a flux, kept in motion by the strife of a fire-principle and a water-principle. Stars governed it to some extent, so that astrology was a valid science. Gods and demigods and demons and spirits carved out local empires and aided or afflicted mankind. The gods were tyrannous powers responsible for whatever order the cosmos possessed. They had to be propitiated with human sacrifice. They made their will known to human beings, always, of course, through druid interpreters, who alone understood their language. They appeared in human shape; some druids professed to be gods incarnate. The incarnation theme showed itself under another aspect in the fertility ritual, when the druids killed a male victim personating the god of life. The god was said to be reborn in another victim. This perpetual cycle of death and renewal maintained the rotation of the seasons and made the crops grow. To some participants the ritual was pure magic, to others it may have been more in the nature of a prayer. Local customs were to prolong it in milder versions for centuries; in the druidical prime the killing was indispensable.

Death by religion being common, and death by miscellaneous violence being commoner, the druids fortified their flocks with the doctrine of immortality. They taught it more forthrightly and dogmatically than any other priesthood in Europe. A Briton could never die. All being well, he slipped away to Avalon or some similar retreat, dwelt there not too frustratingly for a long time, and then, perhaps, returned to earth. Spells and dooms might affect his wanderings, but his survival was so fully assured that he could raise money on an IOU payable in the next world. The druids presided at the ceremonies of birth and death. It has been suggested that the terraces on the slope of Glastonbury Tor are the remains of a spiral pathway by which they scaled it in procession, blessing or cursing the shades which had passed below.

A druid combined the roles of poet, prophet, and medicine-man. In every capacity he was more of a magician than anything. Poetry consisted mostly of riddles and charms. Prophecy was oracular divination or fortune-telling. Even medicine hardly counted as such. The druids prescribed various herbs, but the actual herb was far less important than the ritual they enjoined for its use, which belonged to exactly the same plane of human behaviour as their famous veneration of oak and mistletoe. You had to gather the herb at the proper hour, dressed wholly in white, with unshod feet . . . and so forth. All this minor magic had a feminine air, and there actually were druidesses as well as druids. But the men stood higher.

Their power, overt in Gaul and disguised in Britain, was in some ways superior to the power of kings. They formed the minds of their aristocratic students. They acted as judges in criminal and civil cases. They advised officials, and presided over the rite governing administrative appointments. This was curious: the chief minister took a ceremonial sleep in which he was expected to have a dream about the right candidate for the post. A little knowledge of hypnosis doubtless enabled the attendant druid to control his selection.

All dissent was crushed by a sentence of excommunication. Those who disobeyed the druids became taboo. They were sent to Coventry and deprived of the benefits of magic.

This power proved self-destructive. When the Romans occupied Gaul the druids effectively opposed them. Roman religious tolerance had its limits. Opposition was bad enough, terrorism enforced by superstition and ritual murder could not be suffered to continue. The Romans set up schools for the Gauls, breaking the druid monopoly of education, and Tiberius published edicts against the darker practices. But beyond Gaul Britain remained unconquered, a base for sorcery and subversion. Augustus talked of an expedition but never sent one. Caligula brought an army to the Straits of Dover but never embarked. When the Emperor Claudius at last

27

undertook to invade the island, the extirpation of Druidism was very likely one of his main objects. He had no strong economic or political motive, and his personal tastes were scholarly rather than military.

Claudius took the field himself and defeated the British leader Caradoc or Caractacus in a battle near London. After his departure the Roman advance faltered. Caractacus was captured and taken to Rome, but other leaders kept up the war, and the druids encouraged them. In 61 the legionaries finally came to the Menai Strait; and across the water, in Anglesey, they witnessed the last stand of the hated cult. Druids and druidesses marched back and forth, chanting spells and waving branches and torches. Their parade accomplished nothing. The invaders poured over the narrow channel, dispersed the marchers, and burned the sacred groves.

Celtic paganism survived, and a tamer Druidism persisted. But the hierarchy collapsed. Roman law, and later the Christian Church, drew the teeth of the cult. What Britain retained was not Druidism but an atmosphere that went with it. Nothing could undo the effect of the island's eminence – or imagined eminence – as the headquarters of a great mystical company, potent enough to sway western Europe and provoke Rome into her only religious warfare. A late comer to the Empire, absorbed under exceptional circumstances, Britain took her place at the Roman table with a head full of dreams and reservations.

5

While Avalon's priests vaticinated about the comings and goings of their murky sub-deities, a distant province was generating another priesthood, predestined to transform Avalon with a still more outrageous tale about a personal visit from God Himself.

Midway in time between the two Roman attacks on Britain, at a moment foreshadowed by Jewish rabbis and eastern astrologers, a carpenter's wife in Palestine bore a male child. The boy grew up in the family trade, came almost uneventfully to the age of thirty, and then began to startle the neighbourhood with wild prophecies and alarming threats. It was easy to dismiss him as a crazy fanatic, but not at close quarters. He made stupendously arrogant assertions about his own future role as Judge of Mankind. He accepted homage as the Messiah, and claimed to have existed before Abraham. But he combined all this with a disconcerting practical wisdom and a moral teaching rooted in love and forgiveness. Much of the teaching was adapted from the rabbis and mystics, but on the lips of this astonishing prophet even the familiar exploded into something entirely new. Strange things happened in his presence: miraculous cures, miraculous catches of fish, miraculous changes in the weather. Respectable artisans and civil servants left all to follow him.

He appointed twelve apostles, the chief being the fisherman Simon Peter, and he sent out seventy other disciples to preach a message of repentance and divine judgment. In the light-ning-illuminated landscape of his ministry, the outlines of a sort of organisation began to emerge. That was a threat to the Roman government and the religious officialdom of his own people. Entering Jerusalem, he was betrayed and executed. There was no doubt as to his death. Yet he came out of the tomb alive, showed himself to the disciples who had for-saken him, and then . . . vanished.

From that moment they knew once again that they must live for their Lord's purposes, even though they still did not know very exactly who he was or what his purposes were. He had called himself the Son of Man and the Son of God. He had uttered various commands with a terrifying air of authority. His atrocious death had apparently been a sacrifice of some kind; his return had been a triumph over the grave, revelatory and symbolic. The Apostles, to whose spiritual care he had entrusted his flock, resolved at last that he could only be looked upon as a being hitherto undreamt-of: the Creator of the World historically and humbly made man. Through the society he had founded, the Church built on a rock, the human race was to be liberated from the bondage of death. And the Church would endure for ever, worthily or unworthily doing his work.

But before, at the black hour when the Lord hung dead upon the cross with a gash in his side, few or none of the disciples foresaw this. They felt themselves the victims of a blasphemous fraud. Some ran away and hid, others watched in thunderstruck misery. The tragedy was played out, as it seemed then, and only a single stage-direction remained. The corpse had to be disposed of. Without political influence there was no chance of getting it back from the Romans, and the dead man had practically no friends with money or standing. As it turned out, however, he did have one or two, though they had not figured openly in his disreputable band.

A man came forward by name Joseph, a rich man from Arimathea, one of the councillors. And Joseph, who was a disciple of Jesus, but in secret, for fear of the Jews, asked Pilate to let him take away the body of Jesus. Pilate gave him leave; so he came and took Jesus' body away; and with him was Nicodemus, the same who made his first visit to Jesus by night. Joseph took possession of the body, and wrapped it in a clean winding-sheet; then he buried it in a new grave, which he had fashioned for himself out of the rock, and left it there, rolling a great stone against the grave-door.[1]

This was the stone that played such a dramatic part in the Resurrection.

Joseph, so they say, was helped in taking the body from the cross by his son Josephes. And some of the blood about the Lord's heart dripped down mingled with sweat into Josephes's shirt and clung to his chest. Before he wiped it off, his father took two small vials or cruets, and in those cruets he saved some of the drops, the first and holiest of all holy relics. After which they laid Jesus away.

But now Joseph's colleagues called him to order. Let the author of the apocryphal *Acts of Pilate* take up the story:

When the Jews heard that Joseph had begged the body of Jesus, they sought for him, and for Nicodemus and many others which had come forth before Pilate and declared his good works. Joseph said unto them: Why is it that ye are vexed against me, for that I begged the body of Jesus? Behold I have laid it in my new tomb, having wrapped it in clean linen, and I rolled a stone over the door of the cave. And ye have not dealt well with the just one, for ye repented not when ye had crucified him, but ye also pierced him with a spear.

But the Jews took hold on Joseph and commanded him to be put in safeguard until the first day of the week; and they said unto him: Know thou that the time alloweth us not to do anything against thee, because the sabbath dawn-

[1] I have combined the slightly different Gospel accounts into a single paragraph.

eth; but know that thou shalt not obtain burial, but we will give thy flesh unto the fowls of heaven. Joseph saith unto them: This is the word of Goliath the boastful which reproached the living God and the holy David. When the Jews heard these words they waxed bitter in soul, and caught hold on Joseph and took him and shut him up in an house wherein was no window, and guards were set at the door; and they sealed the door of the place where Joseph was shut up.

But when the prison was opened the prisoner had vanished. Messengers who went to seek him found him at his own home in Arimathea. So the priests ordered him to come, and he met them again at the house of Nicodemus.

Joseph said: Why is it that ye have called me? And Annas and Caiaphas took the book of the law and adjured Joseph, saying, Give glory to the God of Israel and make confession unto him. We were greatly vexed because thou didst beg the body of Jesus and wrappedst it in a clean linen cloth and didst lay him in a tomb. And for this cause we put thee in safeguard in an house wherein was no window, and we put keys and seals upon the doors, and guards did keep the place wherein thou wast shut up. And on the first day of the week we opened it and found thee not, and we were sore troubled, and amazement fell upon all the people of the Lord until yesterday. Now, therefore, declare unto us what befell thee.

And Joseph said: On the preparation day about the tenth hour ye did shut me up, and I continued there the whole sabbath. And at midnight as I stood and prayed the house wherein ye shut me up was taken up by the four corners, and I saw as it were a flashing of light in mine eyes, and being filled with fear I fell to the earth. And one took me by the hand and removed me from the place wherein I had fallen; and moisture of water was shed on me from my head unto my feet, and an odour of ointment came about my nostrils. And he wiped my face and kissed me and said unto me: Fear not, Joseph; open thine eyes and see who it is that speaketh with thee. And I looked up and saw Jesus, and I trembled, and supposed that it was a spirit: and I said the Commandments: and he said them with me. And ye are not ignorant that a spirit, if it meet any man and hear the Commandments, straightway fleeth. And when I perceived that he said them with me, I said unto him: Rabbi Elias? And he said unto me, I am not Elias. And I said unto him: Who art thou, Lord? And he said unto me, I am Jesus, whose body thou didst beg of Pilate. And I said to him that spake with me: Show me the place where I laid thee. And he brought me and showed me the place where I had laid him, and the linen cloth that lay therein, and the napkin that was upon his face. And I knew that it was Jesus. And he took me by the hand and set me in the midst of mine house, the doors being shut, and laid me upon my bed and said unto me: Peace be unto thee.

Joseph added that the Lord told him to remain in his house for forty days; and after the interrogation he went back to it unmolested. When the term expired he joined the other disciples, all of them rapturous over the news of the Resurrection. They walked together to Olivet where the Lord showed himself for the last time. Joseph saw him speak a few words to his bewildered Apostles, and turn from them and go up the hill. After that no one saw him again.

So the disciples returned into Jerusalem, where they waited for the message from heaven which would mark out their path. A day came when the Holy Spirit descended on them, and their tongues were loosened, and Peter sent them forth to preach. At first their preaching was to the Jews in Judea, but Christ had said 'to all nations,' and a few Gentiles, indeed, began to listen. Savage persecution broke out, but Saul, the most violent of the persecutors, surrendered to Christ on the Damascus road and became the Church's most ardent missionary and first theologian. Under the new name of Paul, he swept aside the Jewish exclusiveness which still restrained many believers, and set off to convert Gentiles in Asia Minor. He crossed to Macedonia; he harangued the philosophers in Athens; before his martyrdom, Italians and Spaniards had heard his voice. Others followed in Paul's track. Peter, still chief among the Apostles, established himself in Rome, launching the Roman Church on its career of pre-eminence.

Meanwhile, according to report, Philip made his way to Gaul with a great company of disciples, and among these were Joseph of Arimathea and his son Josephes with their two precious vials. Up from the Mediterranean to the Channel the Christians spread, planting the seeds of the mighty

Church of Gaul. But was the Channel the limit of the world? Had not the Lord said *all* nations? In the year 63, when Peter and Paul were still in Rome untroubled by Nero, Philip set Joseph over a group of twelve and dispatched them to Britain.

Carried by a miraculous wind – the story continues – their ship rounded the Cornish promontory in one night and made a landfall in Wales. The local chiefs being inhospitable, they passed on into a part of Britain where a king still reigned not yet subject to Rome. Though King Arviragus heard them respectfully, he refused baptism. But because they were upright and holy men, he invited them to stay in his kingdom, and offered them the Isle of Glass as a dwelling-place. It was unpopulated but fertile.

So they set out for Glastonbury. And when they came to a hill half a mile from the Tor, they were all weary: so the hill is called Weary-all. The day was near the end of December, the dead of winter. And Joseph, seeking a sign to cheer his dejected followers, planted his staff in the earth and knelt down and prayed; and Christ heard his prayer, and the staff turned into a thorn-tree like no other thorn-tree, which blossomed ever after on Christmas Day. Thereupon they went over rejoicing into Avalon.

Here they lived as hermits. But the angel Gabriel appeared and commanded them to build a church. And the church that they made of wattles was the first in Britain. It was dedicated to St Mary the Blessed Virgin. Joseph himself carved an image of her and set it there. Nearby a spring welled from the hillside, and its water healed the sick.

After King Arviragus died, the next two kings were his son Coillus and Coillus's son Marius. They confirmed the first grant, and they added twelve hides of adjoining land. A hide was as much as a man could cultivate in a year with an ox-drawn plough. In that country it was about a hundred and twenty acres. For many generations the land round the Tor was called the *Twelve Hides*. Joseph and his son Josephes and the rest of the hermits lived on in their domain till they died, perpetually occupied with works of piety. Joseph was buried near the church, the two cruets with the Lord's blood being laid beside him. His companions died also, one by one, and their graves were not far from his. Their cells stood abandoned, no priest officiated at the altar, and for a space the wilderness returned.

Such is the legend of the founding of Christian Glastonbury. Any monk in the Abbey at the dissolution would have told you most of this, with perhaps a hint or two at the Holy Grail. How and why the legend grew, and when and under what circumstances, and how much truth may underlie it, are proper themes for dispassionate inquiry.

Chapter Two

ROMA SECUNDA

In A.D. 658 the Anglo-Saxons, ponderously accomplishing the conquest of Britain, arrived at Glastonbury. They found within its natural moat an odd little church or chapel which no one could adequately account for. Sixty feet by twenty-six, it had a window at the end and three in the side. Basically it was a wattle structure, made of twigs twisted together and bound with clay. But some careful person had reinforced it. Wooden planks and pieces of lead kept the weather at arm's length. The local Britons offered an explanation: the patching-up had been ordered by no less a man than that famous missionary Paulinus, who, after lately converting so many Anglo-Saxons, had passed through into this West Country where Celtic Christianity lingered. Surely the newcomers had heard of him? Yes, yes, of course they had. So much, then, for the reinforcement. But as for the church itself, little transpired except that it was exceedingly old and much patronised by Irish pilgrims.

Attached to the church there was a monastic community of sorts. That too seemed rooted in antiquity. The monks, however, proved uncommunicative. Or perhaps they were genuinely forgetful. Or perhaps they put off the Anglo-Saxons with a mystification aimed at the superstitious piety of barbarous converts. At any rate, if they gave any account at all of the Old Church's origin or the birth of their community, it was not what we should now call credible.

Time passed, an English king reconstituted the monastery, and an English element overlaid the Celtic. If there ever were any traditions, they died now; the ruling nation could never ascertain the truth about its puzzling ecclesiastical capture. Yet a story did circulate. By the year 1000 such scribes as the biographer of Dunstan felt able to commit themselves to an authorised version which ran somewhat in these terms:

> There is on the confines of western Britain a certain royal island, called in the ancient speech Glastonia, marked out by broad boundaries, girt round with water rich in

fish, and stagnant rivers, fitted for many uses of human futility, but dedicated to the most sacred of deities. In it the earliest (English) neophytes of the Catholic rule, God guiding them, found a church, not built by art of man, they say, but prepared by God himself for the salvation of mankind, which church the heavenly Builder himself declared – by many miracles and many mysteries of healing – he had consecrated to himself and to holy Mary, Mother of God.

Behind this myth of a miraculous foundation before all record, there was certainly a belief that the church dated from the original coming of Christianity to Britain, an event assigned to the first century A.D.

The proper prelude to an examination of the problem is to find out what was thought about that event by people nearer to it. We can then see how they applied their concepts to Glastonbury, in so far as they did, and assess their views in the light of later research.

2

The earliest clues of all take us back to the second century only. Some time before 200 the great controversialist Tertullian, erupting a pamphlet against the Jewish religion, throws in the Britons among a list of peoples who have already responded to Christian teaching.

For on whom have all nations believed, except Christ, who is already come? On whom also other nations have believed . . . the different nations of Gaul, and of the British isles, places inaccessible to the Romans, but in submission to Christ.

Origen, a few years later, speaks of the supersession of polytheism in Britain.

When did the land of Britain ever unite in the belief of one God, before Christ came?

Eusebius, about 330, is supposed to indicate in vague language that the Apostles themselves – or perhaps only contemporaries of the Apostles – journeyed as far as Britain. His statement, however, melts like mist when you try to catch hold of it.

In any case the rhetorical flourishes of far-off Africans and Levantines do not carry much weight. Closer to the purpose is Gildas, a native British writer and one of the earliest. A sixth-century monk, he allegedly lived at Glastonbury for several years and was buried there. Both facts are uncertain, though the former is probable. But between his residence, if it happened, and his burial, if that happened, Gildas did other things which are better established. He went to Brittany, to the monastery of Ruys, and at Ruys he wrote a book on the troubles of Britain. He called it his *liber querulus* or Complaining Book, an exceptionally honest title. While Gildas's historical retrospect is confused, inaccurate, and maddeningly reticent just where we could most do with information, he does show a certain casual acquaintance with his country's past. He fails to mention the foundation of Glastonbury, but that means nothing; he fails to mention other important facts which he can hardly have been ignorant of. Though silent on that particular issue, he transmits a most remarkable notion about the advent of the Faith in Britain.

> Meanwhile these islands, stiff with cold and frost, and in a distant region of the world, remote from the visible sun, received the beams of light, that is the holy precepts of Christ, the true Sun . . . in the latter part, as we know, of the reign of Tiberius Cæsar.

In other words, before A.D. 37! The Latin is bad, and has been construed with a pause at 'Sun' to mean only that the religion reached Britain during the events Gildas has just described – 'meanwhile' – with the 'Tiberius' part absorbed into what follows. But the events in any case belong to the first century. Gildas has been discussing the Roman conquest and Boadicea. One does not get the impression that he is merely speculating. It sounds more as if he were referring to a familiar idea. The inference is easier to draw than to reject. Sixth-century Britons in the unconquered west, with a continuity of tradition back to the first Christian landing, held this to have taken place extremely early.

The time apparently given by Gildas is before the final Roman conquest. Such a priority suggests that the story known to him, whatever it was, did not involve any representatives of the Imperial régime. It cannot have portrayed the first missionaries as coming to a Romanised land. If it had, even so irresponsible a writer as Gildas would have had to reconsider the date. The underlying historical fact may be that the Faith did come over in the phase of transition, when Roman rule was still largely a matter of garrisons, and wide territories remained almost untouched.

Nobody knows what Gildas heard. But in the Dark Ages, a number of legends were taking shape.

The first story, or group of stories, had St Paul for its central figure. There was evidence – of a sort – that he himself visited Britain. Clement of Rome, as early as A.D. 100, spoke of Paul as 'arriving at the extremity of the west.' Clement probably meant Spain, but Theodoret (unfortunately a much later writer) said he passed on from Spain to 'the islands which are situated in the sea,' including Britain. Presumably he followed the tin route to Cornwall.

Report, however, made more of his friend Aristobulus. 'My greetings,' says Paul in *Romans* xvi. 10, 'to those of Aristobulus's household.' For some reason this personage's name became associated with Britain. He is 'Bishop of Britain' in a text dubiously ascribed to Dorotheus, a fourth-century Tyrian ecclesiastic. There are several other allusions to him in this capacity, the fullest being in a Greek martyrology.

Aristobulus was one of the seventy disciples, and a follower of St Paul the Apostle, along with whom he preached the Gospel. . . . He was chosen by St Paul to be the missionary bishop to the land of Britain, inhabited by a very fierce and warlike race. By them he was often scourged, and repeatedly dragged as a criminal through their towns. Yet he converted many of them. He was there martyred after he had built churches and ordained deacons and priests for the island.

A more interesting related story grew up round Claudia Rufina, a British lady mentioned by Martial, the Roman epigrammatist.

Claudia, of azure-painted Britons born,
What Latian wit and Latian grace adorn!

38

She lived in Rome with a husband named Pudens, who advised the poet to censor his more daring verses.

> Pudens, at thy request again,
> O how can I refuse
> To take up my correcting pen
> And check my erring muse!

Now St Paul, in the second Epistle to Timothy (iv. 21), does actually refer to a Pudens and a Claudia, together with Linus, who succeeded Peter as Bishop of Rome. Claudia is credited by the hagiographers with a daughter Pudentiana, to whom a church in Rome is dedicated. Some of the modern Catholic Archbishops of Westminster have been styled 'Cardinal of St Pudentiana.'

Did Claudia's conversion have repercussions in her own country? Welshmen, as custodians of British antiquity, eventually maintained that it did. Some said Claudia's 'azure-painted' father was Caradoc or Caractacus, the British prince whom Claudius Cæsar extradited to Rome.[1] Caractacus figures in a related Welsh conversion story which represents him as accompanied by his own father, Bran the Blessed. Bran received baptism from St Paul and returned to Britain. He brought with him 'Arwystli Hen, and Ilid and Cyndaf, men of Israel.' Arwystli has been equated by some with Aristobulus, though this will not work etymologically. Ilid turns up in several other contexts. He and his companions only occur in late and suspect documents, influenced by the Glastonbury lore, but there may be a traditional nucleus. Claudia herself is a theme of academic speculation rather than legend.

The hardy tale of the British King Lucius was known to historians such as Bede in the eighth century and Nennius in the ninth. Lucius is said to have become interested in the Christian religion about 170, and to have sent a message to Pope Eleutherius inviting missionaries to visit his realm. The Pope gave him two, Faganus and Deruvianus, who received him into the Church, baptised numerous Britons, and set up ecclesiastical organisation throughout most of the island.

As it stands this is manifestly a blunder. There was no independent British king at the date given. Moreover, comparison with other records suggests that somebody has

[1] Said to have been buried at Glastonbury.

confused Britain with a place in the Edessa neighbourhood. Yet the date may not be far wrong for the establishment of the Church in Britain as a functioning institution. Tertullian and Origen point the same way. That is what the tale of Faganus and Deruvianus really commemorates, and indeed the authors who pass it on do not claim in so many words that the papal emissaries were the first to bring Christianity.

The third legend, by contrast with the others, is slight. Whether it embodies anything authentic there is no telling. About 638 Isidore of Seville declared that the Apostle Philip visited Gaul. Freculfus, a compiler of general history two hundred years later, repeated Isidore's statement. The idea of a vigorous apostolic mission in Gaul under Philip's leadership became a part of the western Christian tradition. Had the Apostle's followers taken the further step across the Channel? For a while no articulate person made that claim. But the possibility was there, guesswork cost nothing, and eventually the claim was made.

Finally, there were stories current in the Dark Ages about voyages to Britain by St Simon Zelotes and by St Peter himself.

Thus the notion of a mission to Britain in early times was nebulous and ill-founded, but persistent. Its vitality was such that many different attempts were made to supply details. Nor was it really so preposterous. Claudius's conquest, during the 40s of the Christian era, brought Britain forcibly into the Roman orbit and into the news. Imperial enterprise opened up the island to a rapid economic invasion. The Romans' quarrel with Druidism gave their new province a special religious interest, and Boadicea's rising excited the capital itself. Neither St Paul nor St Peter nor any other alert resident in Rome could have helped hearing constantly about British affairs. That a mission was at least contemplated is very likely. That it actually happened within the Apostles' lifetimes we have no good reason to affirm, but only a negative reason to deny. There are only rumours, no record worth calling a record. But, after all, plenty of real happenings fail to get recorded.

3

By the eleventh century the position at Glastonbury was

this. The Old Church stood there like a part of the landscape, with its door and its little windows and its reinforcements of wood and metal. No one remembered how it had come to be there. The fable of the miraculous founding is evidence of two things – first, antiquity: and second, oblivion. The comings and goings, the raids and wars of eight or nine hundred years had blotted out every intelligible tradition, at least in the English regions.

While the Glastonbury fable passed dimly from mouth to mouth and from pen to pen, all the stories outlined in the foregoing pages continued in currency. People at one place or another in Britain were ready with versions of the first coming of the Faith, which had supposedly occurred at a time not too remote from the building of the Old Church. St Paul or Aristobulus; or Faganus and Deruvianus; or followers of St Philip – somebody, at any rate, had crossed over the Channel bringing the Gospel, and with that advent (the more rational began to argue) the dawn of Glastonbury as a Christian shrine must surely be connected.

The interweaving of the traditions, and their application rightly or wrongly to Glastonbury, started at an unknown date and had made considerable progress by the twelfth century. The church's history began to creep into daylight through the devoted labours of a monk, England's first eminent historian after the Norman landing: William of Malmesbury.

Born about 1090 of mixed Norman and English blood, William came from Somerset. His father recognised his scholarly bent and placed him as soon as possible in Malmesbury Abbey, where he studied logic, medicine, ethics and history, and became librarian, to the library's immense advantage. In 1125 he visited Glastonbury and stayed for several weeks at the monastery, exploring the manuscripts and talking to the monks. Afterwards he travelled widely through England, compiled chronicles, took part in important deliberations of Church and State, courteously declined the office of Abbot of Malmesbury, and died middle-aged enjoying a respect which all subsequent scholars have perpetuated.

The fruit of William's research at Glastonbury was a book *De Antiquitate Glastoniensis Ecclesiæ*, which he dedicated to Henry de Blois, who had just been installed as Abbot. Our oldest surviving copy is unfortunately corrupt. The opening paragraphs, and a number of later sections, look like interpolations belonging to the thirteenth century. What William concluded in 1125 can, however, be disinterred from a long digression in his *Acts of the Kings of England*, a digression which is simply another form of the *De Antiquitate* account. First he mentions Faganus and Deruvianus, the mythical papal envoys, and quotes a theory that they travelled westward in 170 and built Glastonbury's Old Church. Then he speaks of a further tradition implying that they did not build it, but only restored it.

There are documents of no small credit, which have been discovered in certain places to the following effect: 'No other hands than those of the disciples of Christ erected the church of Glastonbury.' Nor is it dissonant from probability: for if Philip, the Apostle, preached to the Gauls, as Freculfus relates in the fourth chapter of his seventh book, it may be believed that he planted the word on this side of the Channel also. But, that I may not seem to balk the expectations of my readers by vain imaginations, I shall leave all doubtful matter and proceed to the relation of substantial truths.

This is clear enough. William, and the monks, recognised the existence of a belief in a Christian advent during the first century. Unspecified documents connected it with the foundation of the Old Church. But no information survived about it, or none worth reporting. William, a critical investigator, preferred not to name a specific person.

Our text of *De Antiquitate* itself dates from a period long after William's death. It may be as late as 1240. In the opening chapter, superimposed by another hand, a long-anticipated figure at last makes his entry.

St Philip . . . coming into the country of the Franks to preach converted many to the Faith, and baptised them. Working to spread Christ's word, he chose twelve from among his disciples, and sent them into Britain.

Their leader, it is said, was Philip's dearest friend, Joseph of Arimathea, who buried the Lord.

Coming therefore into Britain 63 years from the Incarnation of the Lord, and 15 from the Assumption of Blessed Mary, they began faithfully to preach the Faith of Christ. But the barbaric king and his people, hearing such novel and unaccustomed things, absolutely refused to consent to their preaching, neither did he wish to change the traditions of his ancestors, yet, because they came from far, and merely required a modest competence for their life, at their request he granted them a certain island, surrounded by woods, thickets and marshes, called by its inhabitants Ynys – witrin, on the confines of the kingdom. Moreover, later on, two other successive kings, although pagans, observing their pious mode of life, presented to each of them a portion of land, and, at their request, confirmed the twelve portions to them after the heathen manner; and it is believed that the Twelve Hides got their name from them to this day.

Thereupon the said twelve saints residing in this desert, were in a very short time warned by a vision of the angel Gabriel to build a church in honour of the Holy Mother of God and Virgin Mary in a place shown to them from heaven, and they, quick to obey the divine precepts, completed a certain chapel according to what had been shown them, fashioning its walls below, circular-wise, of twisted twigs, in the thirty-first year after the Passion of the Lord, and the fifteenth after the Assumption of the Glorious Virgin, a chapel, it is true, of uncouth form, but to God adorned richly with virtue. And as it was the first in the kingdom, God's Son distinguished it with greater dignity by dedicating it in honour of his Mother.

Thereupon the twelve saints – so often mentioned – paying devout homage in that same spot to God and the Blessed Virgin, spending the time in vigils, fasts, and prayers, were constantly sustained – 'tis pious to believe – in all their needs by the same Virgin's help and presence. . . .

The said saints continued to live in the same hermitage for many years, and were at last liberated from the prison of the flesh. The place then began to be a covert for wild beasts – the spot which had before been the habitation of saints – until the Blessed Virgin was pleased to recall her house of prayer to the memory of the faithful.

And the narrative goes on to Faganus and Deruvianus, their restoration of the church, and the rebirth of the community.

In this manuscript occurs the splendid title ROMA SECUNDA, which clung to Glastonbury during the Middle Ages.

So here we encounter Joseph of Arimathea, who is for ever Glastonbury's peculiar saint, but whose arrival on the scene strikes us as alarmingly tardy. It is not quite his first entry into British literature. The Arthurian romancers of the late twelfth century and early thirteenth made him the bringer of the Holy Grail and the first Christian to touch on British coasts, though the Christianity he allegedly brought was somewhat irregular. These romancers wrote with a motive in the back of their minds. It was a time of ecclesiastical strife, and influential members of the romancers' public would have been glad to bolster the British Church against the Roman by proving it to be equally old and independent of Rome. Hence these stories of Christian origins had a fresh and urgent importance, and a specific legend about specific characters could be a valuable weapon in the ideological armoury.

We shall go into this later. The crucial fact for the moment is the emergence and exaltation of Joseph, first in the Grail romances and then in a more explicit association with Glastonbury.[1] He is brought forward at least partly for a purpose, the promotion of 'British Christianity' against Roman, though after a while Glastonbury Abbey appropriates his prestige and softens the nationalism. It is easy to regard him as a pure interloper with no genuine tradition behind him, as a twelfth-century figment. That is the course taken by most modern scholars.

Yet a question remains: Why Joseph of Arimathea?

Why not St Paul? or Aristobulus? or St Philip? or St Simon Zelotes? or St Peter? All these were available. Yet the story-tellers passed them by. For whatever reason, they made Joseph their protagonist. And Joseph, on the face of it, was a nobody. He had never found his way into popular legend or the cult of the saints. Few apocryphal writers had broken the silence of the New Testament about his career after the Resurrection. But here we meet him in the Plantagenet age, wafted from one end of the Roman world to the other, credited with the founding of Glastonbury, and, in some quarters, exalted as a counterpoise to St Peter himself: as the pontiff or patron of a branch of the Christian Church in no way subordinate to Rome.

[1] I am aware of the theory that Joseph was merely taken over by Glastonbury after the Grail romances had popularised him, and that the romances themselves did not connect him with the place at all. Those who maintain this view sometimes add that the Joseph story was an adaptation of a French legend about the 'Holy Blood of Fêcamp.' This raises some complicated questions best postponed till we come to the Grail (Chapter Seven). Here it is enough to say that the theory does not cover the facts, or invalidate the main argument of this chapter.

It is hard to explain this choice of hero on the theory that the Grail romances and the *De Antiquitate* chapter are pure invention, springing from the whim of a Christian chauvinist. There must surely have been a prior belief lurking somewhere, a belief too stubborn to dismiss, a belief which there was good reason to use. In 1125 William of Malmesbury did not hear it in any form circumstantial enough to justify a detailed account. Because of his silence, the scholars have imagined that the tale of St Joseph must have been concocted after William carried out his researches. But this inference is not safe at all. The case is that of Avalon over again. The Joseph story took literary shape as a part of the Arthurian cycle, and that cycle arose from an event subsequent to William's death: the Anglo-French discovery of Celtic traditions preserved in Wales and Brittany. Arthur himself, indeed, supplies a more telling parallel than Avalon. Throughout the Dark Ages the English had many scribes and scholars, but not one so much as hints at the existence of Arthur, or even at the existence of an Arthurian legend. Yet there was such a legend: the Welsh hoarded it for six hundred years before the English discovered it; and few historians now would deny that there was a real Arthur behind it.

So with Joseph of Arimathea. It is at least arguable that a legend on the subject came down unobtrusively from the Britons. Some such travelling Celtic priest as St David, who visited Glastonbury before the English conquest, may have told his disciples a version of the Old Church's origin which the British monks of that time preserved but the English monks of a later age did not. William of Malmesbury therefore missed it when he came to the Abbey, whereas the Celtic revivalists, a little while afterwards, received it by a circuitous route from the Welsh or the Bretons. This legend need not have been more than the airiest of fancies, never put forward very seriously or propagated very widely. Anglo-Saxon ecclesiastics, writing much closer to the British era than William of Malmesbury, admittedly do not mention St Joseph any more than William does. Yet I find it easier to believe that such a fancy existed from early times than to accept the sudden contrivance of the whole business in the Middle Ages.

There is a 'prophecy' attributed to Melkin or Maelgwn, a fifth-century bard described (unconvincingly) as St David's uncle. Its oracular Latin has been Englished as follows:

> Avalon's island, with avidity
> Claiming the death of pagans,
> More than all the world beside,
> For the entombment of them all,
> Honoured by chanting spheres of prophecy:
> And for all time to come
> Adornèd shall be
> By them that praise the Highest.
> Abbadarè, mighty in Saphat,
> Noblest of pagans,
> With countless thousands
> There hath fallen on sleep.
> Amid these Joseph in marble,
> Of Arimathea by name,
> Hath found perpetual sleep:
> And he lies on a two-forked line
> Next the south corner of an oratory
> Fashioned of wattles
> For the adoring of a mighty Virgin
> By the aforesaid sphere-betokened
> Dwellers in that place, thirteen in all.
> For Joseph hath with him
> In his sarcophagus
> Two cruets, white and silver,
> Filled with blood and sweat
> Of the Prophet Jesus.
> When his sarcophagus
> Shall be found entire, intact,
> In time to come, it shall be seen
> And shall be open unto all the world;
> Thenceforth nor water nor the dew of heaven
> Shall fail the dwellers in that ancient isle,
> For a long while before
> The day of judgment in Josaphat
> Open shall these things be
> And declared to living men.

If we could accept this as a proved Celtic fragment, it would practically settle the matter. Unluckily it has not been traced farther back than a chronicle written by a Glastonbury monk named John, which belongs to the fourteenth century and gives the final official version. John's narrative borrows from the Grail romances, but leaves out the Grail itself. The two small vessels or cruets replace it.

Whatever the truth regarding sources, one point is most curious: that the legend about the first church in Britain should have attached itself to a saint unconnected with any known mission. In view of the journey involved, such a comparatively unadventurous soul as Joseph – who feared even to confess Christ openly – is the very last Gospel convert we should expect to meet in Somerset. Again it is hard to avoid the feeling of an obstinate fact underlying the fable. This time it is not only the fact of a tradition, but the fact of an event behind the tradition. St Joseph's presence on British soil is too odd, under the circumstances, to have quite the air of pure invention.

We possess, I think, two clues worth following. One is St Joseph's reputation for wealth. Could it be that the pioneer Glastonbury Christian was unusually rich, a great man in the vulgar sense? As his memory died away, this perhaps was the sole detail which survived. A large house, or the ruins of a large house, may have stood as a reminder. When the fabulists tried to identify him, of course as honourably as possible, the only Biblical magnate who qualified was Joseph of Arimathea. The virtual absence of legends about St Joseph left a welcome and challenging gap into which his exploit could be fitted. (And the guess *may* have been right!) As a supplement, or alternative, to this theory, we could suppose that the name of Joseph was suggested by a misunderstood inscription.

In the second place, while this proto-Christian may have arrived as early as the stories allege, and may have been the pioneer of his religion in Britain, neither he nor any missionary associated with him achieved much success among the Britons. We are free to believe in Aristobulus, or in someone whom we may call Aristobulus. But there is no trace of effective preaching or Church organisation before the latter half of the second century. The tale of Faganus and Deruvianus is right symbolically even though it is wrong historically. If we adopt an early date for Glastonbury, we must picture something lonely and uninfluential, perhaps not even aspiring to influence, yet softly building a reputation that proved potent when the Roman Empire turned Christian and the age of monasticism set in.

This could have been the way of it. After Claudius's conquest, the swarm of civilians who followed the Roman army included a merchant from Judea. He came to Glaston-bury for business reasons, he set up his household there, and he *happened* to be a Christian. Men of substance were exceptional in the early Church, but they did exist, and some carried on as usual after conversion. Business activity was never held incompatible with the Faith. If a wealthy Christian had settled on Ynys-witrin, his house would have become a hostel for the occasional Christian preacher or traveller (Aristobulus, for example), and might well have continued thus for as long as his descendants remained. The foundation of a church on the spot, and the choice of that area by hermits or monks, would have ensued quite naturally, encouraged by the desire to purify a druidical shrine.

Our hypothetical merchant is not too monstrously unlikely. Immigrants did pour into Britain in the wake of the legions, and they did come from every part of the Empire. The historian Collingwood estimates their number at 100,000. Archæologists have found tomb inscriptions dating from the first century, which show that there were many traders among them, and an appreciable sprinkling of people from the eastern end of the Mediterranean. Collingwood's figure, therefore, does give room for an eastern Christian or two.

As to the motive which might have induced a rich Jew to come all the way to Glastonbury, several speculative authors have hit on the tin trade. This idea seems to have occurred also to the anonymous creators of folk-lore. The Reverend L. S. Lewis, one of Glastonbury's most loyal if uncritical champions, claims to have heard a rhyme with some such refrain as 'Joseph was in the tin trade,' and he adds that tin-workers in the West Country used to repeat the same formula for luck on the job. Perhaps. But the tin mines were not in Somerset, and by the middle of the first century, as we saw, continental competition had almost ruined them. Though the Romans tried to revive the industry, it never recovered sufficiently to attract investment or justify a rich man's personal exodus from one end of the Empire to the other.

While the Grail romances have little direct value as history, they do hint by chance at an intriguing line of thought. One of their chief characters is Vespasian, who commanded the troops in Judea under Nero and afterwards became Emperor himself. His attributed actions in the romances are of small consequence. But the curious thing is that before coming to Judea he was in Britain, and in just the right part of

Britain. He served in the army under Claudius. When the Emperor wound up his personal campaign and went home, the Roman forces split into columns radiating from London. Vespasian commanded the Second Legion, which moved south-westward. Subduing the Isle of Wight and the British hill-forts, he struck out over Salisbury Plain into the less populous land beyond. He may have advanced as far as Devon; he indubitably advanced as far as Somerset. Then he returned to Italy, and, after holding intermediate posts, took up the Judean command. It was essentially a job for a practical soldier. Jewish rebels had won control of part of the country, and Vespasian's commission was to restore order.

Before leaving Britain, Vespasian may well have been responsible for one of the first Roman measures of economic development there. In the Mendip hills north of Glastonbury, the Britons turned out to be mining lead, after a desultory fashion. The mines were promptly expropriated, and assigned to the Second Legion as a source of State revenue. Lead pigs discovered by archæologists show that the Legion was still exporting lead via Southampton in Nero's reign, when Vespasian was in Judea. Now Vespasian seems to have been a good business man, likely to find friends among the mercantile set and encourage them to call on him for advice. He was also interested in eastern religion, and he set great store by a prophecy that 'men coming from Judea' would rule in Rome (though he eventually applied it to himself and his sons). We have been wading altogether too long through a mire of rumours and arguments: here, to wind up the discussion, is a little fantasy which at least accounts for everything we want to account for.

One evening, when the fighting in Judea was nearly over, Vespasian gave a reception for important provincials in the pacified zone. Wandering from group to group, he noticed half a dozen merchants talking more seriously and vehemently than is usual on such occasions. Stray sentences which he caught arrested his attention: something about prophecies and the Jewish Messiah. He strolled over and joined in the conversation, showing enough sympathy and comprehension to avert a change of subject. The merchants were all slightly known to him, and all but one were orthodox Jews. The other, however, spoke in a most peculiar way, giving his nation's prophecies an entirely different application. It transpired that he belonged to the 'Christian' sect. Vespasian listened to his opinions, and thought him puzzling but impressive, the sort of person he would respect and remember. Dinner interrupted the argument. During the meal Vespasian spoke of the vast opportunities in Britain for enterprising citizens. He had just received a letter from an old comrade of his in the Second Legion, stationed in Somerset. The Mendip mines were flourishing, slaves were plentiful, and the Legion could use more contractors to transport and market the lead. As he talked, he saw the 'Christian' listening a few places off.

The next day the man presented himself at Headquarters. He was thinking of going over to Britain, to try his luck in a fresh field. Could Vespasian oblige him with an introduction to the Commander of the Second Legion . . .?

4

Whoever the first Glastonbury Christian was, and whatever he did, one thing we can be fairly sure he did not do. He did not plant the Holy Thorn.

This botanical wonder is a late accretion to the legend, probably inserted by guides for the benefit of visitors. There is no sufficient ground for the supposition that the monks felt the need to Christianise a pagan tree-cult. Even the fourteenth-century chronicler John of Glastonbury does not refer to the Thorn, and John is far from sceptical. We find no clear allusion earlier than a poem entitled 'Joseph of Armathia,' printed in 1520. At that date a giant thorn-tree had stood on Wearyall Hill from time immemorial. It blossomed at Christmas, and nobody recalled having seen a thorn-tree exactly like it. The material for a miracle had proved too alluring to resist. Even so the fancy took another two centuries to reach its full stature.

Puritan zeal was fatal to the original tree, but shoots of it survived transplantation. To-day the best specimen is in front of the Church of St John the Baptist. The Abbey has a smaller tree. The Thorn is a freak hawthorn or applewort, *Cratægus oxyacantha*. Its large leaves are toothed, with tiny appendages at the base. It puts out blossoms early in January, at a date roughly answering to Christmas before the reform of the calendar. In a severe winter the blossoms are said to appear earlier. There is no fruit. While the Thorn is genuinely native to Glastonbury, it has no necessary bond with its original soil. Gardeners have grown it in other places.

A subsidiary fable concerns a walnut-tree in the Abbey grounds, which never buds till St Barnabas (11th June), but then bursts out suddenly. Joseph had something to do with this as well. It is hardly worth asking what.

5

We can now finally retrace our steps and take up history again in the first century.

The revolution which the Romans imposed on Britain was too violent to proceed smoothly. Colonists poured across the Channel, town-building spread like an epidemic, native institutions were dashed to pieces. Before long a dangerous reaction set in. While the Celtic religious powers were collapsing in Anglesey, the Celtic political powers were rallying. Queen Boadicea of the Iceni, exasperated by Roman insults, led a rising accompanied by horrible massacres, which laid waste the new settlements and checked the growth of the towns. After her defeat the invaders moved carefully, consolidating their conquests. They penetrated and circumnavigated Scotland. They put up walls to keep out the Highlanders. Meanwhile, they pressed urbanisation forward in such a way as to transform British society. The wealthier Celts acquired central heating and public baths; their sons learned the advantages of a Classical education. After a few generations the province possessed a Romano-British aristocracy, entirely wedded, for the moment, to the Imperial scheme.

While the Meare village may have lasted well into this period, Glastonbury was not a Roman town. People lived there, however. The proofs of their residence are perplexing. Excavators have found a coin of Vespasian by the Tor and an early Roman *fibula* in the Abbey grounds. Then there is a virtual gap, followed by a series of coins dating from the latter part of the third century. During the era of those coins the Empire was passing through a critical phase, of decisive though indirect importance to Glastonbury.

The most obvious cause was uncertainty about the succes-

51

sion. Emperors were not chosen constitutionally. Any adventurer with strong military backing could make a bid for the purple, and the soldiers had a vested interest in frequent changes, since the pretenders paid them for their support and the civil wars gave rich opportunities for plunder. Coup after coup disorganised the life of the Empire; plagues and famines reduced the population; Germans and Persians cascaded over the frontiers. The dislocation, moreover, had lasting economic effects. Most of the legionaries were peasants, and the irresponsible barrack Cæsars frequently financed their rule by taxing the towns and sparing the country. This policy, coupled with the looting and political chaos, crippled town life and infected urban civilisation with mortal disillusionment. When Diocletian eventually pulled the Empire together, it was not the same Empire. Order depended on an Asiatic system of despotism buttressed by the worship of Cæsar as a god, the Unconquered Sun. Urban life revived, but without its earlier energy. Inflation was murderous. Capital migrated to rural districts. The Villa rose into prominence as an institution: farming settlements based on a solitary large house dotted the landscape and restored agriculture, which had not, in the end, escaped the general decay. Society in Britain as elsewhere moved into a subdued, rustic, culturally sterile phase. Its Roman backbone had long since gone. The world was drearily cosmopolitan. Even the Emperors were no longer Italians. The shell of the State endured for a few years more, but at last the barbarians cracked it open.

During the crisis of the third century public disgust took spiritually radical forms. The Empire, as Belloc remarked with somewhat more than his usual accuracy, was dying of despair. New religions throve, and one in particular, the Christian, advanced like an avalanche. The next topic that we have to consider is its progress in Britain, leading to the foundation of the monastic colony which we may, for convenience, begin at once to call Glastonbury Abbey.

William of Malmesbury's story about Faganus and Deruvianus, the missionaries in A.D. 170, is on the whole the standard medieval account of the way in which the Church was established on British territory. According to *De Antiquitate*, the pair travelled from King Lucius's court to the Isle of Avalon and built an oratory dedicated to Peter and Paul – the wattle chapel, of course, being already there. King Lucius is incredible, even if regarded as a mere honorary monarch or Romano-British bureaucrat, but by 200 the British

Church was firmly entrenched. In the next century it expanded. A legendary hero whom Evelyn Waugh has found irresistible is Coel, alias Old King Cole.[1] His daughter was Helena, the sainted discoverer of the True Cross, who married Constantius Cæsar. Their son Constantine proclaimed himself Emperor at York, overthrew his rivals by Christ's aid, and gave the Church his official backing. Thus Britain made a notable contribution to the Faith. Helena and Constantine are historical enough. It is a pity we cannot feel the same confidence about Old King Cole.

In 303 the Christians' refusal to worship Diocletian touched off an appalling persecution throughout the Empire. This dragged the British Church into daylight. Three victims – Alban of Verulam, Aaron and Julius of Caerleon – won fame by martyrdom. Numerous churches, it is said, were destroyed: proof that numerous churches existed. Constantine's accession brought in a reign of toleration followed by favour. In 314 three British bishops attended an ecclesiastical council at Arles. Their names are given as Restitutus of London, Eborius of York, and Adelphius, town unspecified. The British Church was poor. As late as 360, several bishops who came to the Council of Rimini could not afford their travelling expenses. One envisages a church rooted in the humbler, less Romanised classes. The aristocracy conformed if an Emperor required it, but at the close of the fourth century, despite the general triumph of Christianity, pagan temples were still going up.

Glastonbury played no discernible part in public events. Its career as a Christian holy place began under the inspiration of a movement within the Church, a movement reflecting not only the disillusionment of the age but a growing disquiet over the Christian community itself, which was felt to be getting contaminated.

This movement was monasticism. As a Christian thing, it started almost by chance in Egypt. Devout Egyptians used to retire to hermitages for prayer and meditation. In 270 a youth named Anthony resolved to do this himself. He called on several hermits, learning from each, and then shut himself in a tomb near his home. Satan recognised a saint and assaulted him with temptations. After a frightful struggle he drove the Adversary off. When thirty-five years old, having realised the possibilities of the contemplative life, he moved to a more secluded retreat in a disused fort close to the Nile. Here he

[1] Said to have been buried at Glastonbury.

53

lived absolutely alone for many years. Even the friends who brought him food never saw him; they passed it in over the wall. His reputation spread, and hermits collected in the neighbourhood. At their entreaty he finally came out, still young-looking and in excellent health. Confronted with a kind of spontaneous monastery, he drew up rules for it, and instructed the hermits in the spiritual life. Then he withdrew to Mount Colzim near the Red Sea, and remained there till his death as a centenarian.

St Anthony of the Desert never mixed in the world. He twice went to Alexandria at critical junctures in Church affairs, but he did not stay long, and when Constantine sent him an invitation he politely declined. He was no gloomy fanatic. Though without formal education, he conducted himself with urbanity and good sense, emphasising the virtue of discretion. When he died he wanted his grave kept secret to avoid superstitious homage.

The monasteries founded by Anthony, or under his direct ægis, were simply assemblages of hermits who came together for worship in a communal chapel. His example, however, inspired Pachomius, who launched the main movement, inaugurating nine houses for men and one for women. A wave of enthusiasm resulted. Village-communities of hundreds and thousands of religious, complete with libraries and churches and hospitals, began to spring up along the Nile Valley and in the wilderness. Each had an abbot and a more or less rigid organisation. The Church's hierarchy found the phenomenon perplexing. At first the bishops distrusted it, but later they capitulated, and St Athanasius published a book about Anthony which set the seal of approval on his work. A party of Egyptian monks came to settle in Rome. When the initial shock was over the Romans got used to them, and then learned to admire them. The new mode of devotion spread everywhere. Hilarion founded monasteries in Palestine, Basil in Asia Minor, Martin of Tours in Gaul.

The movement sprang from a civilisation in despair. Yet it was no mere wave of irresponsible cowardice. In the first place, monastic life was austere and demanding. Richly endowed foundations were a thing of the future, and fourth-century monks lived by their hands. Some worked in the fields, often bringing waste ground under cultivation. Some made sandals or mats or baskets. A few were already copying out manuscripts; to them and their successors we owe practically all that has survived of Classical literature. Nor was the atmosphere pleasant or easy-going. The rules required the most exact and humiliating obedience to one's abbot. Fasts were rigorous and penances brutal. A verminous poverty was the norm. It was no life for runaways or idlers. The vast majority of monks had powerful convictions.

Furthermore, monasticism was not a mere selfish quest for personal purity. It could be that, but it could also be much else. To borrow a phrase from the American Syndicalists, the monks built a new society in the shell of the old. Theocratic communities stood beside Imperial cities, witnessing to the world's corruption and drawing off many of its best citizens. They effaced social distinctions and gave fresh scope to ability. Regardless of birth, monks were invited from their cells to become bishops and politicians, and gained a respect which the extortionate lay officials had long since forfeited. The process weakened the State, but the State was weakening itself. The monks, with all their dirt and illiteracy and superstition, built well enough to save Europe from complete ruin when the State collapsed.

Monasticism was slow to reach Britain, and probably rather tepid in its first manifestations. But there was no reason why Anthony's institution should not take root there, in very much its primitive form. Celtic Christianity did vaguely ally itself with the east and respond to eastern influences. Later, as the Church extended itself through Ireland and Scotland, some districts received their ecclesiastical books from the Greeks and Egyptians rather than the Romans. The Celts fixed the date of Easter after the Oriental manner. And when Celtic monasteries emerge plainly into sight, they tend to be like St Anthony's rather than the more formal communities of the Latin West. Their monks are solitaries, meeting for worship in a communal church. The question is, when and where in the British Isles did the practice originate?

Nobody knows. It must have existed by 429. Bishop Germanus of Auxerre, who visited Britain in that year, is stated to have brought over monastic regulations drawn up at the great Riviera community of Lérins. Where were these regulations applied? One of the old Welsh 'triads' – formalised summaries of historical tradition – runs as follows:

The Three Perpetual Choirs of Britain: the choir of Llan Iltud Vawr in Glamorganshire, the choir of Ambrosius in Ambresbury, and the choir of Glastonbury. In each of these choirs there were 2400 saints, that is there were a hundred for every hour of the day and night in rotation.

This gives us the names of three ancient monasteries apparently thought of as having flourished at the same time. Ambresbury is Amesbury, and in the 550's the pagan Saxons destroyed it. Hence Glastonbury must be prior to that; and several allusions in other contexts confirm the inference. The number of inmates is exaggerated, but it at least implies a famous and firmly-grounded establishment, as indeed does Glastonbury's inclusion in the triad. A history going back to 429 or farther would, on the face of it, be credible for any of the three monasteries. But it is in fact inadmissible for Llan Iltud Vawr and Amesbury. Both came into being about 500. Glastonbury, therefore, is left as the sole candidate for the recipient of Germanus's rules, and there is no significant tradition apart from this triad to suggest any other. Little weight can be given to a legend about Bangor, which absurdly introduces St Paul.

The story in *De Antiquitate* (for what it is worth) makes Faganus and Deruvianus form a community on the primitive pattern.

> Preaching and baptising, they went through all parts of Britain until they reached the Isle of Avallonia. . . . Examining the spot diligently, they discovered the sign of our redemption and other manifest marks by which they plainly saw that Christians had formerly inhabited the place. . . . On that account they loved this spot above all others, and they also, in memory of the first twelve, chose twelve of their own, and caused them to live on the said island with the approval of King Lucius. These twelve thereafter abode in divers spots as anchorites – in the same spots, indeed, which the first twelve inhabited. Yet they used to meet together continually in the Old Church, in order to celebrate divine worship more devoutly. . . . Thus, many succeeding these – but always twelve in number – abode in the same island during many years.

No such foundation can have occurred at the attributed date, 170, but the sketch of the hermits is surprisingly probable.

St Collen, the same who banished King Gwyn, has also been cited as a possible founder. Collen comes on the scene too late rather than too soon. Perhaps it was really in the fourth century that Christian ascetics began to settle on Ynys-witrin. It is tempting to connect their arrival with the abrupt numismatic manifestation mentioned above, but that will hardly do. They are not likely to have come before 340, when monastic principles first percolated into the western Empire. But, equally, they are not likely to have come later than 388. That year saw the beginning of seaborne assaults on the British coastline by raiding barbarians – Irish, Scottish, Saxon. The attacks were so frequent and ferocious that Britons in quest of peace would scarcely have formed a new settlement at the head of an exposed inlet.[1]

It is in the 360s or thereabouts that serious possibilities begin to emerge. Britain's ecclesiastical contact with the heart of the Empire had by then been solidly established by the attendance of her three bishops at the Council of Rimini, an event which led to an increased volume of correspondence and pilgrimage. From 360 onward Athanasius's *Life of St Anthony* was enjoying an immense vogue in the West. This, too, was the period of St Martin's work in Gaul, and Glastonbury's inception is more likely to have followed that than preceded it.

On the whole 385 seems a plausible date for the pioneers. The background, I would suggest, was the political upheaval of 383, when a pretender named Maximus was proclaimed Emperor in Britain. Though a Spaniard himself, he probably married a local wife, and to judge from Welsh chronicles the Britons accepted him as one of themselves. At any rate the expeditionary force with which he asserted his claims was largely composed of native troops with a strong personal loyalty to him. He controlled Gaul for several years, and the occupation, some say, was the beginning of British settlement in Armorica, afterwards called Brittany. The amount of coming and going across the Channel during Maximus's reign must have been considerable, and Christian soldiers and officials would certainly have sought out Martin of Tours, whose reputation was enormous. Ninian, a Briton who sailed north to preach to the Picts, lived in Gaul for some time as a disciple of Martin. Very likely the founder of Glastonbury did the same.

One wild conjecture may be just worth putting in. Martin was Bishop of Tours from 372 onwards. A century and a

[1] I have been told that later English and Scottish monks did plant themselves in the path of the Vikings, inviting martyrdom. But I have the impression that the Britons were much less heroic.

half later the city had another great bishop, the historian Gregory of Tours. Gregory, in his history, records the legend of Joseph of Arimathea's release from prison by the risen Christ. He took it from the apocryphal *Acts of Pilate* or *Gospel of Nicodemus*, and this book, owing to papal censure, had never been widely circulated. In fact Gregory is the only Gallic author who shows any acquaintance with it up to the time of the medieval Grail cycle. Yet it was known in England and Ireland in the eighth century. The poet Cynewulf paraphrased part of it. The source of the copies which the English and Irish used may well have been a transcript from a unique Gallic manuscript found by Gregory in the episcopal library at Tours. Now this manuscript could have been there already during St Martin's episcopate; the book is early enough. If we were to suppose that Glastonbury was founded by a disciple of St Martin, who made and imported a copy of the *Acts of Pilate*, we would provide simultaneously for the existence of the texts in the British Isles and for an awareness of the otherwise obscure Joseph of Arimathea at the Abbey before the Saxon conquest. The guess is a topic for romance rather than history, but a wise historian will not wholly neglect any talent he may possess for romance.

Whoever brought the first hermits together at Glastonbury, he doubtless had some special motive for choosing the spot: the wish to dispel pagan superstition, the wish to honour the memory of Christians who had once lived there, or both. When ten or twelve were assembled, they built the wattle church and secured recognition as a community, a tiny group in a remote indifferent land. Some considerable time later, their successors adopted a more highly organised monasticism. Thereupon we may say that Glastonbury possessed an Abbey. As to this last important step, the testimony of William of Malmesbury and his interpolator is clear and circumstantial. It passes Germanus by. Whatever minor changes occurred in the interval, the hermits did not actually have an abbot till the middle of the fifth century. Their abbot was . . . St Patrick.

Such flagrant annexation of the Apostle of Ireland is not so ridiculous as one might suppose. Patrick was the real if unintentional founder of that aloof Celtic Church in which Glastonbury was to figure until the English captured it; and, after all, he was not an Irishman. As for his missionary career, two things are certain. Because of its results it is relevant to our story, and because of its poor documentation it cannot be dogmatised about. Strictly speaking, Abbot Patrick of Glastonbury would be neither inappropriate nor impossible.

6

Patrick was a Briton, born between 370 and 390. Dumbarton has been picked out as his original home. There is also a case, however, for South Wales. A third theory, far more intriguing, makes him a native of Somerset, and therefore, conceivably, a friend of the hermits of Ynys-witrin. When he was in his teens Irish buccaneers carried him off. Irish raids on Wales and the West Country were very formidable at this time, amounting almost to invasion. Adventurers stayed for long periods on British soil, and their presence had to be reckoned with as a permanent factor in society. Patrick was kidnapped, and sold in slavery to a chief named Miliuc, who made him a shepherd. He learned the Irish language, but his work often took him away from human company, and he devoted himself to prayer and contemplation. After six years he escaped and made his way home.

Convinced by a dream that God had chosen him to convert the Irish, he travelled through Gaul and Italy studying, and took priest's orders. He may now have made a first attempt at conversion. His life has a blank in it. But if he did, the attempt was unsuccessful, and he reappears in Gaul aged forty or so as a kind of secretary to Germanus of Auxerre. When Pope Celestine sent the Irish another missionary who failed and perished, Germanus told Patrick to seize the opportunity. Consecrated a bishop, and assured of papal support, he set sail for the country of his bondage. The year was 432.

Ireland had never belonged to Rome. Roman organisation and urbanisation had never come there as they had come to Britain. The Celts of the smaller island lived a simple, unlettered, parochial existence in circular huts. Their amusements were feasts and fairs and juggling. Their weights and measures were taken from parts of the body. They were unsystematically governed by tribal chiefs, with a not very effective over-king at Tara. Druidism persisted among them, and druidical idols received human sacrifices. But there seem to have been a few Christians already, though nothing is known about them.

Patrick addressed himself at once to the chiefs and nobles. At Tara he preached before the over-king Loiguire. It was here that he illustrated the Trinity by a shamrock (if he did.) Loiguire's daughters questioned him charmingly about God, and about God's wife and children. Two princes of Leinster and the king of Munster submitted to baptism. What the nobles did, the commoners, generally speaking, felt bound to imitate. Churches sprang up all over Ulster. After many years of travel and triumph, the saint crowned his labours by founding the archbishopric of Armagh. He had ordained enough priests to keep the Irish Church alive. But he had not really converted Ireland. The Christianity of the convert rulers' subjects was superficial and insecure. The druids fought bitterly. To the end of his life Patrick expected martyrdom. Once he was gone, the ecclesiastical structure visibly tottered, and when it recovered it was changed.

Pictures of Patrick are usually forbidding. Yet he never gave that impression himself. He was brave, enthusiastic, large-hearted. When he heard that his old master Miliuc was still alive, he went to offer a ransom in reparation for his flight thirty-odd years before. (Miliuc, who had undergone druidical training, carried out a ritual suicide rather than face him). Success never turned his head. He was always profoundly humble, and took pains not to spare himself, camping out in a tent and sleeping on rock. Thanks to him the young Christianity of Ireland had a freshness and freedom which the Christians of the decadent Empire had almost lost. In the Dark Ages the Irish Church was to prove enterprising. A Celtic Christianity barely conscious of Rome was to kindle the human spirit in far-off places. And when the heathens drove a wedge between Britain and Europe, the British Church, including Glastonbury, swung into the Irish orbit.

St Patrick is held usually to have died among his flock, aged about ninety or a hundred. Ireland claims his grave as a matter of course. But the two Malmesburian books give him a strange and honourable retirement. He crosses to Cornwall, comes to Glastonbury, and reforms the community, composing a Charter for it.

In this document he is made to give an account of his actions.

By the guidance of God, who is the life and the way, I chanced upon the isle of Ynys-witrin, wherein I found a place holy and ancient, chosen and sanctified by God in honour of Mary the pure Virgin, the Mother of God: and there I found certain brethren imbued with the rudiments of the Catholic faith, and of pious conversation, who were successors of the disciples of Saints Faganus and Deruvianus. . . . I have thought good to record their names in this my writing. And they are these: Brumban, Hyregaan, Brenwal, Wencreth, Bamtonmeweng, Adelwalred, Lothor, Wellias, Breden, Swelwes, Hin Loernius, and another Hin. These men, being of noble birth and wishing to crown their nobleness with deeds of faith, had chosen to lead a hermit's life; and when I found them meek and gentle, I chose to be in low estate with them, rather than to dwell in kings' palaces. And, since we were all of one heart and one mind, we chose to dwell together, and eat and drink in common, and sleep in the same house. And so they set me, though unwilling, at their head.

He goes on to relate how he explored Ynys-witrin.

After some time had passed I took with me my brother Wellias, and with great difficulty we climbed up through the dense wood to the summit of the mount which stands forth in that island. And when we were come there we saw an ancient oratory, wellnigh ruined, yet fitting for Christian devotion. . . . We searched the whole place diligently; and we found a volume in which were written Acts of Apostles, along with Acts and Deeds of Saints Faganus and Deruvianus. It was in great part destroyed, but at the end thereof we found a writing which said that Saints Faganus and Deruvianus, by revelation of Our Lord Jesus Christ, had built that oratory in honour of St Michael the Archangel. . . . Having found therefore this great treasure of divine goodness, I and brother Wellias fasted three months, engaged in prayer and watching.

He tells further how Christ appeared to him and approved the choice of this place in honour of Michael. It was thereupon appointed that two brethren should always live on the for and maintain divine worship in the chapel. Arnulf and Ogmar, Irishmen who had come with Patrick, were the first pair to undertake the charge, and to them Patrick entrusted the charter, leaving a duplicate in the Old Church.

The text of the charter as a whole is undoubtedly bogus. It even speaks of indulgences to be gained by visitors. Here, of course, we detect a medieval attempt to encourage the tourist traffic. Nevertheless there are interesting touches. A curious detail is the list of hermits. The names are not pure gibberish. They do bear some resemblance to British names. It is barely possible that the forger has preserved a trace of some genuine record. Interesting also is the reference to a 'dense wood' on the Tor.

After these episodes Patrick is alleged to have governed the monks for nine years. Gifts from his aristocratic friends enriched the Abbey. He died in 472 and was buried in the Old Church at the right-hand side of the altar, an angel designating the spot with an outrush of flames. His monument was a pyramid embellished with gold and silver.

The tale is admittedly as unconvincing as it is adverse to good relations with Ireland. Cornish folk-lore feebly confirms Patrick's voyage, or return, to the West Country; it might be more helpful if it did not insist that he floated over to Padstow on his own altar. The date of the saint's death has been fixed by adding nine years to a date sometimes quoted for his death in Ireland, the implication being that the people at Glastonbury accepted the orthodox version of his career, but imagined him to have left Ireland instead of dying. Here again there is a fragile support for them, in the ambiguity concerning the age he lived to. But none of the evidence amounts to an arguable case. A manuscript purporting to be the charter itself, which existed in the reign of Henry VIII, cannot be taken seriously.

What we can accept as the factual substratum is the institution of Glastonbury Abbey in the fifth century, with a monastic rule on the continental model. The area which it covered, to judge from archæological clues, was a rough rectangle, with the wattle church to the north-west on the site of the present Lady Chapel. We must not picture a dignified medieval structure. The monks lived very simply in thatched cabins resembling the church. Excavators have discerned traces of one of their buildings a few yards from the Lady Chapel: bits of wattle-work, post-holes, and odds and ends of pottery compatible with a date in the fifth century. The original chapel of St Michael may already have been raised on the Tor by some anchorite living at a little distance. On the other hand the Life of St Collen portrays an empty summit, and Michael's cult had no widespread vogue until the eighth century. Whatever the truth about the chapel, the Abbey itself grew vigorously in size and fame.

Patrick's term as Abbot is not beyond credence. We are still free to suppose that the Apostle of Ireland did have some connection with the community. If he was born in Somerset he may have combined business with pleasure by paying a visit to his home country and trying to convert the piratical Irish settlers. As an alternative we could postulate another Patrick as the pioneer Abbot. Postulating other Patricks is, of course, dangerous. Among Victorian scholars (that critical and disintegratory crew) the concoction of 'other men of the same name' was an occupational disease, and in this instance it produced, not merely one, but four or five. Granted the ability to keep clear of such extravagances, it is fair to put forward an *ad hoc* Patrick as Abbot. The strange thing is that the Irish themselves were doing this as early as the ninth century. In a contemporaneous commentary on a text of that date, the writer asserts that 'Old Patrick' or Patrick Senior is buried at Glastonbury-of-the-Gaels, where the Irish, presumably either pilgrims or buccaneers, used to resort. 'Old Patrick' seems to have been invented solely to account for the Glastonbury tradition, which must therefore have already entrenched itself, and become too potent to brush aside.

A reasonable explanation would be that the Abbey possessed a relic supposed to prove that the saint had dwelt there. Given such a relic, the monks might have garnered up a few bones from their graveyard, called them the remains of St Patrick, and raised a monument over them. As to the relic itself, something of a documentary type would fit best. An ecclesiastic of Patrick's amazing stature must have had many friends and been much sought after. When his patron Germanus went to Britain and expounded the Lérins rule, Patrick is thought to have gone there too. Perhaps it was from him that Glastonbury's actual reforming abbot learned the latest news about the monastic practice of Europe. A letter or memorandum, treasured without being fully understood, is surely the most plausible basis for the legend of

7

Hagiography furnishes two sequels. The first has St Bridget for its protagonist. She was an Irishwoman of boundless vigour and charity, born illegitimately about 453. Concerned with a phase of spiritual vocation which Patrick and his disciples had rather neglected, Bridget took the veil at sixteen and persuaded other girls to join her. She spent the rest of a long life in semi-political activity and the foundation of convents, Kildare being the chief. Her tact and humour seem to have been extraordinarily endearing, and her special ministry to lepers, whom she washed with her own hands, helped to canonise her at once in public esteem. There is no trustworthy evidence that Bridget ever left Ireland, but when her cult penetrated Britain, a story grew up that she came to Bekery or Brideshay in Somerset, died there, and was buried at Glastonbury. In view of the Irish colonisation of that area the tale was not entirely fantastic, but it was, and is, most improbable. The monks doughtily exhibited relics – the foundress's necklace, her scrip, her distaff – and attracted a steady trickle of Irish pilgrims, who tested the relics' efficacy in curing their ailments, and did not always retire disappointed. Anybody who cares to invent a second Bridget, and locate her grave in the Abbey cemetery, is of course at liberty to do so.

More relevant is St Beon, whom the medieval writers identify with Benignus, Archbishop of Armagh in succession to Patrick. The identification will not stand up, since the Irish form of Benignus is Benen, and Beon is a distinct name. St Beon, however, still deserves our attention. While he belongs in the same little legendary constellation as Patrick and Bridget, his legend has a different shape from theirs. Patrick and Bridget are eminent figures in Ireland's history whom fabulists have dragged into a dubious association with Glastonbury. Beon, on the other hand, is a figure in Glastonbury's history whom fabulists have raised to a dubious eminence in Ireland. Regarding his alleged career, opinions may vary, but his right to a place here is incontestable. He is the first real Glastonbury character whom we can get more or less in focus and put a name to. With Beon's entry the purely legendary period ends.

In all likelihood Beon actually was an Irishman. According to his biographers an angel called him to Somerset in the 460s. Proceeding to Glastonbury Abbey he met St Patrick there. The great missionary advised him to become a hermit. He was to walk through the country till his staff put forth buds, and settle wherever the miracle occurred. So Beon set off accompanied by a young servant named Pincius. He did not have to walk far. At Meare he planted his staff, and it budded and swelled, and expanded into a tree. The place proved satisfactory in every respect but one. It was too far from the nearest drinkable water. Pincius had to make long journeys with a pitcher. When returning on a hot afternoon he lay down for a nap. Some facetious person removed the pitcher, but brought it back when the boy woke and grew genuinely alarmed. Pincius told his master a yarn to the effect that the pitcher had been concealed by the Devil, who, however, had failed to hang on to it when rebuked in the name of the Christian God. Beon decided that the water-carrying ought to stop. He commanded a spring to rise out of the ground beside his cell; and so it did.

The energetic hermit banked up a causeway through the marshes to Ynys-witrin, and often passed along it at night to say his prayers in the Old Church. On one of these trips he found his progress barred by a frightful demon. 'Bloody beast!' he shouted (the Latin is *cruentia bestia*), 'what are you doing here?' 'Waiting for you,' the demon retorted. Beon undauntedly advanced on him, brandishing a stick, and thrashed him so soundly that he tumbled into a bottomless pool and never came up.

Beon died in his Meare retreat. His remains lay there undisturbed till 1091, when the monks transferred them to the Abbey. The venerable skeleton cured several bystanders of intestinal worms. Shortly afterwards one of the brethren caught a fever. Somebody advised him to pray to Beon. He replied with a jocular remark, but soon regretted it. The saint pounced on him in a vision and boxed his ears, adding that a tooth had been stolen from his, Beon's, skull, and that if the thief did not put it back the Abbey would suffer. This affair seems to have been smoothed out, and we hear no more of St Beon. Disguised as 'St Benignus,' however, he continued to haunt the Abbey chronicles, and gave his name to a church in the town.

Chapter Three

ARTHUR

While Patrick with his humility came and went, the British province, abandoned by Rome, stood faltering on the edge of Europe in a somnambulistic independence. Years passed, and it stumbled and righted itself and stumbled again. Before the heathen broke through, however, one commanding leader arose, Glastonbury's eternal hero. According to report Arthur lies buried there; and the holy place may have meant more to him than a grave. Medieval romancers were to set the place and the hero side by side in a reciprocal splendour, the splendour of a Cup and a Crown. But in the fifth century that transfiguration was still far distant. Our immediate concern is to discover Britain's protector as he lived.

By 410 the Roman garrison had withdrawn, intent on continental business. An Empire distracted at the heart could no longer hold its outworks. Despite barbarian raids, the Britain which the legions resigned to fate was a civilised province. Local aristocrats, intermarried with Roman officials, formed a well-educated governing class. They spoke their own language, essentially Old Welsh, and also an oddly academic Latin, not yet vulgarised like the Latin of Gaul. They did not travel much; they regarded a journey overseas as an adventure – which indeed the Gothic and Vandal inroads had made it. They wrote elegant letters. Those which have survived are gentlemanly but rather cold-blooded. No mass wave of Mediterranean zeal, dynastic or monastic or theological, had thus far swept beyond the Channel. As the Roman glare faded, nevertheless, a frigid rival light began to gleam through the fog. The island was becoming itself, and making its first contribution to Christian thought and literature. Characteristically, this was a heresy; characteristically too, it was a tolerant, commonsensible-sounding heresy, which tried to dodge the Catholic mysteries and the accompanying historical issues.

Pelagius was the heresiarch whom Britain produced. He denied the Fall and the Atonement. Man, he declared, has neither a bias toward good nor a bias toward evil, and needs no supernatural intervention to save him. No act of Adam, no act of Christ, has essential meaning as an event. Anybody who does the best he can in obedience to Christ's moral teaching will go to everlasting beatitude. In England at least, after fifteen hundred years, it seems that Pelagius has made his point. At the time he encountered difficulties. His theory demanded a bolder break with Scripture and Christian origins than he or his contemporaries felt able to risk. Still, he won himself disciples in Britain, Gaul, and Italy, so that in 418 the Emperor banished him from Rome. In 421 that sentence was extended to all Pelagians. The terrible Augustine entered the controversy; Catholic writers denounced Pelagius as 'the enemy of grace'; and his following dwindled to a group in his native Britain, though, curiously enough, he had never preached there in person. The British group remained influential for several decades. By refusing significance to the localised facts which the Church built on, the heretics helped to foster a cloudiness and rootlessness in the British soul that affected the island's relationship with Christendom ever afterwards. Like an insecurely moored balloon, Britain constantly threatened to drift away. In that phenomenon Glastonbury had an ambiguous share; as we shall see.

The islanders themselves took over the stranded administration. Gradually the shortcomings of their centreless, un-institutionalised culture and outlook became apparent. A young Welsh chief named Vortigern asserted his sovereignty over all the ex-Roman land, through a feeble hereditary claim based on marriage to a descendant of the Emperor Maximus. Anxious for order, a faction saluted him as king. For a little while Roman legions reoccupied the south-east and his position was dubious, but then they sailed away for the last time, leaving Kent under a local ruler who submitted to him.

Vortigern was not yet in undisputed control, but he was probably the dominant figure in a more or less coherent governing body. His reign was the only epoch of united Celtic supremacy over anything like the whole of what is now England. The chroniclers represent him as proud, lecherous, and fundamentally cowardly. There is some reason to think that he was the nominee of a rich Celtic Nationalist group which aimed at a total rupture with the Roman tradition. He and his friends tried to curtail the influence of the Romano-British aristocracy – the men of mixed blood and imperial sentiment and ultramontane religion. Under Vortigern there was a weak revival of the old non-representative Celtic art. The source of inspiration has not been traced. Possibly a school or workshop in Wales, founded by refugee craftsmen from the Lake Village, had hung on through the Roman period far from the interference of interlopers. But the Neo-Celtic civilisation was decadent even in its youth. We get an impression of ostentation mingled with squalor; of elaborately dressed people in filthy tumbledown houses.

The Nationalists gave support to the Pelagian heresy, so that the bishops grew alarmed. This crisis was the primary reason for the arrival of Germanus of Auxerre, who came over as the personal envoy of Pope Celestine. Germanus combined a Christian vocation with a military and administrative background. The Imperial court, disturbed over barbarian raids, may have swayed the Pope's choice. On his advent in 429 the envoy summoned the chief heretics to a conference at St Albans. They came somewhat pompously, with all the marks of royal favour, but got the worst of the debate and lost prestige. Meanwhile savage bandits from Scotland and Germany were swooping into southern Britain. Led by the military apostle, the Britons routed one such mob mainly by shouting 'Hallelujah.' Germanus went home satisfied – prematurely.

The realm staggered on. In 446 an appeal for more Roman aid against the barbarians met with no response. The pro-Roman party suffered a temporary eclipse. Nationalism advanced. Pelagianism revived. Germanus revisited the island, in the teeth of bitter opposition from Vortigern. When he left he left for ever, and there were no more hallelujahs. Vortigern's monarchy was now fully established, but the foreign danger was growing worse. Unable to hold his borders against the raiding bands, the King convoked a council and offered a desperate proposal for playing off one foe against another. He would invite the pagan Angles and Saxons from Germany, and allot them land in Britain in return for their undertaking to keep out the northern marauders.

The council ingloriously agreed. Their chief was following Roman precedents, but without Roman experience or capacity. Very soon Hengist settled in Thanet with a fierce crew of warriors. At first he adhered to Vortigern's treaty, and chased the Picts back across the wall. Britain momentarily prospered. But Hengist saw the King's weaknesses, and skilfully exploited their social contacts. He handed over his beautiful daughter Rowena in exchange for Kent; he locked

Vortigern up after a banquet and extorted more territory still. So at any rate the chroniclers tell us, and they are right in principle. Six or seven years from the first landing, Angles, Saxons, and Jutes began to pour over the eastern coast by thousands, battering down resistance wherever they went. Initially they did not go far in serious numbers, but they went inexorably, and more and more colonists reinforced them. Flying parties of scouts roamed across the country at will, reaching the Irish Sea and the Bristol Channel before they turned back.

King Vortigern's death took place in the 460s. He had outlived his authority. If he really married Rowena as his second wife, his kinsfolk may have taken alarm at the prospect of a mongrel succession. Four or five upstarts divided the British realm. And then the unlooked-for thing happened. Rome returned.

She returned in the person of Ambrosius Aurelianus. His patrician family, though long domiciled in Britain, was more Roman than Celtic, and had steadily opposed the Vortigern clique. The utter discrediting of that clique gave him his opportunity. Acclaimed by patriots as king, he imposed a rough unity for military action at least, and took the field against the heathen. There are indications that he even organised a navy. The astonished invaders no longer had it all their own way. When they pushed Ambrosius back he pushed forward again. Heartened by his success, the Catholic foes of Pelagianism and Celtic Nationalism gathered round him. It would be an anachronism to speak of constitutional theory; but Ambrosius's followers did see Britain as in some hazy sense a part of the Roman Empire, even though the Empire itself had become largely nominal. They stamped that notion into the British soul. Rome's prestige unexpectedly recovered. After Ambrosius we find the title 'tribune' used as a name, Triphun; we find the legionary device of the Dragon adopted in Wales, and Welsh princes referred to, like some of the Emperors, as 'Draco'; we find even the far-away Britons of Strathclyde, in the Scottish Lowlands, calling themselves Romans.

Ambrosius's active life must have ended before the year 500. After his retirement the British kinglets continued to act in concert. They entrusted the overall command to a chief captain drawn from the Romano-British aristocracy, who had risen to distinction under Ambrosius. He gave the enemy a beating which discouraged them from further conquest. Afterwards a day came when the effort flagged, the Britons fell out among themselves, and the barbarians flowed westward to stay. But between Ambrosius's first counter-stroke and the final disintegration, there was a spell of sunshine lasting fifty or sixty years; and its light glinted on the armour of Arthur. For that, it seems, was the chief captain's name.

2

The only distinct contemporaneous voice is a voice associated with Glastonbury, that of the monk Gildas, whose acquaintance we have already made. From the cat's-cradle of denunciations and exhortations in his *liber querulus* we can disentangle a vague story. The rally begun by Ambrosius Aurelianus led, after many changes of fortune extending over forty-four years,[1] to a climactic victory at the 'siege of Mount Badon.' The Anglo-Saxon forces withdrew to the coast and the British confederacy took breath. A phase of peace and order ensued. But then a generation grew up who failed to appreciate what their fathers had done. (Gildas's voice has here an authentic ring.) Moral and political unity foundered. At the moment of writing, says the querulous monk, there are five contemptible principalities, and internal strife is fast ruining the island. Gildas's moment of writing is somewhere in the 540s.

Subsequent historians were to name Arthur as the victor of Badon. Yet Gildas does not mention him. The silence is peculiar and rather disturbing. Psychologically it may be no worse a puzzle than Aristotle's silence about his pupil Alexander the Great; but then we know about Alexander from so many other sources. What is the explanation? That Arthur never existed? But somebody must have led the Britons. Romancers long afterwards, trying to account for the slight to their hero, saw fit to invent a personal feud. There is no evidence for this view. Gildas's biographer, Caradoc of Llancarfan, mentions a rift but also a reconciliation. He adds that Gildas was at Glastonbury when Melwas imprisoned Guinevere on the Tor (an episode we have noted), and that

[1] This passage is obscure, but no other interpretation fits the course of events, or accommodates a related statement made by Gildas about his own birth.

when Arthur came with soldiers to rescue her, Gildas negotiated a treaty in Arthur's favour. Caradoc's is the sole arguably genuine tradition that brings them together, and it does not support the notion of a permanent spite.

A modern explanation of Gildas's silence is ecclesiastical rancour. It is alleged that when he wrote he had given up the British chiefs as fundamentally a bad lot and not worth commemorating. Gildas's Christianity was, indeed, aggressively Roman, and in some respects the British Church was still wandering away from Rome. The link had never been strong. The only serious papal dealing with Britain had been Celestine's not very successful assault on heresy in high places. In 500, despite the ascendancy of Ambrosius's party, the Church's Celtic provinces were almost adrift, and quite uninterested, moreover, in converting the heathen. By Gildas's time the British princes had added irresponsible ambition to heresy, and treason to schism, with such pertinacity that they were fearfully easy to despair of. Gildas saw the renewed invasion or threat of it as a judgment upon his fellow-countrymen, and his main purpose, unfortunately or otherwise, was not to write history but to bring this home to them.

Doubtless the interpretation is sound. Yet it falls short of explaining his Arthurian taciturnity. For Gildas does not assail the chiefs of the Badon period. He gives them credit for their success, and treats the rally as a last gleam of light before the darkness. His major targets are his mid-century contemporaries, whom, incidentally, he does name. Of course Arthur personally may have come under his theological disapproval. Even that does not seem to fit: Arthur belongs so clearly to the 'Roman' revival, not to the 'Celtic' Pelagian separatist movement. However, the religious theory will serve as a stop-gap. We may perhaps imagine some sort of apostasy or revolt which made Arthur unmentionable, and it is a fact that two or three Saints' Lives portray him as anti-clerical. Farther on I offer another suggestion. Gildas's Complaining Book does at any rate show us the outlines of the last effort, and does record the enigmatic engagement at 'Mount Badon,' where the British army must have been led by somebody.

For the same phase of operations there is also the important negative witness of the *Anglo-Saxon Chronicle*. This gives an account of the invaders' progress in Britain. 'Progress' is the operative word. Reverses and retreats are omitted, though scholarly English historians such as the Venerable Bede admit that they happened. The entries from 456 to 530 concern the affairs of Kent, Sussex, and Hampshire or Wessex. In 473 Hengist and Aesc win a victory in Kent; in 488 Aesc becomes King of Kent, beginning a 24-year reign . . . and then we hear nothing more of Kent within the period stated. In 477 Aelle lands near Selsey and chases the Britons into the Sussex Weald; in 491 he takes Pevensey . . . and then we hear nothing more of Sussex. In 495 Cerdic and Cynric, with five ships, disembark in Hampshire; in 501 another chief lands at Portsmouth; in 508 Cerdic and Cynric win a major victory. There is one last Hampshire landing in 514. Some fighting occurs on the Wessex front during 519 and 527, but nothing decisive and nothing that need be more than the skirmishing of advance parties. Clearly the West Saxon settlement does not extend far as an effective political entity. It is not till 530 that the conquerors occupy the Isle of Wight. As late at 552 they are still battling with Britons at Salisbury.

That is the *Chronicle* picture, and, broadly speaking, archæology has not yet supplanted it, though we now know of other settlements round the Wash and the Humber. The invaders overrun Kent, but after 473 they make no substantial advances from it from many years. They inaugurate Sussex, but fail to push far beyond the Downs, or to break through toward London along the Roman road from Chichester. They establish an embryonic Wessex, but from 514 till 530 or later it has only a nuisance value on the British flank. Moreover, each major shift in area comes fairly soon after the last victory recorded in the previous area. The Kentish chiefs apparently cease to gain ground in 473, and in 477 Aelle tries Sussex. Aelle's last success is in 491, and in 495 Cerdic tries Hampshire. The actual dates will not bear much emphasis, but there is a clear impression of British counter-measures discouraging the heathen, first in Kent, then in Sussex, and after 514 everywhere. The date indicated by Welsh annals for Badon is 518. Subtracting Gildas's forty-four years, we get 474 for Ambrosius's first victory, presumably against Hengist in Kent. Both dates fit the *Chronicle* remarkably well.

British history dives underground for a long time and bobs up again in the *Historia Brittonum*. The extant text of this work is a revision made by Nennius, a cleric in the household of the Bishop of Bangor, around 800. The scribe gives a fantastic account of Vortigern – it even has dragons in it – and proceeds to the campaign after his death. Nennius is the first historian to name the officer who took over the command from Ambrosius.

Arthur fought against the Saxons alongside the kings of the Britons, but he himself was the leader in the battles (*dux bellorum*). The first battle was at the mouth of the river which is called Glein. The next four were on the banks of another river, which is called Dubglas and is in the region Linnuis. The sixth was upon the river which is called Bassas. The seventh was in the wood of Celidon; that is, Cat Coit Celidon. The eighth was by Castle Guinnion, in which Arthur carried on his shoulders an image of St Mary Ever-Virgin, and on that day the pagans were put to flight, and there was a great slaughter of them, through the strength of Our Lord Jesus Christ and of the holy Mary his maiden-mother. The ninth was in the City of the Legion. The tenth was on the bank of the river which is called Tribruit. The eleventh was on the hill called Agned. The twelfth was on Mount Badon, in which – on that one day – there fell in one onslaught of Arthur's nine hundred and sixty men; and none slew them but he alone, and in all his battles he remained victor.

One manuscript tells about a pilgrimage made by Arthur just before the Badon campaign.

Arthur had gone to Jerusalem, where he had caused to be made a cross of the same size as the life-giving Cross, and after it had been consecrated he had fasted and kept vigil and prayed by it for three days together, asking that by this wood the Lord would give him victory over the pagans, which was so done. And he carried with him the image of St Mary.

If that reverence for the Cross is a fact, Arthur was assuredly no Pelagian. However, the addition is probably medieval.

As an appendix to his book Nennius subjoins what he describes as *Mirabilia* – Marvels. Here he mentions . . .

. . . a marvel in the region which they call Buelt. For there is a heap of stones, and on the top of the heap one stone bearing the footprint of a dog. When they hunted the boar Troit, Cabal which was the dog of Arthur the soldier, put his foot on that stone and marked it; and Arthur afterwards piled up a heap of stones and that stone on top, on which was the dog's footprint, and called it Carn Cabal. And men will come and carry away that stone for a day and a night, and the next morning there it is back again on its heap.

In Ercing or Herefordshire . . .

There is a burial mound near a spring which is known as Licat Anir, and the name of the man who is buried in the mound is Anir. He was the son of Arthur the soldier, and Arthur himself killed him there and buried him. And when men come to measure the length of the mound, they find it sometimes six feet, sometimes nine, sometimes twelve, and sometimes fifteen. Whatever length you find it at one time, you will find it different at another, and I myself have proved this to be true.

Whatever the explanation of the last overwhelming statement, two points emerge. First, Arthur was not a king but a general. Secondly, there was some grim tradition about a murderous quarrel with his son.

Sceptics have tried to undermine Nennius's testimony, but as regards the main story there are considerations in his favour. On his own showing he is utterly artless, a compiler and nothing more. His history is a pile of bric-à-brac heaped up virtually anyhow. He is so patently not a literary contriver that we can be fairly sure he is really collecting older materials, not inventing the narrative himself. Also, the queer list of battles is to some extent its own confirmation. The place-names are unrecognisable now, and even in those days they can hardly have been familiar. A fabricator would have given familiar names and a comprehensible account, as Geoffrey of Monmouth did when he took up the theme. Very possibly Nennius has lumped together several separate items under the single evocative name of Arthur. But the likelihood of a certain correspondence to fact can scarcely be dodged.

The tenth-century *Annales Cambriæ*[1] have two Arthurian entries.

[1] See preface.

518: The battle of Badon in which Arthur carried the cross of Our Lord Jesus Christ, for three days and three nights, on his shoulders, and the Britons were the victors.
539: The battle of Camlaun in which Arthur and Medraut were slain; and there was death in England and Ireland.

Lastly, our friend William of Malmesbury has this to say:

The strength of the Britons decayed, their diminished hopes went backwards; and straightway they would have come to ruin, had not Ambrosius, the sole survivor of the Romans, who was monarch of the realm after Vortigern, repressed the overweening barbarians through the distinguished achievement of the warlike Arthur. This is that Arthur of whom the trifling of the Britons talks so much nonsense even to-day; a man clearly worthy not to be dreamed of in fallacious fables, but to be proclaimed in veracious histories, as one who long sustained his tottering country, and gave the shattered minds of his fellow-citizens an edge for war. Finally, at the siege of Mount Badon, relying upon the image of the mother of the Lord which he had sewn upon his armour, he made head single-handed against nine hundred of the enemy and routed them with incredible slaughter.

That is succinct and surely rather agreeable. It is also valuable as proof of the existence of an Arthurian cycle, at least in oral form, before Geoffrey of Monmouth. William brings us to the lifetime of Geoffrey himself, whose loquacity about Arthur is all too notorious. But we cannot set him alongside the historians.

Who, then, was Arthur?

All modern conjecture starts from the phrase *dux bellorum* which Nennius applies to him. The most fruitful explanation is that of Sir John Rhys. Nennius's phrase represents an old Roman military title which the British administration kept up. Rome's defensive system in Britain provided for three permanent generals. There was the Dux Britanniarum, who had charge in the north; there was the Comes Littoris Saxonici, who protected the south-east coast; and towards the end there was the Comes Britanniarum, who could go anywhere with a mobile field-army whenever an emergency threatened. When the legions left, the first title was in abeyance, but the other two persisted. Ambrosius Aurelianus may have exercised one of his few rights as king to appoint a Comes Britanniarum as Captain-General for the province.

This was Arthur or Artorius, now held to have been a Roman-blooded aristocrat born about 470. In his perilous office he commanded regular contingents supplied by the princes. But he also formed a picked company of his own, trained in the Roman arts of war, and above all (here is Professor Collingwood's brilliant surmise) in cavalry fighting. During the Empire's long decline the Roman mailed horseman had risen to lordship of the field. When available, he dominated all battles. His spectre was to haunt Europe a thousand years, losing Agincourt for the French. The last Imperial Comes Britanniarum had six mounted regiments. Hengist's followers and immediate successors had nothing comparable, nor did they know much about armour, or about the disciplined tactics that go with cavalry fighting. Arthur scraped together the last remnants of Roman skill, taught the smiths to forge armour and the troops to manage their horses, and instituted a mobile squadron that could hurtle from place to place carrying all before it. Hence the knights. Arthur's Badon exploit is exaggerated, but not senselessly exaggerated. Constantine the Great is said to have routed an army with only twelve horsemen. Panic once let loose can easily get a hold on superstitious barbarians.

As to the geography of the twelve battles, there has been much debate. One theory places them all in Scotland. It is claimed that the victories of a northern Arthur have been superimposed on those of the southern leaders. This would be more plausible if Nennius had been a Scotsman. There is a case for the view that part of the story belongs to Sussex. But the City of the Legion would seem to be Caerleon or Chester. Caerleon is too far west, unless we postulate a very roundabout sea-raid. Given a fluid situation in Yorkshire or Lincolnshire, which the *Anglo-Saxon Chronicle* does not cover, a vanguard action at Chester is not impossible. It might have been a renewal of early raids 'as far as to the western sea,' which Gildas mentions as happening before the rally. Linnuis could be Lindsey, adjoining the Humber. These are mere guesses. For the present the problem of the minor battles is best abandoned, with the bare note that they probably cover a wide area, and confirm the concept of Arthur's mobility.

Mount Badon, however, looms so much larger than the

rest in Gildas and Nennius – as also in Bede, who draws on Gildas – that it does call for identification. We would expect it to be a hill-fort. There are two favourite candidates, Badbury Rings in Dorset, and Liddington Castle just south of Swindon, which has another Badbury close beside it. The objection to the first is political. Arthur might have come there to defeat a foray by Cerdic, but the West Saxons were not yet important enough for their vicissitudes to affect the position as a whole. The various groups of settlers were not united. There is no serious question of concerted action on their part, or of a treaty in one zone imposing a truce on others. What we have to envisage is the defeat of one or two elements in the Anglo-Saxon complex, those being such that the defeat was a major military event and a heavy blow to the morale of all the colonists.

In the period from 500 to 520, only two groups answered to that requirement. The Kentish community was senior to the rest, wealthy, firmly consolidated, and governed by a king of recognised rank. It is quite likely that only the Kentish-men were capable of a regular campaign large enough for the immediate fate of the invasion to turn on it. Conversely, any fighting which did not involve them could scarcely have had Badonic results. Aelle's coastal kingdom in Sussex was less powerful, but its head, according to Bede, enjoyed a primacy of honour and was acknowledged as Bretwalda, or paramount chief of all his compatriots in the island.

These facts transfer the focus of our attention to the Liddington Badon. It is far over, but not too far, and it belongs in the strategic picture as we know this to have presented itself to British minds. The enormous defensive line called the Wansdyke was almost certainly constructed under Ambrosius, to defend the south-west against an army marching from the Thames Valley. The wild Saxon raiding of the early years seems to have planted a few short-lived settlements in Berkshire. Ambrosius apparently feared that Hengist would move up from Kent to reinforce these advanced posts, and then swing left into Wilts and Somerset, the heartland of British territory. One of his first measures, therefore, was to order the making of the Dyke. Its impressive ditch and rampart run fifty miles from Inkpen through Savernake Forest, along the Marlborough Downs, past Bath and Stantonbury and thence brokenly to the Bristol Channel. It faces north, it belongs to the right period, and history records no other strategic situation which would account

77

for it. The dreaded offensive did not at once materialise, and the Berkshire outposts presumably fell to the Britons during the 470s. But a later thrust from Kent along the anticipated route would have been likely enough.

Liddington Hill itself is a ridge rising nine hundred feet above sea-level. From the railway it is a conspicuous landmark just before the train enters Swindon; it is at the western end – or rather angle – of the range which forms the south side of the Vale of the White Horse. An army from the lower Thames trying to break into central Wiltshire, and thence into Somerset, would have advanced along the range or the Vale itself and turned left near Swindon to march through the gap to Marlborough by the Roman road. And it is here precisely that we strike the fortifications. 'Liddington Castle' is a huge ramparted earthwork at the western shoulder of Liddington Hill, commanding the entrance to the gap. It is the highest and nearly the foremost point of a system of defence in depth; there are many earthworks in the district, but the Castle is the most formidable, and overlooks the most country. Toward Swindon it is precipitous. Round by the gap, however, there are gentler slopes well suited to a cavalry sortie. We may leave it an open question whether or not British contingents would have engaged the approaching Saxons in the debatable land farther down the Thames. What is certain is that Liddington would have been exactly the spot for Arthur to await the invaders with his main mobile force, ready to pounce as they crowded into the gap on their way to Marlborough.

The following, then, could have been the shape of the British rally from Ambrosius onward. The picture fits the records, such as they are, and the archæological evidence, for what it is worth.

By 473 or thereabouts the Angles, Saxons, and Jutes had established a large colony in Kent and a number of smaller ones elsewhere in eastern England, not specified in the *Chronicle*. Parties of spoilers made raids in all directions. But Ambrosius checked the raids, and then moved victoriously south-eastward to seal off Kent. Hengist and his successor, who had inherited that civilised county almost intact, henceforth confined their efforts to organising a kingdom there, the first coherent political unit in Anglo-Saxondom. Learning that the free-for-all scramble by way of Kent had come to an end, the next migrant chief of any consequence, Aelle, landed farther west near Selsey. He too made progress, but a British counter-attack eventually hemmed him in to a coastal strip. It was in the Sussex campaign that Arthur first distinguished himself. The shift was now repeated. By-passing Sussex as unprofitable, Cerdic and other leaders occupied Southampton and Portsmouth. Over the next fifteen years these colonists received reinforcements and encroached very gradually on Hampshire. Arthur meanwhile, as Comes Britanniarum, was developing his cavalry army elsewhere, but it seemed only a question of time before he turned south.

During the second decade of the sixth century the Sussex Bretwalda or his colleague in Kent, foreseeing the British counter-offensive, resolved on a march in force into enemy territory. For this project the resources and population of the south-eastern kingdoms were now adequate. The plan was to advance up the Thames and penetrate the British heartland by way of the south side of the White Horse Vale, as the Danes were to do many years later. Some time after 515 a combined host assembled and began to push up the river, gathering reinforcements among the small tribes which (to judge from archæology) had crept into Middlesex. British infantry manned the Wansdyke, while a detachment in the rear contained Cerdic. Arthur himself waited with his knights in the Liddington fort. The allies besieged it, but the knights made a sortie, threw them into confusion, and chased the survivors home again. The effort had been too great to repeat, and the Bretwalda's miscalculation so discouraged the colonists elsewhere that until 530 they made no further significant progress.

It was victory, but it was still not enough. The Britons complacently forgot how to conquer. Fewer and fewer soldiers learned to train horses or to fight from the saddle, and in peacetime Arthur had no control over the military curriculum. The shadow of a mysterious failure overhangs him. He saved Britain, yet he never achieved recognised power in the State. He was sincerely Christian, yet the Church had little love for him. At length he was summoned from the twilight of an honourable but helpless retirement to take part in a civil war. And Medraut or Modred proved his death.

Such, more or less, must be the historical Arthur. There is also the traditional Arthur. But indeed the distinction is artificial. Traditions are evidence, and they grow in a historical context. To the context and the traditions we may turn.

3

Arthur's rally failed and the Anglo-Saxons resumed their
westward march. They moved slowly, consolidating their
gains and imposing their language as they went. No historian
believes nowadays that the Britons were merely exterminated;
but they were thrust down into a very subordinate position,
and dubbed 'Welshmen' or foreigners. Wedges of Anglo-
Saxondom split British territory into three zones. There
was a Strathclyde Wales extending northward from Lanca-
shire into Scotland, and a West Wales or Dumnonia stretch-
ing from Somerset to Land's End. Between came Wales
proper. It clung to its nationhood, and indeed has never lost
it. Princes reigned, bishops upheld the Cross, merchants
and missionaries travelled, warrior chieftains carried on a
delaying warfare. Ireland, Cornwall and the Celtic outpost
of Brittany lay within the purview of the sea-going Welshmen.
Most of our relics of British civilisation have come down to
us from Wales.

Despite all the public and private crimes castigated by
Gildas, the staunch little courts that nestled among the hills
had some ground for their pride. They clung to the Christian
heritage, less and less confused by expiring Pelagianism, and
alone in the island they supported a scholarly class. Con-
noisseurs of law declare themselves profoundly impressed by
the lucid language and rich vocabulary of the Welsh codes.
The explanation is that the legal writers, official secretaries
and bards worked in comradeship. Their functions overlapped.
History and genealogy, for instance, were studies necessary in
common. It was chiefly the bards who transmitted the praises
of the famous. Later came the authors of saints' lives. Out of
the fragments descending from that stubborn age, together
with a few allied fragments from Celtic backwaters, there
emerges a bardic and hagiographic Arthur whom we must
now try to assimilate to the *dux bellorum*.

This Arthur is manifestly a human being, though seen
through an enchanted haze. But some have alleged that the
pagan Britons worshipped a god or demigod with the same
name, and that myths about the god Arthur, lingering into

Christian times, transferred themselves to the man Arthur. Modern explorers of the Celtic arcana have described this deity in so many different ways that it is hard to take him seriously. However, the traces of him in poetry and folk-lore are not absolutely nil, and this is the place to examine his pretensions, since, if they are once admitted, all further reconstruction is hopeless.

We catch a glimpse of him as a wind-god: he is Arthur o' Bower, best known to the public nowadays through the improbable medium of *Squirrel Nutkin*. We catch another glimpse of him as a bird-god: according to *Notes and Queries*, an old gentleman at Marazion once advised a visitor not to shoot at a raven because it might be Arthur. We see him – possibly – as a leader of the Wild Hunt, in the fellowship of Gwyn ap Nudd, whom we encountered on Glastonbury Tor. This 'Arthur' rides through the thunderclouds mustering the souls of the dead, and penetrates into Annwn or Hades. Anthropologists, of course, have embroidered him vastly. Earlier ones identified him with the Gaulish Artæan Mercury, a culture-hero who taught mankind useful arts such as farming. Later ones, emphasising the story of the deadly wound and destined return, have made him a dying-and-reviving spirit of vegetation, figuring in peasant fertility rites.

While most of the data and most of the speculations are reconcilable, it is vital to realise that there are no ancient documents or explicit traditions which even begin to reconcile them. The supernatural Arthur is almost wholly a reconstruction, a Piltdown God. Admittedly he can be strung together after a fashion. As a wind-spirit he is appropriate to the Wild Hunt; and birds are at least airborne. Then again, there is a curious link between the tales told of him in association with Gwyn and the nature myths personified in fertility demons. When the Celts connected a spot with death, they sometimes also connected it with life. Ghost-lore merged into agricultural magic. Departed heroes and their tutelary spirits, to whom the secrets of life and death were an open book, became associated and even equated with the genii of fertility. Standing stones – such as those noted in Gwyn's neighbourhood at Pembrey – seem particularly to attract such beliefs. Gwyn himself pretty certainly has a spring-ritual aspect. In one Arthurian legend he is introduced fighting a rival every May Day for the love of a damsel. To quote Professor Krappe:

The chthonic powers, i.e. the dead, are in fact instrumental in the production of grain and fruit. . . . The souls of the dead may go into trees, becoming indistinguishable from genuine vegetation spirits. . . . A mixture of ancestor cult and worship of vegetation divinities is also represented by certain tale types belonging to the cycle of the Wild Hunt.

Thus we can manœuvre the supernatural Arthur, as Wild Huntsman, into the modern anthropologists' realm of ideas; and if we care to squeeze the last drop out of every possible parallel, we may remark that the Egyptian Osiris was both a fertility spirit and a culture-hero.

But all this is fantasy. Nobody has found a trace in the British pantheon of any such elaborate being. Some scholars boldly interpolate him, and then proceed to deny the human Arthur, attributing his entire legend to the expanding cultus of the god. That is hardly legitimate. Arthur the god, as distinct from Arthur the man, is almost imperceptibly insignificant, and so formless as to elude definition. Moreover, he would have had a stern task growing to a major divinity in the face of the Church. Diluted pagan survival is one thing, creative pagan recovery is another. Even if we were to suppose that 'Arthur' was adopted for cryptic reasons as the divine patron of Ambrosius's rally, we would confront the paradox that the sour, uncompromising Gildas approved of the rally and regarded its leaders as Christian champions. A fair conjecture is that some Britons somewhere did practise the cult of such a deity; that the real Arthur was either named after him, or looked upon (in accord with vestigial Druidism) as an avatar of him; and that the great general's exploits gave an impetus to what was left of the cult, so that it lived on in Christian times as a durable collection of fairy-tales, intermingling with the real Arthur's saga to rough out the figure of a popular hero neither fully human nor fully mythical. All of which may appear more relevant when we come to the Grail. Meanwhile, in evaluating the legends and poems, it is well to remember how faint the impression of this god actually is. It is safest to seek the centre of gravity on the human side. Even in recent times, pretty tall tales have been told about American frontier characters such as Davy Crockett, but nobody feels the need to postulate a celestial Crockett.

During the sixth and seventh centuries, a mass of saga material started gathering round the heroes of Britain. It was purely oral, and at first without any scheme. As it grew, however, it began to make exorbitant demands on the memory. The bards took to organising their repertoire by summing up each story in a key phrase or paragraph and grouping the summaries, probably for ritual reasons, in sets of three. They bound each 'triad' together with a heading that applied in common to all three principal characters, or sometimes to the main themes. A fanciful example may illustrate what a triad was like. If some bard had set himself to recite stories out of Shakespeare, he might have invented something like this: 'Three Jealous Islanders. The first was Othello in Cyprus. The second was Posthumus in Britain. The third was Leontes in Sicily.' Plainly the mere act of devising such a triad would help to fix the plots in the memory, and if the bard, having finished with Othello, recollected that Othello was one of the Three Jealous Islanders, his encore would be ready-made. He could go straight on to Posthumus.

Many triads of undoubted antiquity have survived in medieval Welsh manuscripts. Their corresponding sagas cannot often be reconstructed. The headings are sometimes esoteric, sometimes more or less obvious. We read about the 'Three Pillars of Battle,' the 'Three Faithful Warbands,' and so forth. Arthur's name occurs often. He is well known but by no means purely heroic or invincible. There is possibly the slight suggestion of an early adventurous career as a feuding irregular, with recognised authority coming later. Arthur is one of the Three Red Ravagers and one of the Three Frivolous Bards. He is guilty of one of the Three Wicked Uncoverings – the digging up of a buried human head with miraculous properties. (It was supposed to restrain invaders. Arthur said Britain should rely on valour alone.) But nothing marks him off more clearly than the unique treatment which tacks him on to more than one triad as a climactic interloper. Thus:

Three Very Famous Prisoners of the Island of Britain. Llyr Lledyeith who was imprisoned by Eurosswyd. And the second, Mabon vab Modron. And the third, Gweir vab Gweiryoed. And there was one who was more famous than all three: he was three nights in the prison of Kaer Oeth and Anoeth, and three nights in the prison of Wenn Pendragon, and three nights in the magic prison beneath the flagstone of Echymeint. This famous Prisoner was Arthur. And the same youth released him from each of these three prisons; Goreu vab Custennin, his cousin.

In reading these summaries one gets an impression of vanished legendary cycles and foundered epics.

The triads contain some of the oldest Arthurian allusions, and also some of the most remarkable. Consider, for instance, 'The Three Stout Swineherds of the Island of Britain.' It exists in several forms. Here is the fullest version of the lines about the Stout Swineherd, or rather deputy-swineherd, whose activities involved Arthur.

> The third was Trystan son of Tallwch, who guarded the swine of March son of Meirchion while the swineherd had gone on a message to Essyllt to bid her appoint a meeting with Trystan. Now Arthur and Marchell and Cai and Bedwyr undertook to go and make an attempt on him, but they proved unable to get possession of as much as one porker either as a gift or as a purchase, whether by fraud, by force, or by theft.

In the rustic surroundings, it is quite distressing to find so many friends. Arthur, Kay the Seneschal, Bedevere, Mark, Tristan, and Essyllt or Isolde, the latter already in love with Tristan . . . yet the whole assembly of paladins has no better business than to squabble over Mark's pigs. I do not think there is ground for assuming that the pigs are earth-spirits or symbols or anything more than pigs. In the Celtic economy the pig bulked very large, as he long continued to do among the Celts of Ireland. He was a much more dignified character than the Anglo-Saxons have made him. Hence a pig-raid is not an impossible adventure for a Celtic chief. A parallel occurs in the Hindu epic *Mahabharata*, where all the knights of Hastinapur ride out with their banners and chariots and retainers on a cattle-rustling expedition. Arthur's leadership in this exploit is made clear by the fact that one version of the triad mentions only him, without 'Marchell and Cai and Bedwyr.'

Besides the Tristan triad, there are some other early ones which refer to features of the Arthurian Legend as we know it. One speaks of Arthur's wife Guinevere (Gwenhwyvaer); in fact it credits him with three wives, all named Guinevere. Several deal with the wicked Medraut or Modred, who sounds like a contemporary of Arthur rather than a nephew. Medraut and his followers break into Arthur's castle at Kelliwic in Cornwall and 'consume all.' Medraut drags Guinevere from her chair and strikes her. Arthur makes a retaliatory attack on the castle of Medraut, and leaves neither food nor drink in the castle or the district. Medraut's eventual revenge takes the form of a treacherous treaty with the Saxons. Arthur fights him at Camlan in a complicated battle with many changes of side by combatants. Both leaders fall.

We possess triads about the personages at Arthur's court, but most are too late to be of value. They refer, at best, only to medieval Welsh adaptations of French and English romances. One of them does seem independent, and an interesting triad it is. The 'Three Knights who kept the Grail' are Illtyd, Cadoc, and Peredur. We shall be meeting Illtyd very shortly, and under surprising circumstances.

Not all the bardic poetry perished. Four medieval Welsh books preserve a certain amount of it. The *Book of Taliesin* and the *Book of Aneirin* contain poems attributed to those bards, who lived in Arthur's time or soon after, and a few may be genuine. About Taliesin practically nothing is known. Aneirin was a northerner of Strathclyde who lived dangerously. He marched with the British soldiers on a Yorkshire campaign, and escaped almost alone out of a frightful defeat at Catraeth or Catterick because (so he tells us) 'of my fine songs.' His epic *Gododdin* gives a description of the war, and a glimpse of the late British civilisation. It is quite Arthurian. The young noblemen who intend to fight assemble to the country of Manaw Gododdin – roughly Midlothian – from all parts of Britain, and learn their knighthood in martial exercises. The atmosphere is Christian: warriors go to church before battle, and do penance for their sins. The lord's court where they meet is an imposing institution made up of many buildings. There is a reference to baths of the Roman type. The inmates gather to feast in the great hall round an open fire, by the light of rush candles and pinewood torches. They are dressed in silks and colourful plaids, with brooches and chaplets and amber beads. Their drinking vessels are of silver and gold, horn and glass. Three hundred knights go to Catterick to expel the Saxons, but after a week's fighting against impossible odds hardly any remain save the valiant Aneirin himself.

Besides the pair of books named after the bards, there are two miscellanies, the *Black Book of Carmarthen* and the *Red Book of Hergest*. These four volumes are not easy reading. The sense too often depends on conventionalised hints which no longer hint at anything, and the extreme terseness, the staccato effect, and the violent, disjointed imagery, make prolonged study a painful task. It is unfair to read the poems at all, since the bards meant them to be sung, but no alternative exists.

Arthur does figure, but not prominently. While the scantiness of allusion is disappointing, it at least confirms that the poems are early. If they were forged outgrowths of the twelfth-century Arthur fashion they would give themselves away by saying far more, as the late triads do, and we would have to reject them altogether for the same reason. Actually there are ten or a dozen stray lines about Arthur's horse, his kindred, and his general prowess – comparison to Arthur is the highest praise for a warrior – and there are four poems deserving special attention.

In the *Black Book of Carmarthen*, the 'Song of the Graves' enumerates many fallen heroes. Often a definite spot is given for the burial-place, but one exception catches the eye.

> '*Anoeth bid bet y arthur*'

sings the poet – an obscure line, to be translated, roughly, 'A mystery the grave of Arthur.'

Farther on in the same book is a poem about Geraint of Devon and his valour at the Battle of Llongborth.

> At Llongborth saw I, hewing with steel,
> The brave men of Arthur,
> Emperor and director of toil.

The word 'emperor' (*amherawdyr*) is rather exciting. It is the Latin *imperator*, which did mean 'emperor,' but also had the older meaning of 'commander-in-chief.' By the sixth century the only surviving Emperor was far off in Byzantium. Nobody in the West ventured to use the title till the Pope conferred it on Charlemagne in 800. But during an invasion, under the Roman defensive plan, the Comes Britanniarum would automatically be *imperator* for the whole province, not with any political implications, but in the ancient soldierly sense. Thus the Welsh word applied to Arthur confirms the view that he stepped into a high Roman military office which the British administration kept up. As for the locale of the poem, Llongborth is taken to be Langport in Somerset. The Saxons fought there in 710 against the army of Devon under a Prince Geraint. If this is the right battle, it appears that the West Welsh had a military contingent called 'Arthur's Men' long after his death. But the reference may be contemporary. Welsh commentators say that an earlier Geraint went with Arthur to Langport to intercept a strong party of sea-raiders, either Saxon or more probably Irish.

The last Arthur poem in the *Black Book* is more informative. It looks like a dialogue from a lost epic. Arthur demands admittance to a fortress. The gatekeeper insists that he first name all his followers and give their qualifications.

> 'Who is the porter?'
>
> 'Glewlwyd Gavaelvawr.
>   Who asks it?'
>
> 'Arthur and Cai.'
>
> 'What following hast thou?'
>
> 'The best of men are mine.'
>
> 'Into my house thou shalt not come,
>   Unless thou plead for them.'
>
> 'I will plead for them,
>   And thou shalt see them.'

And so on. Arthur mentions a dozen or so companions, with complimentary phrases about their exploits. 'The accomplished Bedwyr' is one. Cai, however, is chief, next to Arthur himself.

Here we get the picture of Arthur as acknowledged head of a band of knights. He has the same status in the only long poem about him in the *Book of Taliesin*. This is entitled 'The Spoils of Annwn' and is by far the most remarkable of the group. It is a pre-Christian version of the Quest of the Grail. Arthur and his company venture into Annwn or Hades, the realm of Gwyn ap Nudd, to bring back a miraculous cauldron of inspiration and plenty. The bard goes with them, and describes, or rather does not describe, their progress. His meaning is esoteric and often quite uncertain. Here is a stanza:

> Beyond the Glass Fort they had not seen Arthur's valour.
> Three score hundred stood on the wall:
> Hard it was found to converse with the sentinel.

Three freights of Prydwen were they that went with Arthur,
Seven alone did they return from Caer Goludd.

The Glass Fort, which guards the gate to the underworld, supplies another link besides Gwyn with the Glass Island. Prydwen is Arthur's boat, and 'three freights' implies a series of ferryings over a narrow strip of water. Arthur finally reaches Caer Vanddwy, a place which another poem specifically associates with Gwyn. At the end of each stanza comes the statement that only seven returned. Taliesin (or Pseudo-Taliesin) intimates that he was one of the seven. Perhaps, like Aneirin, he escaped because of his fine songs.

In the absence of an agreed interpretation, or even an agreed translation, it is useless to argue about the relationships between Arthur, Annwn, Gwyn, the Glass Fort, Caer Vanddwy, the cauldron of plenty, and Glastonbury. The indisputable thing is that the poem entangles Arthur in a network of otherworldly themes, a network which takes in Glastonbury and the quest for a miraculous vessel. It is just conceivable that both the 'Spoils' poem and the *Life of St Collen* derive from some sort of magic mime or initiation rite anciently performed on the Tor, reflecting the imaginative connection between the personnel of the Wild Hunt and the powers of fertility.

Arthur as the chief of a military order, Arthur as the performer of marvellous labours – the bardic hero emerges much more fully in a prose fairy-tale entitled *Kulhwch and Olwen*. (Kulhwch is pronounced, roughly, Kil-hooch, with the *ch* as in *loch*.) This was first committed to writing in the eleventh century. The present text dates from about 1100, and in it the original story, which is not Arthurian, has been artificially woven into the Arthur mythos: an anticipation of the process that took place a little later when Arthurian romance became fashionable in England.

Kulhwch has a wicked stepmother who lays a spell on him so that he cannot marry unless he wins Olwen, the daughter of Yspydaden the Giant. Yspydaden is destined to die when Olwen weds, hence he tries to delay the marriage by making extravagant conditions. Arthur and his followers come to the suitor's aid. The catalogue of these followers runs to two hundred-odd. Some of them are credible human beings, but some are monstrosities from primitive fable. We hear of Sol, who can stand all day on one foot; of Clust, who can hear an ant fifty miles off; of Medyr, who can shoot an arrow through the legs of a wren in Ireland; of Sgilti, who can run along the tops of trees; of Gwadyn Ossol, who can stamp a mountain out flat; and several more with equally astonishing gifts. Gwyn ap Nudd is on the list. Many of the ensuing adventures unquestionably belong to the Arthur tradition, not to the original tale of Kulhwch. One, the hunting of the boar, is actually mentioned by Nennius as an Arthurian exploit.

Yspydaden imposes twelve labours on his intending son-in-law. Kulhwch must clear the bushes from a large hill, sow it with wheat, and bring in the harvest to make bread for the wedding banquet, all in a single day. He must reap a crop of flax under similar difficulties; he must collect a peculiar kind of honey, and a supposedly unobtainable vessel; he must fetch a magical basket, a magical drinking horn, a magical harp, and a magical cauldron (not from Hades, however, but from Ireland). He must get a monster's tusk, a witch's blood, and a very special set of milk bottles; and he must bring the comb and scissors from between the ears of the boar Twrch Trwyth. These labours entail many subsidiary labours – twenty-five, to be precise – and put Arthur's resources under a heavy strain. However, he triumphs. The climax is the great boar-hunt. With grievous casualties, the knights chase Trwyth from Esgeir Oervel in Ireland to Porth Cleis in Wales, and thence to Preseleu, and to Cwm Kerwyn, and to Pelumyawc, and around the head of the Bristol Channel, where they wrest the scissors from him. He flees to Cornwall and makes a last stand, but at length he loses the comb too and disappears into the sea. The labours accomplished, Kulhwch comes to claim his bride, and one of Yspydaden's enemies cuts the giant's head off.

Kulhwch and Olwen very nearly exhausts what is left to us of the literature. There is a thirteenth-century Welsh work entitled *The Dream of Rhonabwy* which introduces Arthur, but the writer is out of touch with the past. Moreover, after 1170 or thereabouts, those Welshmen who revert to the Arthurian theme are themselves influenced by the outsiders who have taken it over and transformed it. That is the trouble with many triads, and the trouble with *The Dream of Rhonabwy*. The late writers add almost nothing indubitably native.

There remain a few paragraphs in the lives of the saints. These items, however, are among the most intriguing of all. The *Life of Gildas* we have already taken brief notice of. The Breton *Legend of St Goeznovius*, ascribed rightly or wrongly to the year 1019, has a preface telling how the fifth-century Britons fled to Armorica before the Saxon invasion. Arthur, the 'great king of the Britons' (this is the oldest known allusion to him as king), drives the heathen back for a time and apparently leads an expeditionary force. 'But when this same Arthur, after many victories gloriously achieved in British and Gaulish lands, was summoned at last from human activity, the way lay open again for the Saxons.' Whereupon fresh horrors ensued, and the refugee population of Armorica swelled. Here, it will be observed, Arthur almost ostentatiously does not die. It seems as if the orthodox Arthurian Legend, with its coronation and overseas conquests and mysterious evasion of death, first took shape in Brittany.

The *Life of St Cadoc* portrays Arthur in ambiguous colours. Its preface describes how Cadoc's father Gwynnlyw, king of Glamorganshire, carried off a Brecknock princess named Gwladys. Her father Brychan pursued them into Gwynnlyw's own territories. Fleeing over a hill, they encountered Arthur playing at dice with Kay and Bedevere. Arthur was smitten with desire for the lady, but his knights reminded him that it was their custom to succour the afflicted. Thereupon he forced Brychan to return home. Gwynnlyw instantly married Gwladys – being anxious, perhaps, to make the position clear – and Cadoc was their firstborn.

The same *Life* relates how Cadoc became Abbot of Llancarfan. One day a man named Ligessauc arrived begging for sanctuary: he had killed three of Arthur's soldiers. Cadoc kept him concealed for seven years, an unprecedented and doubtfully legal action. Arthur, now in late middle-age, at length discovered the miscreant's hiding-place. He came angrily to the River Usk with his retinue and demanded a public hearing. St Cadoc, with St David and others, argued with him in shouts from the far bank. The judges awarded Arthur a herd of cattle as compensation. Arthur insisted that all the cattle should be part red, part white. When the cattle had been collected, with miraculous aid, the holy men drove them half-way across the ford, and the knights took them from there. Or rather, they tried to. The cattle changed disconcertingly into bundles of fern. Arthur, abashed, granted Cadoc the privilege of extending sanctuary for seven years, seven months, and seven days.

The hard-bargaining Arthur recurs in the quaint *Life of St Carannog*. This Cambrian saint, like many others, had a wonderful floating altar. He launched it in the Bristol Channel, resolving to preach wherever it landed. It ran aground near 'Dindraithov,' Arthur's citadel. Carannog followed and met Arthur looking for a huge serpent which had devastated the district of Carrum. He gave the hero his blessing and asked whether he knew where the altar was. Arthur promised to tell him, if he would help in dealing with the serpent. Carannog prayed. The monster slid submissively to his feet, and he ordered it into banishment. Then Arthur produced the altar. He had tried to use it as a table, but everything which he put on it fell off. In token of gratitude he gave Carrum to the saint, on condition that he stayed in Dumnonia. The location of this tale is the country between the Quantocks and Exmoor. Dindraithov is Dunster.

The *Life of St Padarn*, though written as late as the twelfth century, speaks with amazing disrespect of 'a certain *tyrannus* by the name of Arthur.' *Tyrannus* is Gildas's word for Vortigern. It implies, vaguely, an autocrat with political power but no regal legitimacy. This particular autocrat wandered into Padarn's cell and coveted a handsome tunic presented by the Patriarch of Jerusalem. Padarn refused to surrender it, and when his visitor persisted, the saint caused the earth to open and swallow him up – all but the head. Arthur did not escape till he had craved pardon.

To judge from these stories, if Arthur was not exactly a villain in the eyes of the Church, he was not exactly a favourite either. The Welsh monks kept the river between them. It would be interesting to know why. The parallel which occurs to me is that of Charles Martel, who saved France from the Arabs in 732. Though a Christian warrior and a vanquisher of paynims, he annoyed the clergy by expropriating Church property to finance his wars. He therefore met with rude handling from ecclesiastical scribes. Perhaps the *Life of Padarn* is a far-off echo of a similar move by Arthur.

These passages, however, in no way contradict the essential picture. The Arthur of British literary tradition is a commanding figure in a strange half-mythical country, which nevertheless is still recognisably Britain. *Imperator* or *tyrannus* but not king, he stands out as an unparalleled warrior with a mighty military household. His fame resounds through all the islands; alone among the chiefs, he attracts legends not originally part of his saga. The explicit notion of his return as a Celtic Messiah cannot be proved to have existed before, say, the year 1000. On the other hand there seems always to have been a mystery about his grave.

4

Behind the literature a man surely existed, and a man easily reconciled with historical data. We glimpse him first as an adventurer somewhat in the Rob Roy style, raiding his neighbours, winning and losing, capturing and getting captured. His skilful leadership commends him to the organisers of British resistance. Crisis ennobles him by conferring power and responsibility. He is no saint. His life still has disreputable and violent aspects. But after the military career that culminates at Badon and ends at Camlan, all his people remember him.

There is no doubt about the memory. Lovers of folk-lore have amassed countless Arthurian miscellanea – genealogies, local legends, place-names, allusions, oddments of verse, and reasonable inferences. Also there are fragments of veritable antiquity embedded in medieval romance. Scattered and dim and dubious in themselves, these things can be forceful in combination. They come into their own more especially when we face the problem of beginnings and endings. Where was Arthur's native land? and was he actually buried at Glastonbury?

The answer to the former question is surprisingly clear. Arthur was a West-Countryman. Wales and Scotland have Arthurian place-names and Arthurian folk-fables, but none that so much as hints at fixed residence in Wales or Scotland. Arthur's land is the south-western promontory, West Wales or Dumnonia. Indeed the whole Ambrosian movement seems to have taken shape in Dumnonia: that is precisely the part of Britain which the Wansdyke protects. As for Arthur, they show you his strongholds at Kelliwic in Cornwall and at Cadbury[1] in Somerset. The primitive triads, the ones that echo his fighting apprenticeship, have Cornwall for their setting. Tristan was most assuredly Cornish; his monument near Fowey can still be seen. Medraut, the victim of Arthur's alarming raid, was also a Dumnonian chief. In the civil war he made his last throw at Camlan, and Camlan is either the

[1] See preface, p. 8.

River Camel or the River Cam near Cadbury. When Arthur besieged Glastonbury to rescue Guinevere, according to the *Life of Gildas*, he had the forces of Cornwall and Devon under his orders. The Welsh *Life of Carannog* places him in much the same region. The phrase 'dux bellorum' applied to him by Nennius occurs as a title of the Dumnonian King Constantine, a relative of Ambrosius Aurelianus. The Geraint poem suggests that a contingent of the Dumnonian army was long known as 'Arthur's regiment.' It is a legitimate fancy that the British leader had a home of his own in Cornwall and, later, an operational base at Cadbury, this being Camelot, and commanding the British heartland immediately behind the Wansdyke.

His burial is far more perplexing. Like other parts of the Glastonbury lore, the legend does not come under scrutiny till the Middle Ages. When it does come, it comes in two instalments and presents difficulties.

To begin with, there is the story given by Geoffrey of Monmouth, whose British 'History' was the starting-point of medieval Arthurian romance. This book, based on Welsh traditions extravagantly inflated, appeared between 1135 and 1140 and won general acceptance. In it Geoffrey described how Arthur, after his last battle, was borne away to the Isle of Avalon for the healing of his wounds. There the reader lost sight of him. The Welsh notoriously liked to pretend that Arthur had not died, but was waiting in Avalon or some similar retreat to return and succour his people. Geoffrey left the door open for that belief without affirming it himself. Sceptics might reject the Return, but even they, if they followed the majority in accepting the *British History*, were bound to suppose that 'Avalon' was Arthur's last resting-place. Geoffrey did not say where Avalon was. It is sometimes maintained that his account is incompatible with the Glastonbury identification, and that he could not have known of this. Neither statement is justified by the text of his *History*, but he also introduced Avalon into a poem about Merlin, and there he did speak of it in terms hardly applicable to Somerset. Hence, his contribution to the lore of the Passing was simply this: *Arthur's last earthly destination was Avalon* – geographically unspecified.

The second and more important witness is our friend Giraldus Cambrensis, writing in the 1190s. Giraldus has a keen, restless, critical outlook. He is one of the very few twelfth-century writers with the acumen and audacity to ridicule Geoffrey of Monmouth. Hence he is not predisposed to Arthurian credulity; quite the reverse. When he sets down what he does set down about Glastonbury, he has certainly been convinced of its truth, and convinced by such arguments as a modern mind can respect. The story which he hands on from the monks is this. During a royal progress through Wales, King Henry II learned from a bard that Arthur was buried at a particular spot in Glastonbury Abbey. (The Glass Island, Giraldus explains, is Avalon.) Henry passed the news to the Abbot. Nothing resulted at the time. But in 1190 or thereabouts, after a fire had razed most of the Abbey, excavations were undertaken and the remains of Arthur duly found. The outcome was satisfactory. The monks profited by the publicity, and the English kings were enabled both to claim the Arthurian succession and to laugh at Welsh prophecies of Arthur's return as a Celtic champion.

Just about here in the consideration of Glastonbury the mind begins to writhe. Contending theories charge across it like Wild Huntsmen. The argument moves in cycles and epicycles. Did the monks give out that Glastonbury was Avalon because they found Arthur there? or did they think Arthur worth looking for because Glastonbury's identity with Avalon was already accepted? Did people believe Glastonbury was Avalon because of King Gwyn? or was Gwyn located there because of the Avalonian myth – or because of his comradeship with Arthur? Alternatively, was Arthur located there because of Gwyn? When the Grail enters on the scene the complication redoubles. Fortunately we have not yet reached the Grail. And by keeping our heads, and looking squarely at the facts, we may disperse much of the fog at once.

If we take our authorities at their face value, the order of events in the twelfth century is something like this. First, Geoffrey of Monmouth announces to his readers that the wounded Arthur was taken to an unlocalised Avalon. Then the Welsh bard tells Henry II that Arthur was buried at Glastonbury. Henry tells the Abbot, to whom the information is new. After an interval the monks excavate. Finding, or professing to find, proof of Arthur's interment, they draw the inference. 'Well, that confirms what some of us have suspected for years. This island of ours is Avalon.' Thereupon they inform the world accordingly. On such an interpretation, the movement of thought is loosely syllogistic:

Arthur's last earthly destination was Avalon;
Arthur was buried at Glastonbury;
Therefore Glastonbury=Avalon.[1]

Of course there are other possibilities. Assuming the veracity
of the monks, we might suppose that they had equated
Glastonbury with Avalon before Henry's trip through Wales,
and that the bard's disclosure, whatever it actually amounted
to, only suggested an exact spot to dig. But perhaps, after
adopting a pre-existing equation, they invented the bard.
Or perhaps they invented the bard and the equation together.
Of these three theories the first two seem dubious, because
in Geoffrey's book the equation does not appear. However,
it might have been concocted after he wrote, and appropriated
by the monks in good faith; or the Abbey might have preserved a tradition which he did not know or preferred not
to use. A more forceful objection, which applies to all three
of the alternative theories, is that the monks' announcement
of the Glastonbury-Avalon identification was never disputed.
Despite the fact that Glastonbury was not even in Wales;
despite Avalon's colossal publicity value; despite the exploitation of the discovery by English kings – no Celt or Celtic
enthusiast spoke up in protest, no rival Avalon arose. The
Welsh had their own islands of the dead, their own fairy
hills, their own Arthurian place-names, their own poems and
legends. Yet they made no retort. There were still Celtic
diehards who maintained *a priori* that Arthur could not be
buried at Glastonbury because he had not been buried anywhere. But apart from these distant negative rumblings, the
Abbey's astounding boast went unquestioned.

Under the circumstances I cannot believe in a pure fraud.
The orthodox version of the fraud theory, as set forth by a
recent Dean of Wells, goes far toward refuting itself. Its
advocates urge that the monks concocted Avalon to cash in
on the Arthur vogue. They needed money to rebuild after
the fire. But if Avalon was so potent we would expect to
hear of at least one competitor, at least one challenge, or
at least one expression of cynicism. We never do. (Contrast

[1] It is not actually quite so simple. The monks exhibited a cross
with an inscription in which the name 'Avalon' could be deciphered,
and allowed visitors to suppose that they had dug it up. But
the truth probably is that the cross was an afterthought. See Chapter
Six.

the relative failure of Glastonbury's claims to possess the bones of SS. Patrick and Dunstan. Or contrast what happened at fifteenth-century ecclesiastical councils. The English bishops claimed seniority on the strength of the Glastonbury legends. Their French and Spanish colleagues reacted vigorously and produced legends of their own.)

How are we to account for the silence? Nobody could fairly maintain that Wales was already committed to the identification. If so, Geoffrey of Monmouth would scarcely have handled the story as he did. It is easier to think that at some time after Geoffrey wrote, an event took place which was held to put Glastonbury in a new light. That event could perfectly well have been what Giraldus implies it was, the bard's disclosure to Henry II. I am not suggesting that Arthur necessarily *was* buried at Glastonbury; I am suggesting that the bard gave away an authentic tradition to that effect, which was known to so many Welshmen that when the monks published it neither the tale itself nor the inference could be brushed aside. The syllogism stood. Arthur's last earthly destination was Avalon; Arthur was buried at Glastonbury; and so – once the world learned the truth – Glastonbury had to be Avalon. Probably the same sequence of ideas had occurred before in a dim way. But during the Angevin era the whole pattern became explicit.

Our oldest elucidatory item is that obscure line from the 'Song of the Graves':

Anoeth bid bet y arthur.

It has been translated 'Not wise the thought, a grave for Arthur' and 'A mystery to the world, the grave of Arthur' and 'Concealed till the Judgment Day the grave of Arthur.' Its essential message is clear: 'Don't ask questions.' The poet is aware of a secret. So, by the way, is William of Malmesbury, who also alludes to the unknown grave, and to the long-prophesied Return. In view of the circumstances of Arthur's end – strife among his own people, while the Saxons were building up for a fresh advance – it may be that his lieutenants concealed their loss. Immediate publication would have dealt too heavy a blow to native morale, would have given too much encouragement to the enemy. A few loyal veterans (led, shall we say, by Bedevere, 'the last of all the knights') carried off the leader's body to some remote spot and buried it under cover of darkness, hoping that the heathen might be restrained a little longer by the power of his name and the fear of his return. The mystery of Arthur's grave became a part of the racial mythos. The idea of the great Return eventually took hold of the Britons themselves, or at any rate of their Welsh and Cornish descendants. In poetry, Arthur's place of retirement and healing was inevitably said to be Avalon, the Garden of the Hesperides, the proper place for a hero; and that was the tale that Geoffrey used. But there was also a more mundane tradition, quietly transmitted from story-teller to story-teller, which purported to give the secret of Arthur's grave. He was buried on Ynys-witrin, the Glass Island, within the precinct of the Abbey. And that was the tale which the bard told Henry II.

As to the origin of this Glastonbury tradition, there are two obvious explanations, neither of them entirely satisfying. The first is that the tradition was true. The second is that Arthur became associated with Glastonbury because, in his supernatural character, he had become associated with Gwyn and the Wild Hunt.

I dislike the Gwyn idea. In the first place, the imaginative transition from a semi-divine Arthur on the Tor to a human Arthur buried below is not anthropologically convincing. It is the wrong way round. In the second place, while Gwyn possessed an abode on the Tor, he was never confined to it. He had other homes; Pembrey, for instance. We do in fact encounter the fairy-tale Arthur, Gwyn's companion, in several places. But not one of the corresponding fables has generated a grave for the real Arthur.

The obstacle to accepting the Glastonbury burial as a simple fact is the implied coincidence. It locates Arthur's resting-place in an island suspiciously well qualified to be Avalon when the juxtaposing of traditions compels the identification – an island with a supernatural tinge of just the right kind. To some extent, indeed, the hero might have created his own Avalon. The rumour of his burial might itself have nourished the spell of the place. But that alone is hardly enough. The character of the Abbey supplies a clue. Arthur may well have asked to be laid to rest in the holy place of his own Dumnonia, near his own fort at Cadbury, especially as the region may then have possessed no other Christian foundation of any standing. If it could be shown that the religious community came into being with an eye to the exorcism of occult powers already established, we would have the spectacle of Arthur and Avalon ironically brought together by

D

Christian agency. Or shall we invoke the theory proposed before, that the Island was a time-honoured burial ground? That would sufficiently explain both its mythical aura and its choice for the grave of a Celtic hero, even a Christian Celtic hero. The 'prophecy of Melkin,' whatever its actual source, points to a belief on the subject in the Middle Ages and doubtless earlier. This burial ground accounts for Gwyn, as we saw. With or without it, the rumour of Arthur's ghostly presence accounts for his association with Gwyn and for his adventures in Annwn.

To press the point would be injudicious. I conclude only that there is no decisive reason to reject Glastonbury's claim. If the fatal battle of Camlan was fought on the Cam, near Cadbury, it looks quite reasonable. The funeral scene is admittedly so dramatic as to be perilous for an honest historian – the torchlight, the pale and startled monks, the sad warriors, the bloodstained figure dressed like a Roman officer, the murmured ritual and the pledges of secrecy, and over all the strange haunted hills. But because a scene is dramatic, it does not absolutely follow that it never happened.

A final fancy. Was Gildas present at the graveside? and did he swear secrecy with the rest? and did he avoid mentioning Arthur in his book because he had found that Arthurian reminiscences led to awkward questions?

5

We have a beginning and an end, but Arthur's track in between is fragmentary. For most of the time we catch echoes of his footsteps and that is all. The salient point about the mass of Arthurian oddments is the grandiose geography. Nobody else except the Devil is renowned through so much of Britain. From Land's End to the Grampian foothills, Arthur's name 'cleaves to cairn and cromlech.' We hear of the Cornish fortress at Kelliwic; of a Cornish hill called Bann Arthur and a stream called the River of Arthur's Kitchen; of Cadbury and its noble shades; of the lake Llyn Berfog in Merioneth, where Arthur slew a monster, and his horse left a hoof-print on the rock; of a cave by Marchlyn Mawr in Caernarvon, where his treasure lies hidden (woe to any intruder who touches it); of a cave at Caerleon, and another near Snowdon, where his warriors lie asleep till he needs them; of still another cave in the Eildon hills, close to Melrose Abbey, where some say he is sleeping himself; of the mount outside Edinburgh called Arthur's Seat; of Arthur's Stone, and Arthur's Fold, as far north as Perth; and many more such places. Arthur seems to be everywhere.

The first natural deduction is that Arthur really was everywhere: that he flashed from end to end of his crumbling country on that terrible armoured charger, rallying the fainthearts, reconciling the factions, and pouncing on the bewildered heathen, with Kay and Bedevere riding beside him. And the second deduction, already foreshadowed by the literary evidence, is that the man who bequeathed such a towering legend was no ordinary human being. Even if most of the Arthur stories were borrowed or fabricated, it is still necessary to explain why they should ever have been attached to Arthur. Even if the bards vested him with the attributes of a god, the question still remains: Why him in particular? To which there is no adequate answer but the readiest one – because he deserved it.

Somewhere in Dumnonia, probably close to Glastonbury, he fell at last. But he left a durable achievement which no Celtic degeneracy could efface. He had gained a respite. He had forced the invaders to think again. He had given his own people a legend to keep their culture alive. Thanks to him, by the time the wars drew to an end, Pope Gregory's mission had done its work and civilisation had begun to return to the eastern counties. Night had never extended from sea to sea. England was England, not a wild heathen Anglo-Saxondom; and she was ready to draw on the legacy of Arthurian Britain, and make it splendidly her own.

Chapter Four

THE CELTS

It is time to attempt a retrospect and a prospect. What precisely was Glastonbury? How did it take shape, what did it mean in the age of Arthur, what did it later come to mean? The theory offered in this book may be summed up under seven headings. Conjecture breaks in at every point. All I will seriously urge is that we do find things falling out *as if* my hypotheses were true, and that even if some were to be disproved, the rest would not automatically follow. The degree of interdependence, indeed, is as debatable as the guesses thmselves. An anthropologist might argue that most of the structure stands or falls with the first paragraph. An ecclesiastical historian might feel that the whole story will become unintelligible if research undermines the third or the fourth. My own impression is otherwise. There is no single truth involved, and therefore no single ascent to truth, no single staircase up a toppling pagoda of ideas. I have reconstructed Glastonbury like a small boy building with blocks. One block may rest upon another, and in such a case the removal of the lower one may force a certain redistribution. However, the edifice need not lose all coherence even if the block vanishes into thin air – a thing which notoriously happens to children's toys, and to historians' hypotheses.

To proceed, then . . .

(1) The people of Glastonbury Lake Village buried their dead on the island near the Tor, with a good deal of priestly ceremony. The people of the neighbouring Meare Village continued the custom into Roman times. For the later Celts this burial ground on the Glass Island was awe-inspiring and somewhat uncanny. They quite possibly used it themselves, but the prior use by an alien Celtic stock gave it a peculiar character.

(2) Because of this, tales about fairy folk and the shades of the dead accumulated more thickly at Glastonbury than elsewhere. Gwyn ap Nudd, the lord of Annwn or Hades, was allotted an invisible palace inside the Tor, to which he repaired with his Wild Huntsmen. Geographical accident favoured the

legend-weaving. The Celts believed in hills of the dead and in islands of the dead; here they saw a hill on an island – and a very conspicuous, very odd sort of hill. No general belief was ever held explicitly as a religious tenet. But over a fairly wide tract of country and a fairly long stretch of time, Celts told each other stories about King Gwyn, and the mustering of the ghosts, and the Glass Island with its passageway to the other world. This began to happen before Christianity took deep root in Britain.

(3) Soon after the Roman conquest, when civilians were streaming into Britain from all parts of the Empire, a prosperous Levantine Christian established his household on the Isle. His interests were mercenary rather than missionary. Neither he nor his descendants gave Glastonbury any special significance in the eyes of the early Church. But after the family moved away or died out, a faint recollection of his wealth and his Christianity did persist. Fragments of his house or his tomb-inscription remained.

(4) In the fourth century a few hermits gathered on the isle, choosing that spot partly in honour of the vaguely remembered Christian, partly with a notion of banishing the demons suggested by Celtic fantasy. They built the Old Church, or, conceivably, restored an earlier one. Some time later, on the advice and with the blessing of St Patrick, a more regular community came into being.

(5) Arthur was a Romanised Dumnonian gentleman, either named after, or regarded as an avatar of, a minor Celtic god. His understanding of cavalry warfare raised him to leadership in the struggle against the Anglo-Saxons. At the head of his knights he organised delaying actions in widely separated places, finally repulsing the heathen at the Liddington Badbury. A long armistice followed, but eventually the Britons quarrelled among themselves, and Arthur fell in Somerset fighting a chief who had made a pact with the common enemy. After receiving his mortal wound he asked to be buried in Glastonbury Abbey; perhaps because of the place's nearness and sanctity, perhaps because of the venerable graveyard. This was done in secrecy. Two traditions came down to the Welsh – that Arthur had gone to 'Avalon' and would return; and that Arthur was, in fact, buried at Glastonbury. These were at length reconciled after a fashion by equating Glastonbury with Avalon, an equation already vaguely anticipated owing to the tales noted in (2). The exact nature of Arthur's Christianity must remain uncertain. It was sincere in its way, but it

was not such as to recommend him strongly to Rome, and the English inroads followed by Roman missionary work effaced most of the records about him. The pagan associations of his name, and his ghostly presence at Glastonbury, led to his transformation into a half-mythical figure – a companion of Gwyn, a Wild Huntsman, a Harrower of Hades.

(6) During the life of the British Abbey, some imaginative monk identified the rich proto-Christian with St Joseph of Arimathea. The fable did not then become popular, and little stress was laid on it, but it found its way into oral traditions transmitted to Wales and Brittany. After the English conquest, the Anglicisation of the Abbey, and the Romanisation of its religion, this Celtic legend was entirely lost sight of, but it re-emerged in the Celtic revival of the twelfth century. The prophecy of Melkin – which mentions St Joseph, Avalon, and the use of the Isle for pagan interments – is not totally spurious.

Lastly, to anticipate the ensuing chapter:

(7) Glastonbury's role in pre-Christian folk-lore, plus its superimposed character as a Christian shrine, caused an altogether exceptional concentration of awe. For a while the Abbey was renowned as the holiest and most numinous place in Britain. Its 'perpetual choir' offered up prayers for deliverance from the horrors of further conquest, and for the conversion of the conquerors. These prayers, as we shall see, were to all appearances granted. The Wessex men halted for many years a few miles to the east, and when they at last arrived they were Christians themselves. At Glastonbury, and there alone, there was continuity with the original British Church. At Glastonbury, and there alone, Anglo-Saxon kings recognised a dignity overriding all the distinctions of race and language. They treated the British sanctuary with reverence, enriched it themselves, and used it to bring the peoples together for the first time. Here if anywhere, symbolically at least, modern Britain was born. The welding religious principle was Roman, not Celtic. But Glastonbury's powerful tradition was not easily extinguished. A Celtic strain persisted there – demi-pagan, demi-magical, insular, mysterious – and the same shrine was destined to take on different aspects at different times, reflecting tensions in the nation which sprang from it.

Nothing better attests the strength of the Ambrosian revival in Britain than the sudden blazing up of the British Church. Whereas the military success blew over, the Christian impetus lasted. Out of it sprang an extraordinary phenomenon, Celtic Christianity, and a Celtic island-culture which briefly outshone the Continent. Later came that undying wonder the myth of the Grail.

In the decade of Arthur's apogee Glastonbury was the principal Christian centre, not only of Dumnonia, but of Britain. This is a matter of inference rather than explicit knowledge; but the fact emerges, even if only by way of elimination. Under Roman rule the British Church had been arranged round three bishoprics, all in the more civilised eastern zone. These were London, York, and probably Lincoln. By the date of Mount Badon, enemy action had nullified all three. We cannot tell for sure whether the Anglo-Saxons had already occupied London – owing to their scorn for towns, no record of the capital's fall descended to the compilers of the *Chronicle* – but they almost certainly had, and in any case it appears that about this time the metropolitan clergy deserted their posts and scattered into the west. The other two episcopal cities were far from the centre of resistance, and heathen raids were harassing the whole seaboard. Even before Arthur's day, York and Lincoln had dropped out of ecclesiastical history.

What survived? There was St Albans, the shrine of Britain's first martyr, where Germanus had disputed with the Pelagians. But St Albans lay in a perilous enclave of precariously Christian land, beyond the effective power of the British confederacy. Then again there was Amesbury or Ambresbury, which housed one of the 'perpetual choirs' mentioned in the triad. This was a respected community, but a very young one. Some scholars have tentatively identified its founder Ambrosius with Ambrosius Aurelianus himself, who withdrew, they suggest, into the religious life. The Midlands had nothing of importance. Wales and Cornwall, though astir, were still backward and scarcely Christian at all. But in Somerset stood the Old Church of Ynys-witrin, already old enough for its origin to be doubtful. Round about it clustered the cabins of the monks. There was an abbot, and there was the memory of a hermit-community before the line of abbots began. It is likely also, for a reason which will appear when we revert to Gildas, that the story of the first-century Glastonbury Christian had now taken provisional shape, with all its implications of seniority and peculiar honour. So the Tor rose over the marshes like an Occidental Zion; the Mass continued, the pilgrims came and went; and, if Arthur did indeed make his headquarters at Cadbury Castle, the religious capital of Britain found itself within walking distance of the *de facto* political capital.

Glastonbury's pre-eminence might logically have endured. Historical illogic decreed otherwise. Because of the caprice or conviction of one man, British religion as a positive force migrated beyond the Bristol Channel. Its greatness, which Arthur lived to see with mixed feelings, was a Welsh greatness, and thence in a subsidiary manner a Cornish and a Breton greatness. Welsh missionary activity spread to Ireland, where it restored the frayed frabric of St Patrick's creation. Glastonbury was not passed by. Its strength and glory burned on through the dimmest ages. But in the lives of the British saints it is not chiefly of Glastonbury that we hear, even though some of the most famous were vitally concerned with the place. It remains true that the story of the revived British Church, and of the larger Celtic Church which the Britons did so much to form, is essential to the story of Glastonbury. There are cross-currents, influences back and forth, without which the historic role of the Glass Island would be obscure.

Our main source of knowledge about the ecclesiastical revolution is the bulky mass of Saints' Lives. Most of these were written several centuries afterwards, but their authors used records of intermediate date, and their value is far from negligible. Confronting any one of them, with its anachronisms and bogus miracles and attempts at edification, a modern reader is apt to shy away. Yet they fit together and reinforce each other. We can extract a rough chronology. We can fill out a given saint's career with details about him taken from Lives of contemporary saints. We can correct and supplement the Lives with data from outside sources. When the blunders have been excised, and the marvels discounted, and the inconsistencies allowed for, the residual body of credible and coherent fact is large enough to be of value. Fortunately the Celts bestowed the title of 'saint' very freely, so that the number of Lives available is impressive.

St Illtyd, the revolutionist, was a Breton. Armorica had lately been colonised by the British, and no real distinction had yet arisen between the inhabitants of the two countries. Illtyd himself was apparently an elder cousin of Arthur. He studied in Paris about 470 and heard talk of the monastery of Lérins, which had fired St Patrick's imagination. In due course he sailed over to Britain and served, it is said, under his military relative. But the name 'Arthur' in the account must be a mistake for Ambrosius, whose New Model Army was then gaining its first victories in Kent. Illtyd fought creditably, and the epithet *farchog* (knight) clung to him ever after. When the campaign ended he moved to Glamorgan with his wife Trynihid and joined the court of the local king. One day – so the story goes – he was out fowling in the woods with a party of the king's retainers. His companions grew hungry and extorted food from a pious hermit, who lived there in a hut, and who, presumably, had just replenished his larder. Scarcely had the miscreants eaten when they stumbled into a bog. Several perished. Illtyd was stricken by this event. He found his way back to the denuded hut and asked the hermit for spiritual advice. As a consequence of their talk a religious vocation seized him.

He had played an honourable part in Britain's recovery. But now it dawned on him that the recovery should be spiritual as well as political. God called him to be a monk and a teacher of monks. The monasticism envisaged by Illtyd, and realised in the Celtic Church, had several differences from the kind familiar in western Europe. It was mobile. There was no notion that men under monastic vows should be closely bound to a particular spot. There was benevolent recognition of the freedom to wander. In time to come the more enterprising monks wandered far, preaching and organising and building churches and founding religious houses. It was this itinerant, missionary type which Illtyd was chiefly destined to propagate.

His vocation forced him on to a crisis. Withdrawing from the court, he took his wife and some servants on a holiday by the bank of a river. They put up a shelter and settled down for the night, first turning the horses loose to graze. About sunrise Illtyd asked his wife to go and see to the horses. She went out, found everything in order, and returned shivering and dishevelled. Illtyd would not let her get back into bed. He told her to put some clothes on and go away. He, for his part, was going too. One does not imagine that he really sprang this decision on her without warning, but the method seems a trifle ruthless. Trynihid took her leave and glumly devoted herself to good works. They did meet again, but the meeting was not cordial.

Illtyd received the tonsure and habit from St Dyfrig, the 'Dubricius' whom later romancers represented as crowning Arthur. He retired to a valley, lived alone for a while, and then formed two communities which grew into the monastic colleges of Caldey and Llantwit Major; Llantwit being the Llan Iltud Vawr of the triad about the Three Choirs. It was more than a monastery and more than a college. In its economic usefulness it foreshadowed the Benedictine foundations. The monks rebuilt the Roman sea-walls, reclaimed many acres of alluvial soil, and farmed them vigorously. Illtyd introduced an improved method of ploughing for which all Wales learned to thank him. When he heard of a famine in his native Brittany he shipped over his surplus wheat.

The date of the founder's death is unknown, but he probably lived till at least 520. Among his pupils at Llantwit were St David, St Samson, Gildas, and Prince Maelgwn of Gwynedd. David strode into immortality as patron of Wales; Samson was a principal architect of the restored Church of Ireland; Gildas, whatever his shortcomings, made his indelible mark on history; and Maelgwn became the last King of All Britain with any serious pretensions. What competition could there be? The genius of Illtyd carried all before it. The renewed British Church was irrevocably Welsh. This change, however, meant a breach with the imperial past, and Arthur did not greatly approve of it. As we saw, the Saints' Lives portray him as on bad terms with the holy men of Wales, and as offering inducements to one of them to live in Dumnonia.

But here is a remarkable point. As we saw also, a late triadic series reflects Welsh adaptations of medieval Arthurian romance. That series designates the soldier-saint Illtyd as a Keeper of the Grail. His companions are Peredur and Cadoc. The Peredur of Welsh tradition was only a fairy-tale hero, but Cadoc was an actual saint, contemporary and friendly with Illtyd's pupils. The linkage of ideas would seem to identify the mysterious Grail Castle with Llantwit Major. This is not so preposterous as it sounds. For the situation symbolised by the Quest is clearly authentic. The heart of the Christian life of Britain, represented by the miraculous vessel, is first at Glastonbury and then no longer at Glastonbury. It is somehow transferred to a wild region of sea and mountain resembling Wales. The knights must ride away to find it, and Arthur watches them go with misgiving. To treat the Quest as an allegory of Illtyd's revolution would be fanciful. Yet the evidence of the crucial triad is plain. Some Celtic student, browsing over the lives of the British saints, did associate the two things. It is a reasonable conclusion that to a certain extent fact influenced fiction. The story of the migration of British Christianity, preserved orally and in Saints' Lives, gave the Grail romances a shape which they would never have acquired in its absence.

3

Gildas we have met already. He is an authority of sorts for the early planting of Christian faith in Britain. He is an authority of sorts for the affairs of Ambrosius and Arthur. It remains to carry out a brief survey of his life and work, determining what little can be determined about the years he spent at Glastonbury. He is not an encouraging example of British holiness, but his place is here.

Thanks to the liberality of the Celts in counting people as saints, we possess two Lives of him. The first was composed approximately 880 at the Breton monastery of Ruys, which Gildas founded. The second was composed by a Welsh monk, Caradoc of Llancarfan. It has been assigned to 1156. Caradoc's emphasis on Glastonbury suggests that he wrote it at the Abbey. The two biographers are interested in different aspects of their subject, and the two accounts do not overlap as much as they might. Victorian scholars inevitably constructed a second Gildas. But their victim proliferated like Patrick. Even Caradoc's hero taken alone turned out to be composite. The scholars evoked a third phantom, a fourth, and (I think) a fifth. All of these may be consigned to oblivion. One Gildas is enough. Indeed, more than one Gildas would be intolerable.

In his querulous book on the invasion of Britain, Gildas gives a statement about the date of his birth. Unluckily the text is corrupt. He mentions the event in some sort of relationship with Ambrosius's maiden victory, with the siege of Mount Badon, and with a period of forty-four years. Given a certain liberty of interpretation and emendation we can extract various meanings. However, the only meaning reconcilable with the military facts on the one hand, and with Gildas's adventures on the other, is that the birth occurred in the year of Ambrosius's maiden victory forty-four years before Mount Badon, i.e. about 474. The historian was thus a younger contemporary of Arthur.

He was a North Briton, the son of Caw, a nobleman who lived near the Clyde. According to the Ruys writer he had four brothers; according to Caradoc, twenty-three. Whatever the exact number they were a combative crowd, all except the future monk, who preferred literary pursuits. A Pictish raiding party finally worsted the sons of Caw and made the family home uninhabitable. The brothers emigrated, leaving behind only Huail, the eldest, who embraced the career of piracy. They presented themselves at the court of Gwynedd in North Wales. King Cadwallon and his son Maelgwn greeted them kindly. The King allotted them lands in Anglesey. Gildas married, but lost his wife and took holy orders. He studied under Illtyd at Llantwit Major, stayed for some time, and then went to Ireland, where he made the acquaintance of St Bridget and presented her with a bell. This voyage probably happened in the second decade of the sixth century. Meanwhile the piracies of Huail in the Irish Sea had grown beyond endurance. Arthur in person organised an expedition which led to the outlaw's death. Gildas was overwhelmed with anger and grief. He hurried back from Ireland and acted as the family spokesman in demanding a blood-fine. When Arthur had recompensed the brothers with an estate, Gildas consented to give him the kiss of peace.

(In its broad outlines this dispute is acceptable as a fact – it would be a queer thing to invent – but some of the Welsh authors account for it differently. They say Arthur killed Huail for making love to a woman whom he himself had an eye on. This version puts Arthur more in the wrong and Gildas correspondingly more in the right. The reader can take his choice. Hunting down important pirates, however, would have been part of Arthur's job.)

At some indefinite stage Gildas crossed the Channel. He was abroad for several years and may have paid a visit to Rome. He also spent much of the time in Brittany, where he instituted Ruys. Having done so, he plunged back into the Welsh ecclesiastical ferment. We catch a glimpse of him at loggerheads with the young St David, whom he vainly strove to eject as abbot of a Pembrokeshire monastery. He turned up at Llancarfan and made the acquaintance of St Cadoc, that other Grail-keeper, to whom, as to Bridget, he gave a bell. Cadoc respected him but preferred him at a distance. They used to pass Lent on separate islands in the Bristol Channel. Cadoc made his retreat on Flat Holm, Gildas on Steep Holm, where he ate fish and gulls' eggs. Gildas's fame, however, was always for scholarship rather than asceticism. With later generations 'Gildas the Wise,' meaning 'learned,' became a stock phrase. The compliment was scarcely deserved. A manuscript copy of the Gospels which he made at Llancarfan was preserved for centuries, but there is no hint at notes or a commentary or anything more than the bare copy, and his book on the Anglo-Saxon invasion is not the work of a man of wide reading or even of unusual capacity for verbal inquiry. It is conspicuous only because it stands alone. Many of Gildas's contemporaries were ballad-makers and popular chroniclers, but unfortunately they did not write; in most cases because they could not.

Arthur died in the 530s or early '40s. Before this event, if Caradoc is to be trusted, Gildas attached himself to the Glastonbury community. The Abbot made him welcome. He built a new church (hagiographers are too fond of this facile church-building), and went about in a distinctive goat-hair garment. The chief incident of his stay was the siege provoked by King Melwas of Somerset. Melwas abducted the much-abducted Guinevere and imprisoned her on the Tor. Arthur arrived with levies from the Dumnonian promontory, but owing to the rivers and marshes he failed to close in. The monks detested the business, and Gildas and the Abbot persuaded Melwas to relinquish his prize – whom, perhaps, he had had enough of. Arthur did not seek any indemnity; he was getting on in years and anxious for peace. The opponents put in a joint appearance at church in token of amity.

And here the ways definitely part. Caradoc says Gildas dwelt in the Abbey for the rest of his life and was buried there. The Breton biography, coupled with other notices, pretty well rules this claim out of court. What Gildas almost certainly did was to go over to his Ruys colony with a band of British recruits. There, before 548, he wrote his Complaining Book, a morose and violent denunciation of almost everything British. He was now an old man, but he lived considerably longer. He enlivened his last years by visiting Ireland in the cause of liturgical reform; by quarrelling savagely with Conmore, a Cornish prince; and by composing epistles on the virtue of moderation. Death finally overtook him as an octogenarian at least.

Caradoc's Glastonbury details are suspect, because of his stress on Melwas.[1] He wrote when the tide of Arthurian romance was already flowing, so that the literary fashion gave him a strong motive for putting in an Arthur story. If we cut out that siege of his, the remnant is somewhat meagre. 'King Melwas,' furthermore, must be mythical. There are no traces of a political separation of Somerset from the rest of Dumnonia. The romancers produce variants of the same story, and one of these variants has a patently supernatural setting. Caradoc's version, however, may be true in a way. It may combine two elements. In the first place (we can suppose) bards transmitted a tale about the fabulous Guinevere which was in effect a Celtic Persephone-myth. Arthur's consort was said to have been carried off by a lord of Hades and then conditionally released. Owing to the Tor's otherwordly associations, a late form of the myth centred itself on Glastonbury. But it so happened that near the end of Arthur's life, when the British confederacy was foundering on internal feuds, an adventurer did seize Ynys-witrin and Arthur did besiege it. The enterprise later became confused with a purely mythical exploit.

This much we can positively say about Gildas's term at the Abbey: Caradoc of Llancarfan did not invent it. William of Malmesbury alludes to it in his *Acts of the Kings*, compiled thirty years earlier and before the Arthur craze had confused the issue. The Bosworth Psalter, a volume belonging to St Dunstan, points to a tenth-century belief in it. One argument in favour has not hitherto received much attention. Gildas, it will be recalled, speaks of the pioneer Christian preaching in Britain as having happened very early, perhaps in the reign of Tiberius, or else, if we adopt what is probably a safer interpretation, about the time of Boadicea's rising. He gives no details. But where did he get the story? Surely not from the traditions of the Roman provincial hierarchy. The bishops of London, Lincoln and York never made exalted claims as to the earliness of Christian activity in their sees. Only a single British community ever did make such claims, then or afterwards: namely Glastonbury. Hence it is a fair

[1] See preface, p. 8.

conjecture that when Gildas implies a mission in the era of the Roman conquest, he is recollecting something learnt at the Abbey – a legend which the sixth-century monks told about a primitive Christian whose house or tomb-inscription still fragmentarily remained.

Gildas's reticence is annoying, like his reticence about Arthur. But if his assertion echoes any other legend than that of Glastonbury, it would be interesting to know what this other legend was, and why it expired, when national and local pride furnished such powerful motives for prolonging its life. We have no good reason to think that either the legend of Bran or the legend of Aristobulus existed in Britain in Gildas's day. Residence and inquiry at Ynys-witrin would fully explain his statement, which otherwise presents a problem.

I conclude, then, that Gildas did live at the Abbey in the 530s; that he had dealings with Arthur, and possibly witnessed his furtive burial in the grounds; and that he gathered information there which he put in the book he subsequently wrote at Ruys. Not enough information. Any British historian will agree that Gildas's book is one of the most exasperating sources he has to cope with. He finds the tradition about the Church – with no particulars. He finds what is apparently the reign of King Vortigern – without Vortigern's name. He slithers in a single bewildering sentence from the campaigns of Ambrosius to those of Arthur – and then Arthur is imperceptible. He nearly catches hold of a critical date – and the muddled prose lets him down. Places, events, personages, peep out through the smoke and vanish.

Nothing is clear but Gildas's determination to abuse his own people. From his haven beyond the Channel he assails all the princes for their crimes, vices and lack of co-operation. He includes his old schoolfellow Maelgwn. The princes' subjects are engulfed in the flood. Whatever the justice of his charges, he does not paint anything resembling a fair picture; and, as a scholar familiar with the Welsh Church and its missionaries and teachers and improvers of agriculture, he must have known this. He seems, after his fashion, to have been an upright and ardent soul, but something deranged him. His book is an unlovely specimen of literary treason. When the Anglo-Saxons became literate themselves, they gleefully cited its monotonous diatribes to show the Celts what their own Wise Man really thought of them. Caradoc notwithstanding, the corpse of Gildas is one which Glastonbury can well do without.

4

The Abbey greeted a more distinguished if more tran-
sitory resident in the person of St David himself. He came
during the 530s and left his mark on the landscape. Gildas
may have been present at the time, but the pair did not get on
too well. Hence a certain predisposition in David's favour.

For the biography of the patron of Wales there is a single
major source, and, as with other prominent saints, a considerable number of minor sources. The basic Life is by
Rhygyfarch, who compiled it in 1090 from oral traditions
and early documents now lost. Other Welshmen, Giraldus
Cambrensis among them, drew on Rhygyfarch's work and
incorporated further material. The Lives of David's colleagues
supply still more; and William of Malmesbury tells a story
which raises a question in the history of the Old Church,
bringing the saint into a vital relationship with the Abbey.

David was born in approximately 497[1] in a valley near the
west Pembrokeshire coast, which bore the Latin name of
Menevia. The place to-day is called St David's. According
to Rhygyfarch, the mighty Patrick himself had thought of
settling there, but sailed away when an angel told him the
spot was reserved for another not yet born. As a boy David
walked to school daily at 'Vetus Rubus,' where he learned
the alphabet, the Psalms, and various portions of the missal.
(It is noteworthy how completely the Classical education
had collapsed.) He then studied at a small insular monastic
community under Abbot Paulinus, and afterwards went to
Illtyd. Entering the monastic life, he became abbot of Paulinus's community. Some time subsequent to this honour
he and Gildas had their unedifying dispute. Then David began
a long tour, preaching and restoring worship in various parts
of what is now England. Of his tour more in a moment.
On returning he transplanted his own abbey to Menevia. Here
he imposed rigid rules of self-mortification. He is a leading
exemplar of the tough asceticism which was so marked a
feature of the Christian revival. It was prompted by a desire

[1] The later dates which have been proposed seem to me to involve
too many clashes with evidence in the other Lives.

to do penance for the national sins to which Gildas and other moralists attributed the Saxon inroads. The monks were yoked to the plough like oxen, and subsisted on one meal a day, the menu being confined to bread and herbs. When the see of Menevia was founded, its bishops always abstained from meat out of respect for St David. One of them who at last ventured to eat it was very properly slain by pirates.

From 547 David was travelling abroad accompanied by a monk named Teilo. At some stage he was consecrated a bishop. Rhygyfarch asserts that he went to Jerusalem and received his consecration at the hands of the Patriarch, but that is probably a fiction, devised to prove the separateness of the Welsh hierarchy from that of the English Church. After his return to Britain David presided over a synod which regulated the sacrament of penance. At the synod he is said to have invoked Roman authority: if he did, the action is a reminder that the Celtic Church never entirely broke away from its parent body. He also sent emissaries to Ireland to correct the liturgy – another of the many cases of Welsh co-operation in the advancement of Irish Christianity. His life drew on to a late close (the Celtic saints were a long-lived tribe) in an atmosphere of general homage.

Our main concern is with his tour in England. If it happened, it was astonishing. He went first to Glastonbury and built a church. Then he moved on to Bath and purified the waters, which had hitherto been poisonous, a fact that the Romans would have found mystifying news. After Bath he visited Croyland, Repton, Coldingham and Leominster, founding monasteries at each. After that he journeyed through Cornwall.

This itinerary, of course, really will not do. Croyland was instituted in 716, Repton in 660, Coldingham in 650, Leominster in the eleventh century. Not one of these monasteries was even a Celtic foundation. And the springs at Bath were not poisonous. David's exploits have been sadly exaggerated. However, the visit to Glastonbury is likely enough. William of Malmesbury in the *Acts of the Kings* gives a curious account of it. He says David came to the Abbey with the idea of dedicating the Old Church to the Blessed Virgin. The night before he was to do so, Christ appeared to him in a dream and asked why he had come. David explained, whereupon the Lord answered that he himself had already dedicated the church in his mother's honour, and that although the Welshman showed commendable piety, the ceremony ought not

113

to be repeated. As a token of the truth of this vision, Christ laid his finger on the palm of St David's hand, inflicting a small but uncomfortable wound. The wound, he said, would remain till morning. When David celebrated Mass, and uttered the words 'through him and with him and in him,' it would instantly heal. The saint awoke, and soon verified the prediction. Giving up his plan, he arranged for the building of another church, this being the structure mentioned by Rhygyfarch. William adds that according to tradition David returned to Glastonbury at the end of his life and was interred near St Patrick.

The unknown fabulist who composed William's legend had a pretty obvious motive. He wanted to refute a sceptic who had denied that the Old Church could have originally been dedicated to Mary. It had been so dedicated, indeed, from time immemorial; yet, if it really dated from the first century or even the second, an original dedication in that style was (humanly speaking) incredible. The same preoccupation reveals itself in the opening chapter of the *De Antiquitate* text. During the Middle Ages Glastonbury's monks tried to defend two contradictory propositions – that the Old Church had been built in the apostolic era, and also that it had been a shrine of the Virgin from its inception. In the face of ecclesiastical history there was no method of reconciling the two claims, except by inventing visions and miracles.

But the episode of St David focuses attention on a genuine problem underlying the fancies. Since we may now admit that the Old Church did not exist before the fourth century, the question of its dedication lies open to serious debate. Was it Mary's from the beginning after all? or did she displace another saint? Did her position change at the period of St David's visit? In the light of what has come down to us about her role in the Church at large, what are the probabilities?

The status of Jesus's mother in the early thought and ritual of the Christian community is none too plain. Christian people, including acquaintances of the Holy Family, seem always to have reverenced her as an exceptional person with an exceptional character and career – exceptional in a supernatural sense. The Gospel of St Matthew, which can hardly be later than A.D. 70, gives a version of the miraculous birth. Luke repeats it with augmentations, telling us in a peculiarly emphatic manner that Mary 'found favour with God' and was 'blessed among women.' Over the next hundred years or so several of the Fathers in widely separated countries refer to her as in some way set apart. While the doctrine of her exemption from original sin is not affirmed by these authors, it is compatible with the glowing language they use. Again, there is a recognisable case for the view that a belief in Mary's assumption into heaven was prompt and widespread, not, of course, as a defined dogma, but as a piece of sacrosanct folklore. No place ever claimed to possess her bodily remains. Her sepulchre was assigned to a certain spot, her bones never were. The contrast with the Apostles and other figures of the New Testament is striking. Seemingly the Virgin was held by a decisive number of Christians to have passed physically into another sphere of existence, leaving an empty tomb.

Belief, however, is one thing; a religious cult, complete with prayers and church dedications, is quite another. Apocryphal literature of the third century (not earlier) places Mary on a high plane and counsels the faithful to seek her intercession. In the fourth century (not before) Christian writers of repute begin to approve the practice. The cult thus acknowledged may have been occasioned in part by theological chance. Arius had denied the full godhead of Christ, and the Church, anxious to expunge his teaching, happened at the moment to be laying intense emphasis on that godhead. As a result the Saviour had temporarily grown somewhat remote, and Christians felt the need for an intermediary. His glorified and afflicted mother appealed to their imagination.

Devotion to the Virgin was a popular rather than a theological thing. She was, so to speak, a democratic heroine. The poet Ephrem of Syria extolled her in grandiloquent lines, but the scholarly Augustine had little to say about her. Matters came to a head at Ephesus in 431. There, amid immense public acclamation, a Church council declared against Nestorius and the Nestorian heretics. The affair was notable, not as marking any fresh trend in Marian devotion, but as showing the height it had already unobtrusively reached. For the heresy, on the face of it, did not concern Mary at all, but only her Son. Catholics maintained that Christ was a single person uniting humanity and divinity. Nestorius's disciples contended that he was actually two persons, one human and the other divine, a celestially contrived case of dual personality. The fiercest reaction of the orthodox masses took a form which now seems astonishing. Seizing on a point made by Nestorius in a sermon, they cried out that the doctrine was an affront . . . not to the Christ whom it turned into a kind of madman, but to the Blessed Virgin. She had brought forth a single child, a single person; and this was manifestly the human Jesus, not the deity supposed to have been mysteriously combined with him. Therefore she was not, as the Greeks put it, *theotokos*. She did not deserve the title of Mother of God. That, not the splitting apart of Christ, was the heretics' unforgivable blasphemy.

After this demonstration of Mary's hold on the minds of the people, she advanced from triumph to triumph. Madonnas became a standard product of art. Justinian, early in the sixth century, begged Mary's protection for what was left of the Empire; his general Narses asked her advice on the field of battle; and Heraclius bore a banner with her image on it. Nevertheless, once again, a distinction must be drawn. A cult in Constantinople is one thing, a cult in Britain is another. To complicate matters further, the custom of dedicating churches need not have kept pace with the custom of invocation. Could a British church in the fourth, the fifth, or even the sixth century have been dedicated to Mary?

No straightforward answer presents itself. We possess no record of her entry into the northern island which later prayed to her so devoutly. Arthur's Britain may have been steeped in Byzantine Mariolatry, or it may have been wholly ignorant of it. The uninformative histories of the Welsh, Irish and Scottish saints who followed are no safe guide, for these saints represented a new Christian departure, with a new spirit of simplicity and austerity to which the Blessed Virgin was necessarily something of an alien. Our Welsh chronicler Nennius, listing the twelve Arthurian battles, refers to her image which the *dux bellorum* carried at Castle Guinnion. He may be giving a true picture, he may be echoing a bard's adaptation of the annals of the Byzantine leaders. Gildas, curiously enough, is a little more helpful. In his denunciation of King Constantine of Dumnonia, he speaks of this monarch as calling on the Mother of God to witness an oath. The date of the incident is about 544. The account of the oath itself, and of the sacrilegious murder by which Constantine allegedly broke his faith, seems to me to point fairly clearly to Glastonbury as the scene of the whole episode.

This allusion gives us a limit in one direction. Farther back the silence is absolute. The most promising place to look for the Marian cult would, indeed, undoubtedly be in a monastic settlement. Monasticism came from the East, and its aggressive ideal of chastity propelled those who embraced it into the vanguard of the Virgin's adorers. Well before the Ephesus council this was a familiar phenomenon throughout Christian Asia. Travel, in the fourth century, was still fairly easy. British ecclesiastical envoys roamed widely. No chronologically possible influence can be ruled out on merely geographical grounds. Yet if the Old Church dated from the fourth century, and I do not think we can put it much later, its original consecration in Mary's name is hard to credit.

Moreover, the legend of David and his vision defeats its own purpose. Christ, in heaven, might have dedicated the church to his mother, but manifestly nobody knew this on the terrestrial level. David's project plainly implies that when he went to Glastonbury the church was *not* regarded as Mary's. Otherwise, why the proposed ceremony, and why the apparition?

The truth may be approximately this. Glastonbury's unidentified founder, who brought together a group of hermits for the first time in Britain, was a man under eastern influence importing an eastern mode of life. He imported also the cult which tended to go with it, a cult chiefly prevalent in the eastern part of Christendom. The Glastonbury monks addressed prayers to the Blessed Virgin; they included her in their liturgy; and when Ambrosius revived Imperial sentiment, they acquired and exhibited a madonna in the Byzantine style. It was at Glastonbury that Arthur himself learned to revere her. But the Old Church did not bear her name. Its rededication finally happened in the 520s or '30s, perhaps as a gesture of thanksgiving for Arthur's victories, perhaps also in response to travellers' tales about Justinian and Narses. As to the name or names which it honoured before, we have a clue of sorts. Comparing Rhygyfarch, Caradoc of Llancarfan, and the *De Antiquitate* interpolator, we find agreement that, by 540, at least one subsidiary place of worship had been erected close by. The first two writers simply mention a 'church,' the latter speaks of an 'oratory of Peter and Paul.' According to medieval report the building was scarcely more than an annexe to the Old Church. A guess which covers the data is that the Old Church formerly commemorated the two apostles, and that when it was given over to Mary, the person responsible – St David or another – built them a chapel to avoid the insult of total expulsion.

However, the argument is rather futile. The essential fact is that Ynys-witrin was the first British home of the Virgin's cult. That, at any rate, it would be hypercritical to deny. There is no rival tradition whatsoever. When all the fantastic mists have dispersed, 'Our Lady St Mary of Glastonbury' remains a time-hallowed title.

As for David, it is only necessary to add that he died in the 580s and was buried: some say at Menevia, others at Glastonbury; and that, in either event, his remains do seem to have been shown and venerated at Glastonbury Abbey in 946.

5

After St David the Welsh were less important. They had accomplished their major task by reinvigorating the Church in Ireland. Ireland henceforth became the geographical base of Celtic Christianity, and the main source of its intellectual life wherever it flourished. That life was fiery and perplexing. Irish monastic libraries contained books which Christians elsewhere had almost lost sight of. Among these were several curious apocryphal texts: the *Book of Enoch*, which St Jude quotes in his Epistle; the *Apocalypse of Moses*; and, significantly perhaps, the *Acts of Pilate*, the only ancient book which gives prominence to Joseph of Arimathea. Where did these volumes come from? In some cases one suspects a Byzantine traffic. Rome opposed the circulation of much of this literature, and monks in Ireland knew Greek. A Gaulish writer describes a mass influx of European scholars, refugees from the barbarians. The flowering, whatever its exact cause, was impressive. It produced a surplus for export. Even when England was entirely occupied by the English, learned men from the smaller island kept drifting over St George's Channel and teaching in the monastic schools. As late as the tenth century Glastonbury Abbey had an active contingent of them. Irishmen restored religion in western Cornwall and built many churches there. Conversely, English and even continental clerics went to Ireland to study, acquiring by far the best available grounding in science, mathematics, and Scripture, and often going forth after graduation to evangelise Nordic heathendom.

The main geographic movement of Celtic religion was rotary and clockwise. The migrant people called Scots, who at first lived principally in Ulster, began the colonisation of their own future country as missionaries among the Picts; and from the West Highlands they carried the Faith to the Anglo-Saxons as far as Lincolnshire. The most memorable Scot was Columba, who founded the Iona community. Here the Church of Scotland was born, and here in due course came Oswald, the exiled English prince of Northumbria, to return home converted with Scottish monks in his wake.

William of Malmesbury's interpolator asserts that Columba imitated Patrick and David by going to Glastonbury and dying there. He gives no details, and the assertion is most unlikely. During this phase of history Glastonbury is not conspicuous. However, we do begin to get local names and administrative particulars. William himself says he saw a charter dated 601, in which the King of Dumnonia granted five hides of land to the Abbey. In this concise document William could make out the abbot's name as Worgrez or Worgret, but owing to the age of the manuscript he could not make out the King's. In all probability the charter was genuine. A forgery would have been longer, more explicit, and more legible – witness the outpouring ascribed to St Patrick. Also, it would most likely have mentioned twelve hides instead of five. Twelve was the traditional number, and 'Glastonbury Twelve Hides' was the traditional district, to which the medieval monks were anxious to justify their title.

A map of this Dumnonian grant would be worth looking at. Had any reclamation of marshland occurred?

After Worgret we learn the name of another British abbot, Lademund, but nothing else about him. Vaguely in the same period St Collen belongs. His Life claims that he too was abbot for a few years, retiring voluntarily to live as a hermit on the Tor. But the Life is a foolish piece of work, only valuable for that weird folk-lore episode of King Gwyn, which may disguise an attempt at formal exorcism. The Gwyn affair raises a minor point of interest. Collen is portrayed as hearing about the fairies through a conversation of rustics outside his cell. Who are these rustics? I imagine that other people besides the monks did live in the neighbourhood. Some of them may have cultivated the Abbey's fields. But the origin of the village that spread round the west of Ynys-witrin is completely obscure. No chronicler speaks of any civic charter, as distinct from monastic charters, till the reign of Henry II.

By 650, at any rate, we have the picture of a venerable if

119

visually unimpressive establishment, owning and farming land near the Tor. Though aloof from the main trend of events, Glastonbury Abbey was the senior shrine of the Celtic Church. It is now relevant to ask what that position entailed, what it spelt in terms of historic influence. Here, as with the cult of Mary, the theme chiefly accessible to research is not the course of developments at Glastonbury but the character of the Abbey's heritage. What that could mean to England did not fully appear till the twelfth century.

For a long period of time after St Illtyd the Celtic Church was nearly cut off from Rome and the Continent. For this reason it acquired features differentiating it from the larger Catholic body. Rome recrossed the Channel in 597 when Augustine's mission landed in Kent. Sixty years later the spread of Roman practice among the Anglo-Saxons led to a sharp conflict with the Celts, especially in the north, where Scottish monks had already done the rough spadework of conversion. In 663 the Synod of Whitby was convoked to restore union. A prominent abbot spoke for Rome, presenting the stronger case with needless arrogance and rudeness. The Scottish advocate was Colman. He conducted a dignified but quite fruitless campaign, which a royal arbitrament in Rome's favour brought to a close.

Because of the violence of this dispute, it used to be thought legitimate to write history as if the Celts had anticipated the Greeks in formal schism, or as if they had declined to recognise Rome at all before the Synod of Whitby. They have even been singled out as primitive Protestants. For these views of their status there is no support. If any overt major rebellion had been detected among them, the ruthless ultramontanists would have said so. Beyond doubt the Celtic Church was Catholic and in theory papal. Its priests were validly ordained. They taught Catholic doctrine and dispensed efficacious sacraments. While seldom actively conscious of Rome, they always dimly acknowledged the City as their spiritual capital; the Irish and Scots, who had never lived within the Empire, were no more unorthodox on that score than the Britons who had.

The positive proofs are scanty but adequate. In the fifth century, for example, St Patrick decreed that difficult questions should be referred to Rome, and this rule was subsequently reaffirmed. In the sixth, St Columban (on no account to be confused with Columba) corresponded with the Pope in terms which made his allegiance very clear. In the seventh, at Whitby, Colman himself confessed that Peter alone held the keys of heaven. Thus we possess the testimony of several outstanding and responsible men in different periods, the last of whom would certainly have challenged the Roman claims if any vestige of Celtic ecclesiastical theory had given him the least ground for doing so. Against this evidence nothing concrete has ever been adduced, except a letter from the Abbot of Bangor to the missionary Augustine. In it the Abbot says he has no superior but the Bishop of Llandaff, and denies the authority of the Pope. The letter, however, is now known to be a forgery perpetrated after the Reformation by a Welsh Protestant. Careful study can lead to only one conclusion. While the Holy See was far away and little regarded, it never ceased to be the centre of unity. The Christianity of the British Isles was not schismatic.

Its main visible discrepant features present no problem. They all depend on a single peculiarity. The Celtic Church was based upon monasteries rather than dioceses. The office of Abbot conferred power; that of Bishop conferred hardly any. In fact the Celtic hierarchy could scarcely be disentangled. Room for doubt exists even to-day as to whether St David was ever called an 'archbishop,' and, if so, what his title meant. Bishops were necessary to ordain priests and preserve the apostolic succession. Therefore the Celts had them: but for no other reason. After Illtyd the spirit of their ecclesiastical system was strictly monastic, in sharp contrast with all the rest of Christendom. Once again geography and history counted. It was no accident that this idiosyncrasy arose on the extreme fringe of the former Roman Empire and in the non-Romanised territories beyond. Until Benedict's time the Papacy never quite shook off a distrust of monasticism as too intense, too enthusiastic. In countries under the Roman spell, though individual monks often distinguished themselves, and combinations of monks often exerted influence, a serious challenge to the entrenched Petrine hierarchy was unthinkable. But the Romans had never conquered Ireland, and even in Wales they had practically stuck to garrison duty. While Patrick's archbishopric of Armagh declined in importance, the stream of graduates from Llantwit and other Welsh houses, together with the eruptions of Irish and Scots, ruined the feeble episcopal tradition and set up a novelty in its place.

The rest followed. The monks' freedom to roam, originally perhaps a chance innovation, became essential to the discharge of their heavy responsibilities as supply-priests for the local churches. An abbey like Glastonbury must, in a sense, have covered whole counties, though its own estate was confined to a few acres and the number of monks actually resident was small. The monastic contempt for worldly goods and worldly beauty permeated life with an ideal of holy dreariness. Everybody was either fasting or sinful. The Celts had no significant Christian architecture and no significant Christian art, except for carved crosses and illuminated manuscripts covered with labyrinthine designs. Their weakness in representation, especially in drawing the human figure, was lamentable.

Yet austerity was not the whole story. The Celtic way had its compensations. Convents, as being the monasteries of the opposite sex, enjoyed a high dignity. Women in general seemed closer to the key officialdom of the Church. Hence the paradox that these northern ascetics had less regard for clerical celibacy than the men of the south. Modern misunderstandings have led to exaggeration of the divergence. Much stress has been laid on the fact that in some religious houses the abbot's post was hereditary, with the implication that the abbots had wives. These houses, however, were under the control of rich families which imposed their own members successively as abbot in a purely managerial sense; the inheritors remained laymen. Again, despite statements to the contrary, there is no proof that the Celts anticipated Orthodox Christians by allowing priests to marry and raise families. What they did do was to admit married men very freely to the priesthood . . . on condition that conjugal relations ended. Husbands in their late thirties or forties frequently chose the religious life, once their children were old enough to fend for themselves. That is why Welsh genealogies include numerous people legitimately descended from priests. In a candidate for holy orders the lack of virginity and the existence of a spouse were not the barriers they would have been among the Gauls or Italians. A different conception of the status of women at least encouraged the Celtic practice, if it did not inspire it. The sharply defined 'either-or' attitude never prevailed. This nearer sense of spiritual kinship with the daughters of Eve promoted the curious institution of the mixed house, harbouring both monks and nuns. Occasionally such a house had an abbess as head, with a tame bishop at her call.

Owing to the lack of cohesion, to the weakness of authority, to the ease with which a problem could become nobody's business, the Celtic energy was for long a bounded energy, and in some areas it remained so. Papal Rome could stand on the defensive or wallow in political vileness indefinitely without appearing to have wholly forgotten Christ's injunction to go forth and teach all nations. In tracing her history we never get the impression of a definite shirking, a conscious refusal, a specific limitation of aims. With the Celtic Church, at least in Britain, we do. As various Jeremiahs observed, the Britons made no attempt to preach the Gospel to Anglo-Saxondom. The Llantwit group left the heathen to himself by the North Sea and tried not to think about him. They could not plead the military position as an excuse. Preaching to a triumphant foe might well have been fruitless. But Illtyd's pupils had a full generation of opportunity after Badon, and wasted it. Their missionary labours were entirely a matter of Celts evangelising Celts. Not till a hundred years later, and then only by invitation, and from Iona and not from Wales, did Celtic monks venture on to Saxon soil. Even the great expeditions of the Irish, which extended from Germany to Iceland, did not get fairly under way till Rome had re-entered the British Isles and altered the pattern of affairs.

The Celtic Church had many minor idiosyncrasies – alien customs, curious liturgies, irregular practices. Irishmen might pray with their arms outstretched. Scotsmen might fast on unusual days. But these vagaries had nothing heretical about them. On a crucial disciplinary issue, the abolition of public penance for sin, Celtic example actually swayed the policy of the Roman bishops. It is no use looking for the source of the Whitby quarrel in Columba's missal or Colman's dinner menu. Yet despite the absence of any obvious cause, the quarrel raged with extreme and long-lasting acrimony. When Rome's adherents crossed into Wales the Welsh made them undergo forty days' penance for their religion, refused to sit down to meals with them, and ostentatiously scoured the dishes after the papists had eaten. The word 'heretic' was tossed wrathfully to and fro, but, as honest historians have complained, we never see why. It was the Roman party who took the offensive, and who did most at the outset to embitter relationships. In one Yorkshire monastery they performed a purge.

Their leader's uncompromising demand for submission at Whitby was provoked, I believe, by the very fact that the obstacle which rose in his way was hard to define and hard

123

to grasp. What haunted outsiders in the presence of the Celtic Church, what they continued to feel when its glory had altogether departed, was the Sense of Something Else. This is a state of mind to which even the most sincere Catholics are liable. The core of it may be summed up as follows. The Roman Church is what it professes to be, the unique infallible body instituted by Christ, the agency of salvation even for those outside its conscious membership. The Bishop of Rome, its earthly head, is the vicar of Christ and the successor of Peter. Its teaching is true and apostolic, its sacraments are good and sufficient. Only . . . there is Something Else, a great fact or a great potentiality, which has slipped out of Peter's dogmatic net or slid unnoticed to the bottom.

The root of this feeling, when it occurs on the intellectual level, is probably an impression that Rome has unduly minimised the non-Latin traditions – Greek, Oriental, and so forth. On the popular level, it is enough to note the many vestigial remnants of our pagan inheritance. The Sense of Something Else need not be heretical. A fourth-century outbreak of it very likely explains the discovery of the Virgin's powers as an intercessor. In the crusading era the myth of Prester John embodied the dream of a mighty forgotten Church of Asia with wondrous attributes. In our own time Giovanni Papini has proposed the supplementation of theology by what he calls 'diabology.' The Sense of Something Else expresses itself in a multiplicity of ways. But a recurrent factor is the unsettling notion that the Something Else which Rome overlooks is actually conserved in some local branch of the Church, in some unregarded society, or in some little-known sect. While the Celts trod their own path, they could very easily inspire such a notion in the minds of outsiders. It was practically their manifest destiny to do so. Here were these visionary-eyed wanderers on the misty rim of the world, with their bards and their enchanted islands, their fairy hills and interminable sunset seas: could Rome be sure, could she be quite sure, that they were not hoarding some terrible treasure of the soul? Might not all her pride be confounded by a riddling poem chanted in a remote glen?

That is the misgiving, whether articulate or not, which I think we can discern underlying the obscure vehemence of the papalists. And the vehemence was obscure indeed. For when the clash came, the obedience which they exacted with such ferocity was made to hinge on two apparently minor issues. One was the date of Easter. The other was the shape of the tonsure.

Christian communities up and down the Roman world had formerly employed different methods of identifying Good Friday. The discrepancy could lead to distressing results. Pilgrims might arrive at a shrine for the paschal ceremonies only to learn that they were all over. Christians who observed one rule might hold a banquet while their neighbours who held another were still ploughing hungrily through the Lenten fast. By the fifth century most of the Church had reached agreement, but the Celts deviated for a further two hundred years. In the 630s southern Ireland submitted peaceably to the Roman usage. The Christians of northern Ireland, Scotland, Northumbria, Wales and Cornwall did not. This question generated a truly fantastic amount of heat, and was debated in bewildering terms. When Colman's opponents at the Synod of Whitby urged him to concur in the standard practice of Europe, he cryptically protested that the Celtic method of computation had been handed down from St John the Evangelist. That was his defence.

The argument about the tonsure possessed the same air of unreality, or rather, of things left unspoken. Monks in general shaved a circular patch on top of the head, commemorating the crown of thorns; Celtic monks shaved a strip from ear to ear. The Celtic tonsure was perhaps adapted from the druidic. Rome's representatives, however, assailed it as the 'tonsure of Simon Magus.' The allusion was to the famous wizard and mystagogue, supposed to be identical with the Simon of *Acts* viii. Simon's disciples in the black art did wear a tonsure, which the Roman party accused the Celts of copying. The oddity is that the Celts did not deny the unpleasant charge. Adamnan, a most distinguished Irishman, freely admitted it. To complicate matters further, several Irish asseverated that the tonsure as well as the Easter calculation was due to St John.

What is the inwardness of all this – particularly the Easter business? Colman's protest supplies a clue, which the ambiguity concerning the tonsure reinforces. Both are hints at specific forms which the Sense of Something Else has historically taken. A brief exploration in the twilight regions of Catholic lore will show that any claim to inherit a tradition from John may, in certain contexts, be far more significant than it sounds. The name of the Beloved Disciple tends to be bound up with precisely that hazardous concept of Something Else. He is said, in certain quarters, to have founded a Church-within-the-Church, that works in secret till God chooses to reveal it. The source of the notion is the last chapter of his Gospel. This records a conversation that puzzled the early Christians themselves. Three times Jesus says to Peter, 'Dost thou love me?'

> Peter was deeply moved when he was asked a third time, Dost thou love me? and said to him, Lord, thou knowest all things; thou canst tell that I love thee. Jesus said to him, Feed my sheep. . . . Peter turned, and saw the disciple whom Jesus loved following him. . . . Seeing him, Peter asked Jesus, And what of this man, Lord? Jesus said to him, If it is my will that he should wait till I come, what is it to thee? Do thou follow me.

Here Christ entrusts his flock to Peter, yet he seems to reserve John for some other task. Several mystical writers hint at the continuance of a Johannine succession within the framework of the Petrine succession, preserving doctrines and sacramental principles for which the world is not ready. Conceivably the Celts imagined their Church to contain a Johannine element, which had to be safeguarded, but could not be openly discussed.

The rather spectral Johannine idea is linked historically with a more famous belief concerning the Era of the Holy Spirit. This breaks out at various times and in various places – in the prophecies of the medieval visionary Joachim of Flora, in the speculative flights of Russian Orthodox theologians. Sooner or later, it is held, Peter's commission will expire. The Papacy in its extant form will come to an end. Christendom will move into a new phase, the Era of the Holy Spirit, under the guidance of successors of John. An accurate statement of this belief is in J. K. Huysmans's novel *Là-bas*, which professes to expose modern French witchcraft and diabolism. Huysmans's main theme is the villainy of Canon Docre, a renegade priest. Against this evil character Huysmans counterpoises two or three 'white' magicians. They are Catholics, but adherents of the Secret Church. An astrologer speaks:

'There are three reigns . . . that of the Old Testament, of

the Father, the reign of fear; that of the New Testament, of the Son, the reign of expiation; that of the Johannine Gospel, of the Holy Spirit, which will be the reign of ransom and love. . . . The period from the first appearance of the Messiah is divided, you know, into two epochs, that of the Saviour, as victim and expiation, that in which we now are, and the other, that which we wait for, the epoch of the Christ cleansed of all his impurities. . . . Well, there is a different Pope for each of these eras; the Holy Books announce, as indeed do my horoscopes, these two Sovereign Pontificates. It is an axiom of theology that the spirit of Peter lives in his successors. It will continue to live in them, more or less obliterated, until the wished-for expansion of the Holy Spirit. Then John, who has been held in reserve, will begin his ministry of love and will live in the soul of the new pope.'

Some such theory, of course unacceptable to the Roman party, may have been current among the Celts.

That other uproar over the tonsure points to a similar possibility. For Simon Magus, by universal consent, was no isolated sorcerer. He was the father of Gnosticism, the most subtle and subversive heretical movement of the first Christian centuries. The word 'gnostic' is akin to 'wizard' and 'witch' and perhaps 'druid': it means One Who Knows. Gnosticism in essence was an attempt to fuse Christianity with pagan magic and mystery-cults through the medium of the old, old dream of a Secret Wisdom. It was, in fact, esoteric Christianity. The stress lay on knowledge instead of love. Each of the various Gnostic sects was a clique of initiates grouped round a master, who expanded Scripture into a vast cosmic mythology, fostered an attitude of superior contempt towards most of mankind, and taught how to exist on a more exclusive spiritual plane. The Secret Wisdom involved a good deal of unhealthy spell-weaving, numerology, and conjuration of spirits. By its grotesque inversion of natural meanings (most schools portrayed Jehovah as evil and the Serpent as good), it opened the door to downright Satanism. There were Gnostics and Gnostics, but the Church condemned them all. Whether Simon Magus really originated the movement, we do not know, but Catholics in the Dark Ages believed that he did. Legends told how he came to Rome and challenged Peter to a contest in wonder-working. When the Celts clung to a practice that savoured not only of

Simon but of druidism, the Roman party may have scented a Gnostic recrudescence; and they may have been right.

There is a further ramification still. Although St John, in his own New Testament writings, actually denounces an early type of Gnosticism, the idea of a Secret Wisdom can hardly avoid becoming entangled with the idea of a Secret Church. In Huysmans's guide to French spiritual aberration, we meet the bizarre figure of the priest-magician, manifestly a kind of Gnostic as well as a Johannine. He professes to be on God's side against the devil-worshippers, but his methods are not those canonically approved. Besides extracting omens from jewels and the flight of birds, he performs a Catholic ritual contaminated with occultism, which purports to be a technique of physical and mental healing.

> He had an altar set up formed of a table, and on it a taber-nacle shaped like a little house, surmounted by a cross bearing on the front like a clock face the circular figure of the Tetragram. . . . His costume consisted of a long robe of vermilion cashmere, the waist girt with a red and white cord. Over this he wore a cloak of the same material, cut away on the chest to show a cross upside down. . . . (His ring) is a symbolic circlet of pure gold. It bears the image of a serpent whose heart, in relief and transfixed by a ruby, is attached by a little chain to a miniature ring sealing the snake's jaws.

To read such eccentricities back into the Dark Ages may be an anachronism, at least in part, though the double theory of the tonsure is most suggestive. The traces of the Gnostic tradition are fairly plain, those of the Johannine are doubt-ful. But the Roman-Celtic dispute becomes more intelligible on the view that the Johannine Easter and the Johannine-Magian tonsure were the symbols of a deeper matter which the Celts kept silent about and the papalists had neither the power not the erudition to drag into the open. This deeper matter may have been nothing but a bluff, a hocus-pocus. Yet anthropologists tell us that pre-civilised people often have a remarkable gift for covering up their real religion. The Zulus, for instance, completely hoodwinked early explorers, and the monotheism of some Australian aborigines is a jealously hidden and wellnigh impenetrable mystery. Ireland's tribes were only a few generations away from barbarism. It is possible that currents of a very queer Christianity flowed underground in the Celtic Church. It is probable, whether they did or not, that the ultramontane party suspected they did. Argument proved vain; it led only to crafty evasions. Rome's fire was therefore directed at the two outward signs or rallying points. The Celts took the hint.

There is no need to lay much emphasis on this theory. Of its nature it defies verification. The essential fact is one which the mere virulence of the quarrel goes far to establish, that Celtic Christianity carried a tangible atmosphere of the Odd. Aspects of its oddity peep out in its fragmentary annals. The curriculum of the old Irish schools allots much time to the allegorical interpretation of Scripture, a pursuit which can lead into peculiar byways. Celtic writings contain a swarm of riddles and acrostics and cryptograms, clearly not all devised for amusement only. Complex angelologies, magical formulæ conjuring the seraphim, recall the vapourings of the Gnostic masters. The impression of a lost mystery grows still stronger when we consider the Celtic Church in its broad sweep from the fifth century to the ninth. During half a millennium it plays an active part in the concerns of Christendom. Throughout that time it eludes every attempt to convict it, as a body, of heterodoxy. Yet at the entry stands the heresiarch Pelagius, whose doctrines disturbed the universal Church, and confessedly lingered on in the north till 640. At the exit stands the still more extraordinary figure of John Scotus Erigena, the greatest Christian philosopher of the Dark Ages, whose Neo-Platonism annoyed Rome yet moulded the philosophical system which Rome afterwards endorsed. As Bertrand Russell observes, it is hard to see how Erigena could have sprung out of nowhere. The closest scrutiny of the Celtic Church fails to reveal what he could have sprung out of. But a linkage existed between Neo-Platonism and Gnosticism.

On external issues the Celtic diehards had to give way. After Whitby they fought only rearguard actions. A trend inaugurated at Glastonbury itself was working against them. Step by step the consent to uniformity spread. But when the new Roman Peace prevailed throughout the territory of Roman Britain, and political unity began to emerge, the Celtic mantle descended on Glastonbury Abbey, making it national as no other shrine could be. Its foundations were planted in the roots of the island realm. It attracted scholars from both the occupying races. It claimed the graves of Welsh saints, Irish saints, even Scottish saints. And where

Ynys-witrin rose from the valley floor, the Sense of Something Else brooded as an afterglow, creating now not bitterness but an enrichment of vision, a potentiality of imagination peculiar to this province of Christendom. The English and later the Normans, as heirs of Britain, succeeded to the sanctuary and its ancient enigmas. William of Malmesbury detected hints at a mighty secret in the geometrical pattern of the church's mosaic. A time came at last when the springtides of nationalism lifted Glastonbury to provocative heights; when French courtiers and Sicilian princes became aware of Avalon; when the Sense of Something Else blazed up into the vision of the Holy Grail.

Chapter Five

THE CONQUERORS

We must now retrace our steps and take up the fortunes of Anglo-Saxondom. In 547 an epidemic known as the Yellow Plague swept through the British regions. It carried off King Maelgwn and extinguished the last flicker of nominal unity. Many of his nation died with him, and the flight of several prominent churchmen demoralised the spiritual as well as the political leadership. It was only after this fatal calamity that the heathen English (as we may now finally call them) resumed their inexorable march.

The form of the Heptarchy evolved. A kingdom of 'Northumbria' spread over Yorkshire and the lands up to Scotland. Colonists round the Wash penetrated to Oxfordshire and fanned out: the Midlands became the kingdom ·of 'Mercia.' Political units of fluctuating power arose in East Anglia. Kent remained wealthy and comparatively civilised. Sussex assumed its present shape, but declined. Cerdic's miniature Hampshire domain grew into 'Wessex,' and this kingdom was to prove the most important of all, the nucleus of Great Britain and indeed of the British Commonwealth.

During the years from 550 onward the men of Wessex poured across Wilts, captured Salisbury, abolished Amesbury with its perpetual choir, overran the Badon defensive zone from behind, and emerged on the Thames. In 577 they broke into Somerset and Gloucester, looting and massacring as far as the Severn. To all appearances Glastonbury was doomed. And then, within sight of the Tor, the heathen halted. Some agency interposed. For eighty years English and Welsh patrols watched each other across a stabilised frontier. The Abbey did not fall till Wessex was spiritually prepared to possess it. All the other sanctuaries of Roman and Arthurian Britain – those at London, York, Lincoln, Amesbury, St Albans – underwent an eclipse. Glastonbury alone saw no break in Christian continuity. Delayed capture was the precondition of this phenomenon. But more was involved than mere delay. In a sense Glastonbury created the continuity which it embodied. The peaceful and reverent acquisition of the Celtic monastery by Christianised English was not predictable, it was novel. Prior events in the conversion of England had not foreshadowed it. From the Channel to the Border, the Faith was cruelly jarred in its passionate youthful delicacy by a discord of races and ecclesiastical systems, of which the Easter-tonsure battle was only an aspect. It was the English of Wessex who first resolved the discord. It was at Glastonbury that the resolution began.

Credit for England's conversion usually goes to the lesser of the two Saints Augustine, the one who landed in Kent in 597. School history books have spread the illusion that the entire country was heathen before him and Christian after him. We have seen how absurd the first part of this opinion is. As to the second, his achievement is debatable. For the Anglo-Saxons – not, of course, for the Welsh – he broke the ice. But he also did damage to the Christian cause in the island which a century could scarcely undo.

The real apostle of the new monarchies was Pope Gregory the Great. Converting Anglo-Saxondom was a long-standing project of his. The story about his punning in the slave-market (which, in its full version, describes a much more complicated, far-fetched, and obviously hilarious dialogue than most people imagine) belongs to a period well before his election to Peter's chair. Other business always kept him in Rome, and England lost the services of a brilliant statesman who might have laid the groundwork of civilised unity and averted many decades of war and disorder. The most that Gregory could do when he became Pope was to organise an English mission and entrust it to the monk Augustine, an old friend of his.

Augustine's way was to some extent prepared for him. Ethelbert, the King of Kent, had married a wife from the strongly Catholic Frankish nobility who ruled in Gaul. Since Queen Bertha had brought a private chaplain, her religion was not unknown at the Kentish court. Hitherto there had been no idea of its propagation, and the royal thegns stood by Woden and the old gods. But now Ethelbert, probably flattered by the Pope's overtures, gave his emissary a courteous welcome. Complicated dealings ensued. Rome to-day honours Augustine as a saint, and there is no reason to question his fervour and perseverance; but his virtues were not attained easily, and they did not show in very attractive colours. He was a naturally timid man who over-compensated by arrogance. His enterprise creaked and groaned along to an accompaniment of anxious correspondence with Gregory. Rulings were sought from higher authority on one point after another. It was a weary business. Communications were not what they had been in the Imperial noontide. At last, however, thanks largely to Gregory's judicious guidance, Catholicism achieved official recognition throughout Kent, with an episcopal see at Canterbury. Many pagan temples were turned into churches. King Ethelbert practised his wife's religion conscientiously, but he stayed moderate, and did not persecute those who clung to Woden.

In modern military jargon, Augustine had established a beach-head. He judged rightly that the next step was to reach out across the island, draw the Celts back into relations with Rome, and enlist their aid in the further conversion of the English. Ethelbert tried to act as an intermediary. Though the Easter-tonsure affair had not yet begun, the Welsh abbots and bishops received Augustine's proposition with mixed feelings. They cared little for the barbarians, and probably could not suppress a certain relish at the prospect of their damnation. It was all very well for this Italian to talk about forgiveness of enemies and the duty of conferring the Church's sacraments on those otherwise in danger of endless perdition: the enemies in question had not overrun Italy. Furthermore, the Italian's manner was disrespectful. He hardly seemed aware of the great things which Wales had done without benefit of Roman support. Accredited representatives of the Welsh Church did nevertheless arrive for a conference at Aust on the Severn. After a first fruit-less discussion, they consented grudgingly to another meeting. At this juncture the catastrophe happened. Augustine's overbearing tone when beyond the range of the Pope's directives had proved as bad as expected. The Welsh, in two minds about further negotiation, decided to hang the issue of the conference on a crucial test. When the time came for the next session they would wait till Augustine had gone into the conference room. Then they would enter it themselves. If he rose to greet them, they would try to co-operate. If he remained seated, they would give him up as impossible. He remained seated and the Welsh left him in his chair.

Under the circumstances it is not to be wondered at that Augustine's success was confined to Kent. But his chief follower, Paulinus, carried Roman religion into Northumbria. Northumbria's King Edwin enjoyed a sort of shadowy suzerainty over all Anglo-Saxondom. He claimed to be the true representative of the Imperial system, still very much alive as an ideal, and appeared in public with an appropriate standard carried before him. Hence, perhaps, his willingness to hear Paulinus. There is a well-known anecdote about an assembly of nobles in the King's presence at York. It was late and dark. While Paulinus preached, a sparrow which had flown in through a window darted out of the gloom into the firelight. For a second or two everyone saw it, and then it vanished into the shadows beyond. A courtier friendly to Paulinus compared the momentary illumination to man's life on earth. If Christian doctrine could shed a beam or two on the terrible darkness before and after, he, for his part, was prepared to accept it.

Again a king and his nobles inclined toward the new faith. If William of Malmesbury is to be trusted, Paulinus made a lengthy tour including a visit to Glastonbury, where he reinforced the Old Church with a casing of boards and an improved roof. But the Roman outpost at York was very nearly lost. The conversion of Northumbria took a startling turn which Rome had never anticipated. The sullen and unregenerate Britons of Wales were still by no means conquered; they were still serious contenders for supremacy. In 633 their king Cadwallon, allying himself with the heathen Mercians, overran Northumbria. For a year he oppressed the northern counties with a régime of exterminatory frightfulness. His aim was not so much domination as genocide, a crime, however, for which the techniques of that backward age were inadequate. The English survived, and in 634 they shook off the forces of occupation. Cadwallon fell in battle. For some years longer the Welsh-Mercian alliance maintained the threat of British recovery, but no leader took up Cadwallon's work, and Northumbria rose unmolested to a level of influence which its position and resources would have seemed to preclude.

These Northumbrian affairs had disturbing results for Christian fortunes in England. Most of the Roman missionaries fled from Cadwallon. Into the vacuum left when the Welsh withdrew there stepped a very different figure, the kindly Scottish ascetic Aidan. He came at the invitation of Oswald, Northumbria's new king. Oswald had been living in the Iona community during the recent troubles, and he returned to his kingdom a professed Christian, but on the Celtic model. Determined to spread his faith, he imported Scottish monks into Northumbria. They settled on the islet of Lindisfarne, where they built a monastery, and their leader Aidan accompanied Oswald on his progresses. Aidan preached in Gaelic; the King himself acted as interpreter. Within a short time the Christianity of Iona – humble and simple, in many ways admirable, but shapeless and unconstructive – prevailed throughout the realm.

Aidan, who richly deserved his popular acclaim as a saint, made no effort to spread the Gospel beyond the bounds Oswald assigned to him. After founding monasteries and throwing together a makeshift ecclesiastical structure, he died, and was buried on Lindisfarne. During the Viking raids many years later, Abbot Tican of Whitby attempted to remove his body to a place of safety. Tican came to Glastonbury, as we know from his signature on a charter, and some say that he brought the body of Aidan for re-interment. The choice of the mighty English repository of Celtic tradition would have been fitting, and there is a certain felicity in the image of the completed cycle: in the symbolic home-coming of Celtic Christianity, personified by one of its holiest teachers, after the long journey by way of Wales and Ireland and Scotland and the northern counties.

But the immediate consequence of St Aidan was a perilous problem for the Church in England. With the Roman discipline established in the most civilised kingdom, namely Kent, and the Celtic in the most powerful, namely Northumbria, there were the makings of a genuine schism. This would of course have been encouraged by the Welsh-English antagonism, which no English ruler had ever tried to resolve, and which Augustine had only sharpened. Religion and culture being as intimately bound up as they were, the British Isles might soon have split into a small 'European' portion looking to Rome and a large 'insular' portion looking to Ireland or Scotland, with hopeless cleavages between.

It did not happen. Fresh trends were developing near the Channel. In 635 Oswald stood sponsor at the baptism of another royal convert, Cynegils, King of Wessex. A good deal of mystery still surrounds this event. Somebody named Birinus had arrived from Italy on the advice of the Pope. He may have been an Irishman. Birinus, at any rate, had introduced into Wessex a Christianity best summed up as a *tertium quid*. It was not Celtic, but neither was it aggressively ultramontane, and its priests owed no allegiance to the Roman stronghold of Canterbury. It almost perished in the cradle. Cynegils's successor Cenwalh rejected it. But no sooner had he done so than the Northumbrian episode repeated itself. The restless and predatory heathens of Mercia, turning south after the defeat of their Welsh allies, fell upon Wessex with alarming success. Before the onset of King Penda, Cenwalh fled to East Anglia, and just as Oswald had lived in exile among the monks of Iona, so Cenwalh found refuge at a court which was already Christian. East Anglian Christianity dated from 631. The ruling families had been won over by Felix, a Burgundian missionary who belonged wholly to the Roman party; but his chief assistant was Fursey, an Irish hermit, and the result of Fursey's collaboration was a tempering of partisan zeal.

Felix baptised the fugitive Cenwalh in 646. East Anglia survived an attack by Penda's Mercians, and when the war ended King Cenwalh returned to his own Wessex. One of his first concerns was to revivify the Church. He imported from Gaul a priest who had spent several years in Ireland, and he made him Bishop of Dorchester-on-Thames, still without dependence on Canterbury. The Church of Wessex which the Bishop proceeded to organise was Roman in its obedience and practice. However, its peculiar origin and its injections of Celtic influence helped to give it a special character. Bede remarks on the friendly relations between the Wessex Christians and their almost schismatic co-religionists in Devon and Cornwall. Auguries of reconciliation were beginning to show.

2

And now a door swung open, a door hinged on Glastonbury. The train of events blundered into motion in 655, when pagan Mercia, sprawling over the heart of England like a monstrous amœba, thrust out another pseudopod to the north. King Penda bore down on Yorkshire with thirty auxiliary chieftains. But this time something went wrong. At the Battle of Winwaed his unwieldy army collapsed, and the Northumbrians killed him. It is a notable point about the pre-Christian Anglo-Saxons that they seem to have been incapable of fighting in masses: numerical strength was deprived of efficacy by a loss of control. Their two famous battles involving a large composite army, Mount Badon and the Winwaed, both ended with a rout. In other respects as well as this one, the racial organising abilities lay dormant till Roman influence aroused them. The foundering of Penda's unmanageable heathen host, and its leader's death, gave the final refutation to Woden.

This failure broke off the Mercian alliance with Wales. In so doing it brought the battle for England to a close after two centuries. The Britons' only hope of recovery had been to play off the English against each other. Cadwallon had tried it, and with more statesmanship he might have restored British sovereignty from the Humber to the Cheviots, creating a Wales too big to be subdued. But after Penda's defeat the Britons were no longer competitors for control over England. They skulked in their Cambrian and Devonian principalities, obviously beaten, obviously subordinate. 'Britain' as an entity opposed to the English, excluding the English, had at last vanished. An obstacle in the way of eventual peace had dissolved.

Mercia's military nullification had a further effect. It removed the pressure on Wessex. King Cenwalh no longer feared an attack across the upper Thames. With that danger out of the way he did not sit idle very long. Acting from motives which it would be interesting to fathom, he concentrated an army and marched into central Somerset. The spellbound frontier with its invisible fortifications at last caved in. For 658 the *Anglo-Saxon Chronicle* has a momentous entry:

In this year Cenwalh fought at Penselwood against the Welsh, and drove them in flight as far as the Parret. This battle was fought after his return from East Anglia, where he was for three years in exile.

The advance engulfed Glastonbury Abbey. Cenwalh's infantry, tramping over the lowland toward the Tor, must have wondered whether the enemy would attempt a stand in that natural fortress. But the exploit of Melwas was not repeated. The Isle fell without a siege, and the English soldiers, converts at their King's order to a faith they scarcely understood, found themselves occupying a strange cluster of wattle huts inhabited by gaunt Britons whose relationship with the new God seemed alarmingly close.

The King may well have undertaken this local and strictly limited war with the specific object of annexing the holy place. But whatever his purpose, and whatever he and a few advisers believed, the rank and file of the army must have thought Glastonbury bewildering. Few of them could read, few had travelled, and few had any clear notion of monastic communities. Moreover, there was the language barrier. Out of the hubbub of Welsh and Anglo-Saxon which broke the hush of Avalon, some very odd rumours manifestly emerged. The earliest recorded version of the Old Church's origin, the tale of its not being built by human hands, is also the most extravagant. It is an echo of the conquerors' awe.

Cenwalh annexed the Abbey, but he left the British Abbot in charge, and saw to it that the infiltration of English monks should proceed by stages. His treatment of Glastonbury was one of the truly regal gestures of history. In the words of Armitage Robinson, he made it a temple of reconciliation between the two races and the two Christian traditions. Here, for the first time, the English treated the Britons with respect as potential members of a larger fraternity: here, therefore, we unearth the United Kingdom's foundation-stone. Here also, and also for the first time, the Roman Church gently took to itself a great Celtic sanctuary, neither persecuting nor violently altering, but quietly shaping union in a spirit of reverence. The Church hardly did as well anywhere else in the British Isles. But in so far as it succeeded at all, in so far as it absorbed the medley of outlying islanders into the civilisation it stood for, it did so by following the pattern of Glastonbury. In 658, at this ancient shrine, in the presence of the Blessed Virgin and the Apostles, Cenwalh struck the true chord of harmony, prefiguring a Britain at one with herself and Europe.

The union foreshadowed at Glastonbury hovered for many decades at the symbolic level. The precondition of its emergence as a political or even ecclesiastical fact was harmony among the English themselves. Within fifteen years this harmony was at least perceptible. In 663, at the Synod of Whitby, St Wilfrid of York enforced Roman discipline among the Christians of Northumbria. We have already glanced at this affair, with its queer violence on the one side, its queer evasiveness on the other. The manner of the actual decision remains to be noted. Wilfrid posed his fatal question to Colman the Scot: 'Did Our Lord give the keys of heaven to St Peter or St Columba?' Colman (incidentally annihilating all later theories of a separate Celtic Church) replied, 'To St Peter.' Whereupon the Northumbrian King, who presided over the gathering, gave his decision in favour of the papalist group. If he allowed his subjects to offend against Peter, even in matters which were not indisputably *de fide*, he might find the gate of heaven locked in his face. Colman gave up the contest and returned to Iona.

Wilfrid's triumph doubtless left an unpleasant taste in Northumbrian mouths. But it was not followed up too brashly. Several Celtic institutions, such as the rootless priesthood and the mixed monastery-convents, were allowed to linger and even spread till they died of their own disadvantages. Nor was the Roman victory barren. It opened all England and eventually Scotland to such civilisation as Europe had retrieved from the wreck of the Empire. Wilfrid and his friend Benedict Biscop infused colour and craftsmanship into the dreary spiritual legacy of the northern Celts. They imported books, relics, pictures; they brought over masons and glass-workers from Gaul, and founded schools to train the English in the same arts; they put up churches of stone, with some pretensions to beauty; they even enlisted the arch-chanter of St Peter's, who plodded all the way from Rome to teach English clergy the Roman method of chanting.

In 669 an erudite Greek, Theodore of Tarsus, became Archbishop of Canterbury. He managed without serious trouble to impose a single ecclesiastical government and a single canon law on the English realms. Northumbria was amenable, Wessex raised no objections, and the successors of the terrible Mercian king had submitted to baptism. Whitby shows the inseparability of religion from politics. Though seven heptarchs divided the land between them, their common and conscientious obedience to a unified Church could hardly fail to draw them together. The warfare which had distracted the seventh century died away in the eighth.

3

Our knowledge of Cenwalh's dealings with Glastonbury is scarcely as full as we could wish. Almost the only indubitable fact is that he confirmed the authority of Bregored, the last of the British abbots. As the British monks died off or departed, Englishmen generally took their places. About 669 Bregored died himself. Cenwalh was still on the throne of Wessex.

Benedict Biscop and Theodore of Tarsus were both acquaintances of his, and it was perhaps on the former's recommendation that he appointed Beorhtwald as the first English Abbot. Benedict's artistic zeal had not been lost on this man. He lacked the resources for new monastic building, but thanks to his inspiration a magnificent stone cross, rich with figures and designs in relief, rose among the slovenly cabins of the monks. Crosses of this kind, with intelligible pictures on them instead of meaningless or mysterious linear traceries, were the first products of English Christian art. Glastonbury's specimen must have stood up like a challenge, the visible token of a new era, vivid and uncompromising.

King Cenwalh granted the Abbey some land at Meare, in a charter bearing Beorhtwald's name and the date 671. So at least we may believe if the charter is genuine, and unlike some later ones it probably is. But on the whole Beorhtwald accomplished little. His reign was unsteady, exploratory. He is even said to have abandoned Brent Knoll, a hill near the Bristol Channel, presented to the Abbey in former times by Arthur himself.

Glastonbury was always plainly destined not to belong wholly to the conquerors. The British branch of Celtdom had withered, but now a stronger branch thrust itself into the West Country and changed the face of things. Glastonbury became, and remained, part Irish, and henceforward its Irish scholars and pilgrims kept its peculiar Otherness alive. One of its oldest charters contains a quotation from an Irish text of the Vulgate. The first actual name is that of Hemgisl, who succeeded Beorhtwald as Abbot about 678. Though English, he had studied in Ireland, and there is evidence that the superior learning and culture which he acquired there, and the wealth of monastic experience which he drew on, enabled him to make his mark very soon in his exacting post. As early as 681 Baldred of Mercia signed a charter granting lands to Glastonbury Abbey: its fame, therefore, must now have grown to considerable proportions beyond the borders of Wessex. Meanwhile the graduates of a school in Selwood Forest, conducted by an Irish missionary named Maelduib, were also making their mark. Maelduib had lived in England for most of his life, and had founded Malmesbury. This monastic colony was originally called Maelduib-byrig, the enclosure of Maelduib; then Ealdelmesburg, the borough of Ealdelm or Aldhelm, its first abbot; then Malmesbury, a form combining fragments of both names. Aldhelm himself was the most distinguished of Maelduib's pupils, and, indirectly, the real inaugurator of Glastonbury's greatness.

After the short reign of a king named Centwine, the crown of Wessex passed to Ine, a direct ancestor of the House of Windsor. His much longer reign was glorious in most of the conventional senses. He defeated the West Welsh under Geraint, occupied Taunton in 710, annexed Devon, and entered Cornwall in 722. More creditable than his military career was his policy toward the conquered, in which we catch the first·clear political echo of Cenwalh's action at Glastonbury. The laws of Ine gave the British population of Wessex a recognised, though unequal, status. 'Wergild' was stipulated (120 shillings for a free Welshman, as against 200 for an Englishman), and the King employed the Welsh in his service, even, significantly enough, in his bodyguard.

. Aldhelm, whom Ine installed as Bishop of Sherborne, probably influenced this wise legislation, and he certainly influenced the King in another respect. William of Malmesbury tells us that it was Aldhelm, about the close of the seventh century, who persuaded Ine to rebuild Glastonbury Abbey. The proposal appealed to the King's imagination. He had undergone a change of heart, passing from formal acceptance of Christian dogma to an active and seemingly enlightened piety. A powerful factor in his conversion was his wife Ethelburga. About Ethelburga the chroniclers afterwards told a story, one of those curious edifying stories which we dare not quite dismiss as pure hagiography. She and her husband were making a progress through the kingdom, and stopped for several days at a royal hunting lodge, which was exceptionally comfortable and well appointed. On the next step of the journey they had only gone a short distance when the Queen made some excuse to take Ine back to the lodge. Everything was now in chaos. The servants (at her instigation, of course) had overturned the furniture, torn down the hangings, emptied refuse on the floor, and put a sow in the bed. 'You should take a lesson from this,' murmured Ethelburga to the horrified monarch. 'That is how all earthly delights will pass away.' The incident has somewhat the air of a university rag, and one wonders about the views of the servants who cleaned up the mess after the lady of the house had pointed her moral. It would be pleasant to think that she gave them a day off in recompense. Whatever the truth in that regard, Ine took his wife's parable to heart. Warfare and government no longer contented him. It became his programme to 'lay great bases for eternity.' Glastonbury at last was his sole terrestrial care.

This Abbey to which the two Hibernicised priests had drawn his attention was still nothing remarkable to look at. A shallow ditch or moat seems to have bounded it. Within the precinct, the ancient wattle church was the principal building. It was now cased in boards, and therefore frequently called the wooden church. It occupied the site of the present Lady Chapel. Its interior must have been very plain, with a cross and a madonna but few other adornments. At its eastern end stood the tiny oratory attributed to St David. The two structures extended along the north side of a rectangular enclosure used as a cemetery. On the east side of this enclosure there was, to judge from excavations, another chapel, possibly built by Gildas. The living quarters lay nearer the hill, but a line drawn eastward along the axis of the church would almost certainly have traversed an empty space. Along such an imaginary line, at all events, most of the subsequent church construction occurred.

Ine left the Old Church architecturally alone. He enriched it, but he did not remodel it. He saw it as a thing of untouchable mystery and holiness. Choosing a site closer to the hillside, he ordered the setting up of a fair-sized church of his own, following a compact pattern devised by Kentish builders. In 704 the finished fabric was dedicated to Dominus Salvator and the Apostles Peter and Paul. Abbot Hemgisl only just lived to see the day: he died soon after the dedication and was buried – not in the new church, however, but in the old one. His successors were the confusingly named Beorhwald (705) and Albert (712). Ine, meanwhile, did not rest satisfied with his first achievement. The Devonian wars engrossed him for some time, but when he had beaten King Geraint and confined the West Welsh to Cornwall, he endowed Glastonbury with more lands, perhaps in thanksgiving. The Abbey acquired ten hides at Brent, ten hides at Sowy, and one at Bleadon. Ine also embellished the churches, providing 2640 pounds of silver and 264 of gold.

More favours were to come yet. In the abbacy of Etfrith or Ehfrid, a friend of Aldhelm's who had studied in Ireland like Hemgisl, King Ine conferred on Glastonbury a status which was then quite novel, though it supplied a precedent for similar cases later. Confirming all previous grants, adding more, and listing the churches dependent on the Abbey, he exempted the Abbot's whole domain from episcopal authority. He made it an ecclesiastical island where the bishop of the diocese had no jurisdiction. Then he went to Rome and arranged that Glastonbury should come directly under the Pope.

In later centuries the monks produced a long document

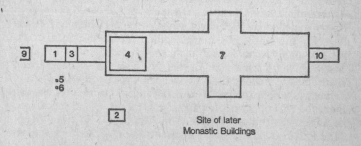

SKETCH PLAN OF ABBEY

1. Site of 'Old Church,' afterwards occupied by Lady Chapel. 2. Approximate site of second chapel (built by Gildas?). 3. Site of third chapel (built by St. David?). 4. Approximate site of Saxon church. 5–6. Pillars. 7. Medieval church. 8. Abbot's kitchen. 9. Chapel of St. John. 10. Edgar Chapel.

purporting to be 'Ine's Charter.' Like Patrick's, it was spurious. The object was to bolster the Abbey's political position. It would be unfair, however, to dismiss the charter as a totally worthless fabrication. The author is trying more or less honestly to express what he believes to be the historical facts. He is trying to reconstruct what Ine's lawyers *must* have written. He embroiders, he fills in gaps, he uses his imagination; but the core of what he writes is authentic tradition.

'In the name of Our Lord Jesus Christ,' the devout monarch is made to begin, 'I, Ine . . . do grant out of those places which I possess by paternal inheritance, and hold in my demesne, they being adjacent and fitting for the purpose, for the maintenance of the monastic institution and the use of the monks, Brent 10 hides, Sowy 10 hides, Pilton 20 hides, Dulting 20 hides, Bleadon 1 hide, together with whatever my predecessors have contributed.' The first of these predecessors is naturally Cenwalh, who gave lands at Meare, Bekery, and elsewhere. The second is Centwine, who 'used to call Glastonbury "the mother of saints,"' who 'liberated it from every secular and ecclesiastical service' (whatever that means), and who authorised the monks to elect their own abbot according to the Rule of St Benedict. Glastonbury may in fact have adopted the Benedictine Rule at this time, but the subject is obscure, and our review of the implications is best postponed till we come to Dunstan. The third benefactor named in the charter is Bishop Hedda, who gave Pennard 6 hides. The fourth is Athelard, who gave 'Poelt', or Poholt, 60 hides, 'I, Ine, permitting and confirming it.'

The author proceeds with the political clauses. 'In order that the church of Our Lord Jesus Christ and the eternal Virgin Mary, as it is the first in the kingdom of Britain and the source and fountain of all religion, may obtain surpassing dignity and privilege . . . I appoint and establish that all lands, places, and possessions of St Mary of Glastonbury be free from all royal taxes and works which are wont to be appointed, that is to say expeditions and the building of bridges and forts, and from the edicts or molestations of all archbishops or bishops. . . . And whatsoever questions shall -arise, whether of homicide, sacrilege, poison, theft, rapine, the disposal and limits of churches, the ordination of clerics, ecclesiastical synods, and all judicial inquiries, they shall be determined by the decision of the Abbot and community, without the interference of any person whatsoever.' The King is made to enjoin the civil authorities not to hold courts, conduct investigations, or seize goods within the charmed circle. He also prohibits 'any bishop, on any account, from presuming to take his episcopal seat, or celebrate divine service, consecrate altars, dedicate churches, or ordain, or do anything whatever, either in the church of Glastonbury itself or its dependent churches . . . unless he be specially invited by the Abbot or brethren of that place.' Two or three obviously bogus articles follow, in which the King appoints two houses for the bishop's residence if he does pass through the Abbey lands, and threatens to take them away if that dignitary fails in treating the Abbey with proper deference. In general, the consequences of violating the charter are most alarming. 'Whosoever shall attempt to pervert or nullify this . . . let him be aware that, with the traitor Judas, he shall perish, to his eternal confusion, in the devouring flames of unspeakable torments.' With these words the charter ends. It is dated 725.

Ine's attributed statements and intentions can be confirmed, to a small extent, from more trustworthy sources. The donations of land at Meare and Poholt, for instance, are not fictitious. Genuine charters have survived to attest to them. As for the Abbey's autonomy, that is more dubious. But until the close of the twelfth century the Bishop of Bath and Wells is never mentioned as exerting any acknowledged control over Glastonbury. Indeed, a serious jealousy arose, best accounted for by a long-standing exemption. After the catastrophe of the Danish raids, an outside authority did take the rifled Abbey in hand; but it was the King's authority, not the Bishop's. On the whole it is rational to conclude that the charter, with all its imaginative accretions, reflects truth.

Having accomplished the glorification of Glastonbury, King Ine considered his earthly task as done. In 725 he abdicated and went back to Rome, where he entered the Benedictine Order and died a monk. His devout queen accompanied him. It is not certain that this was the lady of the lodge episode. There is an interesting story that he also married a Welsh princess. The story is not reliable, but the fact that it could be told is significant.

Strangely enough, Glastonbury's tradition associated this reign with its only pre-dissolution martyrdoms. St Indract, William of Malmesbury relates, was the son of an Irish king. With his sister Dominica and nine companions he set out on a long pilgrimage. The party came to Cornwall and lived for some time near the mouth of the Tamar River in prayer and fasting. Indract, like some others we know, planted his staff, and it grew into an oak. He also made a pond from which he daily drew fish for his small community. But a greedy pilgrim surreptitiously caught a fish for himself, whereupon the supply failed. Relations being strained, the

145

party divided. The prince, his sister, and some of the others left for Rome. They visited the Apostles' tombs and returned, passing through Britain a second time. While they were staying in a cottage at Shapwick, near Glastonbury, one of Ine's officials named Horsa murdered them in their beds and decamped with the money. It so happened that the good King was holding court in the neighbourhood. Unable to sleep that night, he went out for a stroll and saw a light over Shapwick. Horsa had set fire to the cottage; but the glow of the flames aureoled his victims. When Ine heard, he had the bodies buried at Glastonbury.

This is said to have happened in 710. Irish annals fail to mention a martyr who fulfils the conditions. They do name an Indract as Abbot of Iona from 849 till 854, when he was killed by 'Saxons,' presumably on a journey southward. That a holy man called Indract died by violence in the West Country appears from a Cornish church dedication and from the grave at Glastonbury itself. The frightful era of the Danes is certainly more plausible. If Abbot Indract did pass through Somerset, roving warriors could easily have mistaken the Gaelic-speaking traveller for a Dane.

4

While Ine ruled, the military strength of Wessex won general respect. But owing, it may be, to his pious pre-occupations, he did little to safeguard its continuance. By this omission he benefited his people as surely as he had done so by his laws, his religious acts, and his containment of the West Welsh. A powerful Wessex would have prolonged the division of England. In the upshot, within a few years of Ine's withdrawal from the scene, the Christian ruler of Mercia wielded a more than nominal sovereignty over all the English south of the Humber. The kingdoms remained separate, but they looked up to a single overlord.

The eighth century was a fairly peaceful and fairly credit-able epoch. Civilisation seemed to be returning to western Europe. Though the dawn was false, it brought a measure of durable achievement, and the share of the English in that achievement was noteworthy. Their Christianity possessed something of the freshness which had earlier made the Irish so potent a force. One of its products was the Venerable Bede, the foremost scholar of his age. Another was Alcuin. His international reputation for learning brought him an invitation to Charlemagne's court, where he may have been the original advocate of a restored Empire.

Rome recognised the value of these island recruits, and made England her northern base of operations. Germany was still largely heathen; to Germany the evangelists turned. An English mission led by St Boniface established itself beyond the Rhine and toiled bravely through every sort of discouragement. Boniface himself attained the honour of martyrdom. He had started life in Exeter; it is suggested that he was once a Glastonbury monk. Whether or not he himself was at the Abbey, the mission kept in touch with it. A letter from Germany, written by a monk named Wigbert to his Avalonian brethren, gives particulars which he clearly knows will be of the utmost interest to them. These voluntary exiles paved the way for the empire of Charlemagne.

Glastonbury, indeed, repeatedly sent forth active and able sons. We hear of bishops and archbishops – Eanfrid of Elmham, Wigthegn of Winchester. Some of the abbots are scarcely more than names to us, but the record of their sound and unblemished administration is reason enough why their names should live. The list given by Armitage Robinson is: Coengisl, Tumbert, Tica (754), Guba (760), Waldun (762), Beadewulf (794), Muca (800), Guthlac (824), Elmund (851). William of Malmesbury, writing after 1125, describes two memorial pillars or pyramids belonging to this pre-Danish summer.

Willingly would I explain, could I but ascertain the truth, a thing which is almost incomprehensible to all, and that is, the meaning of those pyramids which, situated some few feet from the church, border on the cemetery of the monks. That which is the loftiest and nearest the church, is twenty-eight feet high, and has five storeys: this, though threatening ruin from its extreme age, possesses nevertheless some traces of antiquity which may be clearly read, though not perfectly understood. In the highest storey is an image, in a pontifical habit. In the next, a statue of regal dignity, and the letters HER SEXI and BLISWERH, In the third are the names WENCREST, BANTOMP, WINETHEGN. In the fourth, BATE, WULFRED, and EANFLED. In the fifth, which is the lowest, there is an image, and the words following: LOGOR, WEASLIEAS, BREGDEN, SWELWES, HIWINGENDES BEARN. The other pyramid is twenty-six feet high, and has four storeys, in which are read, CENTWINE, HEDDE the bishop, and BREGORED and BEORWARD. The meaning of these I do not hastily decide, but I shrewdly conjecture that within, in stone coffins, are contained the bones of those persons whose names are inscribed without.

These pillars will confront us again in a more surprising connection.

Royal patronage continued. King Cuthred of Wessex granted another charter. The ostensible text confirms previous grants by kings of Wessex and 'Ethbald King of the Mercias,' and repeats the threats ascribed to Ine. It is marked with a cross and dated 745. The last sentence runs: 'This charter was made and delivered in the aforesaid monastery in the presence of Cuthred the king, who laid it with his princely hand on the altar, in the wooden church in which the brethren of Abbot Hemgisl are buried.'

After 757 Offa of Mercia was 'king of the whole land of the English,' though the royal succession in the other kingdoms did not lapse. The Mercian overlord is said to have added to Glastonbury's buildings. It was a quiet period – the fact deserves re-emphasis – a time of advancing literacy and improving organisation. Christian beliefs were often superficially held, and mixed with the grossest superstition. Yet they were biting deeper, and eliciting excellent results. One feature of the English Church, its meticulous penitential code, is not so purely quaint as it looks. Anybody may smile on reading that a layman who drinks till he is sick must do five days' penance, while a monk guilty of the same lapse must do thirty. But the painstaking and legalistic minds which devised such rules showed symptoms of a capacity for order entirely beyond the Celts. That small England with its million or so inhabitants was enjoying a halcyon phase, happy in the virtual absence of history. When Charlemagne restored the Empire in Europe, with England's Alcuin on the steps of his throne, many must have felt that the dawn was broadening into daylight.

And then the sky darkened, and all went down before a fresh onset of heathendom. The new marauders whom the north had held in reserve are described variously as Danes, Vikings, and Norsemen. The terms are not interchangeable,

148

but they overlap enough to create confusion. In the English connection 'Dane' is the traditional word. From Scandinavia, at any rate, the marauders crossed over. Harmless peasant pioneers who had colonised the Shetlands and Orkneys were followed by war-bands of buccaneering nobles, the armed spearheads of a gaudy, restless, rapacious society. These adventurers poured round Scotland into the Hebrides and Ireland, where they set up lawless principalities. Meanwhile a more deadly horde swarmed over the North Sea directly into England. The British invasion was only part of a demonic outburst of energy that lasted for several lifetimes and spread havoc in every quarter. Vikings terrorised Russia, Vikings besieged Paris, Vikings plundered the Mediterranean. But the English episode was the most frightful. Isolated raids gave place to a permanent, organised, and ever-expanding system of banditry. The Danish groups which might have quarrelled among themselves coalesced instead into a single force, known to historians as the Great Army. While the Army ravaged the land, the long-ships plied to and fro reinforcing it, and darted unchecked about the coast.

Ordinary narrative prose cannot convey the atmosphere of that time. It has been done in poetry (I am thinking of Chesterton's *Ballad of the White Horse*), and perhaps the theme is best left to imaginative writers. An inhuman and implacable doom overhung the whole island. Trying to pierce the murk, we glimpse a kaleidoscope of horrors: ships with devilish prows gliding up quiet estuaries; peasants violently dispossessed by enormous aliens who drank blood and dragged people through fires for sport; horses commandeered in their pastures and ridden madly over the farmlands; churches stripped, crosses cut down for firewood; laughter and learning suddenly struck dumb; refugees streaming one way and slaves streaming the other. The Danish zone in England was not a state, it was the absence of a state, and it spread like a satanic negation. As the ninth century wore its way along, Northumbria vanished from the map; Mercia followed; King Edmund of the East Angles died a martyr for the Faith; London fell and the Danes surged up the Thames toward the White Horse Vale and the West Country.

One of those who fled before them was Abbot Tican of Whitby, bearing, men say, the hallowed bones of St Aidan. To Glastonbury he came and there he buried them. But they still could not repose in safety. At the blackest moment of all, early in 878, a Danish vanguard reached Glastonbury

149

itself. The ordeal was short and fierce. The Danes looted the churches, applied the torch, and withdrew. Christian continuity was not broken. Yet they would have come back and swept the Abbey also into their empire of emptiness, if it had not been for a lonely man in the marshes just to the south, who alone of all English leaders had survived to oppose them. This was Alfred, the King of Wessex.

Before succeeding to the throne he had fought the Danes with success at Ashdown in Berkshire. The victory proving insufficient, he had retired westward. In the west, as a king almost without a kingdom, he had encountered the wonder-working presence of Glastonbury in the person of St Neot.

Neot was Alfred's half-brother, an illegitimate son of the same father. In his youth he wanted to be a soldier, but he was too small even by the lax military standards of the ninth century. He entered Glastonbury Abbey and became notable for his scholarship and devotion. Engaging little stories were told afterwards: how he had to stand on an iron stool to say Mass; how the lock in a door obligingly shifted down so that he could reach it. After being sacristan for some time, he lived for seven years as a hermit in Cornwall. During a pilgrimage to Rome the Pope advised him not to shut himself off but to go about preaching. On his return he founded a small community in the valley of Hamstoke, and perfected his knowledge of the West Welsh speech with the aid of a native hermit. On his first tour the peasants told him they could not stay to listen because they had to chase the crows off their fields. Neot miraculously immobilised the crows while he talked.

Alfred, meanwhile, had kept in touch with his half-brother. In 877 Neot cured him of a chronic complaint, but seized the occasion to remind him of his duty toward his humbler subjects – advice which Alfred, menaced by Danes in Devon and Somerset, had little chance at the moment to profit by. The King, however, promised to send money to Rome to aid the English school founded there by Ine. Soon afterwards Neot died. Alfred was at Athelney in Somerset, barely distinguishable from a refugee, but praying and planning and gathering information as to the possibilities of further resistance. The Danes made their one dreadful appearance at Glastonbury and marched eastward. Alfred pressed after them with his last reserves, arriving at Ethandune, an unidentified spot thought to have been in the north-west corner of Salisbury Plain. There he saw Neot in a dream, dressed in radiant apparel, promising victory; there he engaged the Danish host under Guthrum; and there he routed it. This was 'the high tide and the turn' of the invasion. In May 878 Alfred concluded an agreement with Guthrum by which the enemy chief became a Christian and agreed to confine his nation behind a fixed boundary, leaving Wessex and part of Mercia in Alfred's hands.

By this treaty Alfred laid the foundation of a fully united England capable of absorbing the Danes. More wars were to ensue, and Scandinavian princes were to rule even in Wessex, but not as mere ravagers. Alfred and his successors knocked humanity into them. His own kingdom took in more and more ground till at last it was conterminous with England itself, and the name 'Wessex' became obsolete. Even the Welsh acknowledged the heroic king as Ruler of all Christians of the Island of Britain. The story of his wise government, his erudition, and his foundation of the Navy, is told by a Welsh priest named Asser whom he invited to his court and authorised to write his biography.

The posthumous tribulations of Neot make a sad epilogue. The saint was buried in Cornwall, but his bones, after Alfred's death, were stolen and taken to Eynesbury in Huntingdonshire for a new religious building. His Cornish friends vowed to fetch him back, and an armed band of them actually reached Eynesbury. There, however, the troops of an English monarch dispersed them.

5

As the wave of ruin receded, Glastonbury Abbey lifted its battered head and found itself virtually alone. It was the only religious house of consequence which had survived. Once again, as in the time of the Saxon conquest, Glastonbury stood up as the sole refuge of continuity. At that the continuity was the frailest of threads. Regular monastic life had tailed off. A tiny group of priests lingered, serving Ine's church and looking after a library of disproportionate size. Hermits intermittently settled nearby. While attempts at restoration were going on elsewhere, they were few and feeble. The destruction of books, the looting of treasures, the dispersal of schools, all had combined to impoverish the English

Church and slow down its recovery in every respect. Glastonbury enjoyed two immense advantages, its ancient prestige and its Irish contact. Thanks to the former, aid and protection from the Crown prevented total bankruptcy. During the reign of Edward, in the early part of the tenth century, Avalon seems to have been treated more or less as an estate of the King. Hence the phrase 'royal island' in the mythical account quoted on page 35. Within the enclosure thus protected, a cluster of Irish monks gradually gathered, with access to the stores of books which the flames of invasion had hardly scorched. To call this Glastonbury group the most potent single factor in the revival of learning throughout England would perhaps be an exaggeration. The Irish remained anonymous and unobtrusive; they simply placed what they had to offer at the disposal of Englishmen. Without them, however, the revival would have been immeasurably more difficult. In the library of Corpus Christi, Cambridge, there is an eloquent relic of their labours. It is a *Life of St Cuthbert*, part prose, part verse, written in a beautiful Anglo-Celtic hand. An illustration shows a king presenting a book to a saint. The date is about 937.

Glastonbury's exceptional status and resources were exploited with radical effect by its greatest abbot: St Dunstan.

Railway stations have displayed a poster map of Somerset in which Glastonbury is represented by a picture of Dunstan catching the Devil with a hot pair of tongs. This, apparently, is his chief title to fame, and his Abbey's also, if the choice of the railways' publicity department is anything to go by. The story of the tongs is, as a matter of fact, highly dubious, and much less worthy of record than its companion pieces like Alfred and the Cakes. The Adversary may have pressed Dunstan pretty closely in his assaults, but he would not have done so in a form solid enough to permit so disconcerting a counter-attack.

Dunstan came from an aristocratic Somerset family related to the royal house. He was born about 909 at Baltonsborough, four miles from Glastonbury. His uncle Athelm, educated at the Abbey, was the first Bishop of Bath and Wells. Dunstan also went to school at the Abbey. The half-empty place took hold of his ardent fancy. The scarred and rifled condition in which the Danes had left it inspired him with visions of reconstruction. Once he dreamed that a majestic old man, dressed all in white, stood by him beckoning him to rise and follow. He did so, and his mysterious guide led him slowly through the cloisters and chapels of a new Abbey, nobler than those familiar to him could ever have been. Thus the future Abbot was introduced to his future house; and the prophecy created its own fulfilment. (It would be interesting to know who the old man was, where Dunstan had got the idea of him, and why the dream did not in any way identify him. To those willing to admit such possibilities, I offer the suggestion that this was an authentic apparition on the part of Glastonbury's founder, who went unrecognised because his name had long since been lost. The English of Dunstan's day rested content with the myth about the church not built by human hands.)

Uncle Athelm passed in due course from the see of Bath and Wells to that of Canterbury, and when Athelstan became king, Athelm introduced his promising nephew to the court. Dunstan acquired the status, in effect, of a royal ward. This English court was a volatile institution. It was not fixed at Winchester, the capital of Wessex. It moved from place to place in a constant progress, carrying with it at least three sub-courts belonging to foreign princes in exile. Haakon of Norway, Louis of France, Alan of Brittany, attended the English sovereign and broadened the horizons of others who did the same. Howel the Good, the King of Wales (in so far as anybody was King of Wales), was also an honoured visitor. The company delighted Dunstan and perhaps went a little to his head. He was a gay, artistic, versatile youth, with a fluent tongue and a positive character. Men had strong feelings towards him, whether of like or dislike. They could not ignore him. He read widely, in an age when you had to know the right people to get hold of a book at all. He learned music and rudimentary science. The sequel might have been predicted. When the court was in Somerset, a local deputation approached Athelstan with charges against their former neighbour. He talked to them now, they protested, in a strange manner, taken out of books which they could not read or comprehend. The songs on his lips were not the songs of Somerset. Dunstan was manifestly a sorcerer.

Athelstan, either lacking in judgment or merely weak, allowed himself to be persuaded, and dismissed Dunstan from the court. Somewhere near Glastonbury the victim's accusers pounced on him. No longer afraid of the King's vengeance, they bound him with ropes, tossed him in the mud and jumped on him. After they had gone he managed to crawl to a friend's house. He reached it covered with dirt, and the dogs not unnaturally attacked him, but they fell back when he spoke and they knew his voice.

Left in peace for a while, Dunstan gave some serious thought to the problem of his purpose in life. The role of a court butterfly was closed, and he had had an ugly glimpse of the passion and ignorance which prevailed outside the small circle of the literate nobility. Bishop Aelfheah, whom he had met as a courtier, urged him to take monastic vows. For years he refused, mistrusting his ability to endure the fasts and rigours, but at last an illness put an end to his drifting. Aelfheah ordained him about 936, together with a friend, Ethelwold.

His rise was rapid but jerky. Athelstan's successor Edmund recalled him to court and made him his chief counsellor, a sort of Prime Minister. Dunstan held the position, with interludes, for the rest of his life, sometimes officially and sometimes informally. But an extraordinary twist in his fortunes assigned him an additional task. Envious rivals sowed dissension between himself and the King. Dunstan lost favour, and while the court was at Cheddar he planned to leave the country with some ambassadors whom Edmund was entertaining. One day, however, the King rode out hunting. An agile stag lured him to the hilltops over the Cheddar Gorge. There he lost control of his horse, which made straight for the cliff-edge at a gallop. At that moment the thought of Dunstan flashed into the King's mind. He saw their painful relationship without self-deception: he was in the wrong and he would be called to account for it. If God would spare his life he would make amends. The horse bolted on; the edge drew nearer; the King prayed; and, somewhere below, the disheartened Dunstan was packing his bags. Then, with an almost audible snap, the pattern of grief and panic transformed itself. On the brink of the precipice the horse made a sudden swerve and pulled up. Edmund was safe. Shaken, he set off down the hill considering how to discharge his promise. The abbacy of Glastonbury was in his gift. He took Dunstan there and appointed him Abbot.

In the decade from 943 onwards the story of Dunstan is the story of Glastonbury. Edmund was murdered and the Abbot served as chief minister under his brother Edred, who used the Abbey as a treasury, but the political events are of comparatively minor importance. What matters is the growth, there in Somerset, of a religious house without parallel or precedent throughout England – a Benedictine house in the grand manner. The recovery from the Dark Ages had at last fairly begun.

Virtually all western monasticism was now Benedictine, but the potentialities of the system had not everywhere been realised. The major foundations of the Black Monks, to quote a hackneyed metaphor, were spiritual power-houses; as indeed they are still. The strenuous life of the inmates centred in the *Opus Dei*, the communal recitation of the Divine Office, distributed among the eight canonical hours – Matins, Lauds, Prime, Terce, Sexts, Nones, Vespers, Compline. (Hence the renaissance of music.) In addition the monks put in the equivalent of a modern day's work. They dispensed charity, in a very wide sense. Their chief secular concerns were study, education, and farming. Early medieval culture is Benedictine culture at second or third hand. The social institutions, religious orders, and borrowings from Greeks and Arabs which came later, fitted into a spiritual mould for which the monks were largely responsible. Their copying of manuscripts rescued a sizable portion of the Classical heritage. Moreover, the existence of nations well enough nourished to use that heritage was in large degree owing to the monks' cultivation of the land and reclamation of wilderness. Innovations ascribed to them include the scientific improvement of grain, the acclimatisation of several delicate fruits, the brewing of beer from hops, the practice of systematic bee culture, the artificial insemination of fish, and the planting of the vineyards of Burgundy and the Rhine.

The Abbeys governed themselves according to the Rule of St Benedict, handed down from the sixth century. Their moral ideals may be found in the fourth chapter of that Rule, summed up under seventy-two heads. The list gives the Ten Commandments, the spiritual and corporal works of mercy, various points of holy conduct and holy thought, and, of course, precepts touching the three monastic vows of poverty, chastity and obedience.

Glastonbury probably adopted the Rule after Cenwalh's conquest. But the practice in England of the full Benedictine life was retarded till the coming of Dunstan. It is only in fragmentary outbreaks that we find a scholarly vigour and flair for public service like those of the famous continental foundations. Dunstan's work at his own Abbey was now to prove the chief single initiatory step toward all that was best in the Middle Ages. While Edmund lived he looked on with a sympathetic eye. William of Malmesbury quotes another charter, ostensibly granted by him in 944. Its special feature is the attempt of its medieval composer to provide an early sanction for the Abbot's jurisdiction over the town. The same attempt is made in the 'Ine' charter, which, if genuine, would render 'Edmund' superfluous. Hence 'Edmund' was doubtless written before 'Ine,' and not so very far from the real event. Though forged, it is by no means worthless as evidence. It is a retroactive codification of impromptu arrangements which in all probability did grow up when the Abbey had its first head of commanding stature. 'I Edmund,' says the ventriloquist's royal dummy, 'do grant to the church of the Mother of God, Mary of Glastonbury, and the venerable Dunstan,[1] whom I have there constituted Abbot, the franchise and jurisdiction, rights, customs. . . . But more especially shall the town of Glastonbury, in which is situated that most ancient church of the holy Mother of God, together with its bounds, be more free than other places. The Abbot of this place alone shall have power, as well in causes known as unknown, in small and in great . . . he shall have the same authority of punishing or remitting the crimes of delinquents perpetrated within it as my court has . . .'

Aided by royal support and by royal grants, Dunstan proceeded to realise that early dream. His community must be worthily housed. He brought in his brother Wulfric to be provost of the Abbey estates, apparently careless of accusations of nepotism, when he genuinely saw in his brother the sort of ability he wanted. With the routine of temporal management provided for, he set to work as an artist on the grand scale. As his community grew, more and more hands fostered its further growth.

His most spectacular measure was a somewhat ruthless remodelling of King Ine's church. Besides effacing the last scars of Danish ravage, he added side aisles and a tower, and carried the end of the building farther east. The extensions sideways exceeded the extension lengthwise, and, as a result,

[1] The word 'venerable,' supposedly applied to Dunstan at thirty-five, cannot be cited as proof of the writer's ignorance. It only means 'worthy of respect.'

the church was almost square. One gets the impression that Dunstan's church became controversial; like, say, the Stratford Memorial Theatre. William of Malmesbury does not quite know what to say about it. 'The result of Dunstan's labours,' he writes, 'was that as far as the design of the ancient structure allowed, a basilica was produced of great extent in both directions; wherein if aught be lacking in seemliness and beauty there is, at any rate, no want of necessary room.' Probably the Abbot was experimenting, and his design failed to catch on. But the church very soon acquired an unlooked-for distinction in the shape of a royal tomb. In 946, when Edmund was assassinated, they buried him there.

Tombs, graves, and human remains, indeed, were constantly thrusting themselves into Dunstan's affairs. In the year of Edmund's interment an opportunity arose of bringing over the relics of St David. They were placed on view in a portable shrine, and it is not absolutely proved that they ever went back to Wales. Domestic remains presented Dunstan with a more formidable problem. Even in those days, centuries of burials had distributed bones over a considerable part of his Abbey. In lengthening the church he had to dismantle a mausoleum built by King Ine to the east. This contained the skeletons of fifteen previous abbots, and also an empty stone coffin with two drain-holes in the bottom. Ine had perhaps intended it for himself, before his decision to go to Rome. Dunstan meditated what to do with the contents of the mausoleum. At last, with a fine instinct of economy, he had the stone coffin moved into the crypt of the church and enlarged by the addition of a higher rim. Then he packed all the bones of his predecessors into the one coffin, and put a lid on. There they rested undisturbed even by the Reformers, till in 1928 excavators discovered them.

Dunstan also reconstructed the monks' living quarters, using local lias and a hard yellow mortar. Here too he had burials to contend with, but they constituted less of a problem. The graveyard which he worked on hardest was the ancient plot to the south of the Old Church, where the pillars stood. This could not hold more bodies. The clay was crowded. Dunstan, however, did not see why the site should be abandoned. He had earth piled on top to a height of four or five feet, permitting future generations of monks to use the plot all over again, and he built a wall of masonry round it. Thus, says William, 'the area was raised up to form a pleasant meadow, removed from the noise of passers-by, so that it might truly be said of the bodies of the saints lying within that they repose in peace.' Early coffins of stone and later coffins of wood, unearthed in the banked-up area, show that successive generations of monks made good use of their two-storey cemetery.

The Abbot was anxious to enlarge the Abbey's usefulness to the country in an economic sense. He set the brethren to work on a scheme of land reclamation, embanking the Brue and rendering acres of marshland fit for farming. The state of the Vale of Avalon below Glastonbury in those days is far from clear. There would seem to have been a rather indeterminate network of channels and lagoons, with a broad permanent lake in the Meare neighbourhood, the entire region being subject to inundations when rivers swollen by rain met the thirty-five-foot tides of the Bristol Channel. Dunstan had made a sound beginning, which the medieval abbots eventually followed up. He had other material interests. It is likely that he launched – it is morally certain that he encouraged – the monastic manufacture of glassware. Near the cloister a furnace was hollowed out in the clay soil, oval-shaped, four feet by three. The bottom was lined with pieces of Roman tile taken from older structures. In this compact unit a very various industry was carried on. Fragments which slowly accumulated told their own story to modern archæologists: portions of crucibles and green bowls, one striped with maroon; half a bead; a scrap of window; chips of hard clay furnace-wall and solidified ash. The Glass Island was justifying its name.

Amid all this activity Dunstan walked about with a cross-handled staff, inspecting and advising. Biographers record that he rose at dawn and spent hours in the writing-room correcting faulty manuscripts. That touch suggests that he was the sort of administrator who cannot delegate, a dangerous flaw even in the most able man. Yet he was quick enough to delegate the estate management to Wulfric. The point surely is that he liked to take a personal hand in the matters he cared for most, and scholarship was one of these. More generally, he cared for the Benedictine way. And his vision, as befitted a statesman, ranged far beyond Glastonbury. As chief minister of the Crown he sought to build a strong central authority which would, nevertheless, encourage the growth of local authorities; and as a churchman he thought on similar lines. From his Abbey he planned that the Benedictine system should spread through all England, aided and protected by Glastonbury, yet free at all points to grow.

Dunstan's principal helper in realising his aim was his pupil Ethelwold. The Abbot saw the young monk's ability and moved him as fast as possible into a position of trust. Ethelwold was an expert on music. It is an attractive feature of his character that he asked, and obtained, permission to keep his job of abbey gardener, and as such he seems to have impressed himself on the Abbot's unconscious mind in terms of arboreal imagery. Dunstan dreamed again, as he had dreamt to such good purpose in childhood. He saw a splendid tree covering Britain with its branches, but the branches, instead of fruit, bore the cowls of innumerable monks. At the top a larger cowl overpeered all the others, and that was Ethelwold's.

For ten years Glastonbury Abbey was the monastic school of the English nation, and although its achievement subsequently toned down its own pre-eminence, the impetus never slackened. Abbots and bishops poured out of its cloister. The first major success was the restoration of Abingdon, where the Danes had destroyed the monastery during the reign of Alfred. King Edred offered his help; a party of Glastonbury monks led by Ethelwold arrived on the spot; and Abingdon rose again. Ethelwold became the new Abbot. When he passed to the bishopric of Winchester, he was succeeded by a Glastonbury monk named Osgar, and he in turn was succeeded by a Glastonbury monk named Siward. Ethelwold, meanwhile, was sponsoring abbeys at Ely, Peterborough, and Thorney. It was all in keeping with the trend of the times. Even the jealous town of Wells accepted two bishops from the island across the marsh. After 950 the entire English monastic movement looked back to Dunstan of Glastonbury as its originator.

The Abbot's personal career was adventurous. King Edred died and his regrettable nephew Edwy reigned. Dunstan, too outspoken, fell out of favour at court yet again and went to Flanders. Characteristically, he did not waste his time there. He studied continental movements of monastic reform and noted down ideas. His exile was hardly more than a holiday. Before long the Mercians revolted and proclaimed Edgar, Edwy's brother, as King north of the Thames. The pretender acted promptly to win Dunstan for his cause. He recalled him from Flanders and made him simultaneous Bishop of London and Worcester. Then Edwy died himself. Edgar ruled over the whole English territory, and Dunstan emerged from his trials as Archbishop of Canterbury.

His work in clarifying the relations of Church and State, and in organising the abbeys of Bath and Westminster, lies outside our scope. But even as Primate of the Church and Prime Minister of the State, he showed his old personal care for details when he judged them important. Quarrels over drink, for example, were a public scandal. Dunstan ordered that pegs should be fixed in tankards to mark a statutory limit. Nor, amid these preoccupations, did he lose touch with his own Abbey. The psalter known as the Bosworth Psalter, drawn up for Archbishop Dunstan, bears the signs of a Glastonbury origin.

It is a workmanlike volume with a noble simplicity. There are no pictures. The script is graceful and regular. The capitals are majestic and richly coloured, but without the glare of gold. In the front is a calendar of saints' days which supplies fascinating glimpses of the pre-Norman traditions. It mentions two Patricks, one being the Apostle of Ireland, the other that 'Old Patrick' by whom the Irish explained away the tomb at Glastonbury. St Bridget follows. Aidan and Ceolfrid, the Abbot of Jarrow, are both listed, with the words 'in Glaston'; evidently the story of a transfer and reburial during the Danish raids was fully accepted. The names of Wilfrid and Paulinus are perhaps not especially significant. But a purely Avalonian entry is St Gildas. The British Jeremiah was certainly no saint in the eyes of Roman or Saxon Christianity. The calendar entry is a proof of Celtic influence, and a near-proof of the antiquity of the belief that Gildas dwelt at Glastonbury.

The Leofric Missal, another volume deriving from the same source, confirms the evidence of the Bosworth Psalter.

King Edgar granted Glastonbury a charter, duly quoted by William. The surviving text is another falsification, dated 971. It excludes the Bishop of Bath and Wells from jurisdiction over the parish churches of 'Stret, Mirelinch, Budecalage, Sceapwic, Sowy, Beocharic or Little Ireland, Godenie, Mertinesie, Patheneberge, Edredeseie, and Ferramere.' The Abbot is allowed to have his monks ordained by any bishop in the province of Canterbury. An alternative text insists on the right of the community to elect its own head. William adds that Pope John XIII confirmed the charter, and quotes a letter from that pontiff rebuking Earl Aluric for persecuting Glastonbury. These documents, like the rest of the

1 Aerial view of Glastonbury Tor.

2a *Top*   Glastonbury. The remains of the abbey can be seen at the bottom right with Glastonbury Tor in the left background.

2b *Bottom*   The Lady Chapel seen from the south.

3   The south transept and crossing of the abbey.

4a *Top* Cadbury Castle.

4b *Bottom* Liddington Castle, an Iron Age hill-fort near Swindon, which was possibly Mount Badon, the site of Arthur's decisive victory over the Saxons.

forgeries, are neither reliable nor totally negligible.

In 975 Edgar died, and was buried close to Edmund in Dunstan's church. The saint himself died in 988. The last part of his life was devoted less to politics and more to education. At Canterbury Cathedral School the boys afterwards remembered him for his kindness, and passed on anecdotes showing him in an agreeable light. Many years later, when lesser and crueller masters proposed to whip the entire school at Christmas on general principles, the boys gathered at the saint's shrine and prayed to their 'dear father Dunstan.' A quarrel broke out among the masters and the whipping blew over.

As to this shrine, an extraordinary dispute arose. Taking the Glastonbury records at their face value, we must conclude that the sequence of events ran thus. In the twenty-fourth year after Dunstan's death, King Edmund Ironside came to the Abbey and spoke highly of the late Archbishop. The monks begged him to let them bring back the hallowed bones for re-interment. He consented, and four monks who had known Dunstan personally and attended his funeral set off for Canterbury. Their names were Sebricht, Ethelbricht, Bursius and Adelworde. Arriving at the city, they found its cathedral in a battered state from the Danish depredations. Dunstan's sepulchre, however, was clearly marked. They opened it and revealed his skeleton resting on a rich tapestry. One finger bore a ring which they recognised. Satisfied, they collected the bones and returned to Glastonbury. There a wooden casket was made and painted with the initials of the saint. The monks packed the bones into this casket and interred it under a stone in the larger church, near the holy-water stoup on the right of the main entrance. The hiding-place was not publicised for a long while, but late in the twelfth century, during rebuilding operations, the relics were disposed in a gorgeously decorated shrine. Thereafter they effected many miraculous cures.

The only trouble with the story is that Canterbury flatly denied it. Dunstan's coffin, the archbishops always insisted, had remained inviolate. Throughout the Middle Ages neither party would give way. One Abbot of Glastonbury at last put forward the theory that the four monks had not carried off all the bones, so that both churches had bits of Dunstan but neither had the whole of him. This may have been fairly close to the truth. The weight of evidence, however, is in favour of Canterbury as the major possessor.

Probably the Abbot did have a relic or two, and the tale of Sebricht and his brethren grew round them.

7

Peace was still distant. Scandinavia still kept its grip on many counties. There were marches and counter-marches and plots and assassinations. Another king, Edmund Ironside, was laid to rest at Glastonbury. For a time in the eleventh century Canute, a Dane, ruled over the whole of England. He was a devout Christian, and the ascendancy of his nation brought none of the terrors it would have brought in Alfred's day. In 1031 he went to Glastonbury to pay his respects to the remains of Edmund Ironside, whom he called his brother. After praying, he draped the tomb with a magnificent pall embroidered with many-coloured figures of peacocks. Nearby stood Ethelnoth, the Archbishop of Canterbury. Ethelnoth was a former monk of the Abbey, the seventh, according to William of Malmesbury, to achieve the primacy. The other in his list are 'first, Brithwald (i.e. Beorhtwald); second, Athelm; third, his nephew Dunstan; fourth, Ethelgar, first abbot of the Newminster at Winchester, and then bishop of Chichester; fifth, Siric, who when made archbishop gave to this his nursing mother seven palls, with which, upon his anniversary, the whole ancient church is ornamented; sixth, Elfeg, who from prior of Glastonbury was first made abbot of Bath, then bishop of Winchester.' The list is untrustworthy, but modern historians admit – besides Dunstan – Ethelgar or Aethelgar, Aelfstan, and Siric or Sigeric; also at least five bishops of other sees who came from Glastonbury between 960 and 1010. This unquestioned distinction fully explains the reverence Canute showed during his visit. William credits him with yet another charter.

The Abbey, nevertheless, hoped for the replacement of Canute by a native dynasty. Currency was given to the report of a vision seen at Glastonbury by Bishop Brithwin regarding the imminent reign of the English Edward. As foretold, Edward acceded to the throne in 1042. This was the monarch afterwards canonised (unlike his contemporary Macbeth) and known as Edward the Confessor. As to his piety there is no doubt. His most memorable act was the foundation of the church now incorrectly called Westminster Abbey. The virtues of his government are less plain; he seems to have relied too much on unworthy ministers; yet the generations after his death did look back with nostalgia to the good times of King Edward.

At least a part of the explanation lies in the discontent due to another conquest. The intermarriage of Scandinavian settlers with the basic population of northern France had produced the people called Normans. They were fertile hybrids, astonishingly so. Their courage, their enterprise, their genius for organisation, their skill in architecture and engineering, and their solid religious faith, predestined them to the accomplishment of great deeds. King Edward lived on terms of close friendship with their nobility, and it was his wish that Duke William of Normandy should succeed him. After his death in 1066, William displaced the usurper Harold and began to reign as William I. Norman lords, prelates and officials swarmed into the country and parcelled it out among themselves. Archbishop Lanfranc moved into the See of Canterbury. A royal edict reconstructing the hierarchy was assented to by Abbot Ailnoth of Glastonbury among others. Then, without much more delay, Ailnoth's office passed to a Norman.

His name was Thurstan. Lanfranc imported him from Caen. He had the unhappy notion of substituting the Dijon method of chanting for the Gregorian. The monks, with their national resentments fortified by long tradition, proved intractable, and Thurstan could not handle them. After a furious quarrel in the chapter-house he sprang up and summoned men-at-arms. The monks fled into Dunstan's church and barricaded themselves inside, collecting benches and candlesticks as weapons. The soldiers burst into the gallery and shot arrows at the monks near the altar, hitting the crucifix. Others forced an entry into the choir armed with spears. Two monks were killed, twelve wounded.

The outrage shocked public opinion. It was disgracefully untypical of Norman technique. William compelled Thurstan to withdraw, and banished him to Normandy. Under the next King, William Rufus, the Abbot returned (through bribery, according to one version) but kept away from his Abbey and failed to live down the massacre. During his tenure he had inaugurated a fresh programme of building, putting up a small part of a church in the Norman style. His successor Herlewin, who became Abbot in 1101, showed more grandiose ideas. He pulled down Thurstan's fragment and built an entirely new church on a more splendid scale, spending £480 on it. This resembled another lately erected at St Albans; possibly the architect borrowed his design from there. It was cruciform, with transepts occupying the same position as those in the later church of which the ruins still stand. There was an aisled quire of three bays, with probably two side chapels. The most remarkable feature was a kind of huge step. The sanctuary was eight feet above the nave. Over the high altar were pictures of the last British abbots, Worgret, Lademund, and Bregored, and a crucifix believed to have spoken with a miraculous voice. After the building of this church, it was not long before all traces of the Ine-Dunstan fabric had disappeared.

By the 1120s Glastonbury was more impressive than even Dunstan had envisaged. It was at this juncture that the community sent off its momentous invitation to William of Malmesbury. The likeliest explanation is that some dispute had arisen as to origins. Those pictures of the British abbots were distinctly provocative. Herlewin, aware of William's increasing fame as a writer of history, doubtless gave him an informal commission to silence the sceptics. At any rate he came, and gathered together the mass of documents and traditions which has so far been our main source. It went into his treatise *De Antiquitate Glastoniensis Ecclesiae*, there to be broken up and weakened, after his death, by the credulous verbosity of the interpolator. Some of it also went piecemeal into his *Acts of the Kings of England*, and that is the best place to look for the authentic text.

An accompanying note gives a description of Glastonbury as William saw it himself, Roma Secunda, the resting-place of innumerable saints, the goal of innumerable pilgrims. Naturally the Old Church fascinates him most.

This church is certainly the oldest I am acquainted with in England, and from this circumstance derives its name. In it are preserved the mortal remains of many saints, some of whom we shall notice in our progress; nor is any corner of the church destitute of the ashes of the holy. The very floor, inlaid with polished stones, and the sides of the altar, and even the altar itself, above and beneath, are laden with the multitude of relics. Moreover, in the pavement may be remarked on every side stones designedly interlaid in triangles and squares, and sealed with lead, under which if I believe some sacred mystery to be contained, I do no injustice to religion. The antiquity, and the multitude of its saints, have endued the place with so much sanctity, that at night scarcely anyone presumes to keep vigil there, or, during the day, to spit; he who is conscious of pollution shudders throughout his whole frame; no one ever brought hawk or horses within the confines of the neighbouring cemetery, who did not depart injured, either in them or in himself. Those persons who, about to undergo the ordeal of fire or water, did there put up their petitions, have in every instance that can now be recollected, except one, exulted in their escape. If any person erected a building in its vicinity, which by its shade obstructed the light of the church, it forthwith became a ruin. And it is sufficiently evident that the men of that province had no oath more frequent, or more sacred, than to swear by the Old Church, and from fear of swift vengeance avoided nothing so much as perjury in this respect . . .

There are numbers of documents which prove how extremely venerable this place was held by the chief persons of the country, who there more especially chose to await the day of resurrection under the protection of the Mother of God.

The most arresting sentence is the one about the 'sacred mystery' (*arcanum sacrum*). Nobody can say what it means. But it proves that Glastonbury, in William's time, was not simply another Abbey. It possessed an air of mystical strangeness, and potentialities of wonder peculiar to itself. There is no reason to doubt, as some have doubted, the significance of Avalon for the shaping of the imaginative adventures of the twelfth century.

Chapter Six

DOUBLE MAJESTY

William the Conqueror drew England into a mesh of relationships with the Continent, which held without breaking until
the reign of John. A French-speaking nobility took over the
government, and intermarried with the French-speaking nobility throughout what is now France. There were dynastic
contortions and painful transfers of provinces. One princess,
Eleanor of Aquitaine, was Queen of France and then Queen
of England. But the currency of a single culture was legal
tender on both sides of the Channel. In discussing the literary
work of that era, scholars sometimes disagree as to whether a
given book is a continental or an insular text.

As time passed, both the Church and the Monarchy showed
a strength exceptional in the early Middle Ages. England
never suffered from the sheer feudal anarchy of France. The
Church owed its position partly to accident, partly to human
ability, partly to the support of Rome. The Monarchy did
not enjoy the last advantage, but it acquired a mystique which
proved surprisingly potent – the Arthurian mystique. Before
the Middle Ages were far advanced, 'King Arthur' had made
the name of Britain tremendous through all western Christendom, and his supposed successors basked in a reflected
glory.

Glastonbury was the backdrop for all. In so far as any one
man created the ecclesiastical power which Henry II grappled
with and Becket died for, that one man was its Abbot. In
so far as any one place became the shrine and inspiration of
Arthurian legend, Glastonbury was that place. The impact
of the ancient community on twelfth-century England was
truly incalculable.

2

In the Benedictine abbey at Cluny, as the century unrolled

its third decade, they used to point out an intelligent young Norman of royal blood. Henry was the monk's name. His mother was Adela, the Conqueror's daughter, and his father was the Comte de Blois. Adela's brother, a much more celebrated Henry, still wore the crown in England, where his iron justice had won over many Anglo-Saxons to the Norman régime. The whole family formed a vigorous branch of that intertwined society which ruled from the Cheviots to the Pyrenees and the Maritime Alps.

Henry de Blois had been sent to Cluny as the best training-school for an ecclesiastical career. The Abbey was the head-quarters of the New Monasticism and the mainstay of the New Papacy. Its glories dated from Abbot Odo, who had practically founded another Order within the Benedictine Order. The continental religious houses of Odo's day, though they still produced mighty individuals, had too often ceased to be forceful as institutions. After all they reflected the medium they grew in, an unspectacular peasant world. The monks prayed and studied and taught, but, as we saw, they also busied themselves with public services and field labour. Each abbot governed his own monastery, and frequently cut a figure in local affairs as landlord and magistrate. There was no positive Benedictine 'line,' because there was no rigid organisation. Within the walls, moreover, there sometimes reigned a tangible spirit of internal democracy.

Odo judged that problems were gathering in the path of the Church, and that the old system as it stood was too easy-going to roll them back. He began at Cluny by fostering a stricter, more energetic morality. But he went on to change the monastic constitution. He withdrew his monks from contact with everyday life, and laid far more stress on their studies and devotions. If the phrase is forgivable (perhaps it is not), they became specialists in the Faith. Odo persuaded other abbots to adopt his reform. The movement did not halt even there. New houses affiliated to Cluny sprang up all over Europe, to a number in excess of three hundred, and their link with the parent abbey was more than a bond of imitation: it was a bond of obedience. The Abbots of Cluny presided over the whole galaxy. They flooded an amazed Christendom with their graduates – priests who were literate and better than literate, priests who kept their vows, priests who carried august notions of Christ's authority to the councils of kings and the papal chair itself. Cluny gave Rome Hildebrand, the pope who made an emperor wait in the snow, and Urban II, the pope who launched the Crusades.

A Cluniac monk was seldom a comfortable person to live with. But, by 1125, comfortable people were not what the Church required. The world that awaited Henry de Blois was a single immense growing-pain. Thirty years before, Europe had blazed suddenly with a conscious purpose and snatched Palestine from the infidel. The fall of the Holy Sepulchre inaugurated a vaster upheaval than the fall of the Bastille. Christendom in arms proved to be Christendom transfigured. Arrogant castles arose in east and west, at Kerak and Tripoli and Rochester and Carlisle, revolutionising warfare and concentrating fresh power in their owners' hands. Trade followed the Christian flag and covered the Mediterranean with ships. Half-barbarous Franks and Normans encountered the calm splendours of Byzantium, the luxuries and subtleties of Islam. They learned a new reverence for the Blessed Virgin, which was to change the face of art and society; they also learned to rejoice in silks and spices and scepticism. Before long, unsuspected gates were opening at a dozen points. Greek philosophy nibbled at the Catholic intellect. Dawning intimations of Arab philosophy threatened it with a new subversion. Heretical preachers trudged westward along the Balkan mountains, bringing alien scriptures and a dark Oriental creed. But life beat strongly within the citadel. Men wrote histories and made poems, built churches and founded guilds, resuscitated Roman law and groped toward a just commonwealth. Western society ran to sharp extremes of sanctity and brutality, grandeur and squalor. But on the whole it was alert, prosperous, hopeful and enterprising.

Cluny set itself to bring that society under the Church's guidance. In a sense, of course, Cluny belonged in such a society, and was the instrument of Christian reform proper to it. Monks who did no work in the usual sense could not support themselves. However stern their asceticism, they depended to some extent on the bounty of a world that could accumulate wealth. From that world came the money, and from that world also came the abbots, noblemen like Mayeul, Odilo and Peter the Venerable, who knew the field they cultivated.

So Henry de Blois took holy orders. In 1126 his royal namesake invited him to England and made him Abbot of Glastonbury. For a Norman not yet thirty, without administrative experience, the charge was a heavy one. But he shouldered it honourably, aided by an authoritative manner and an imposing beard. Well aware that Glastonbury was not Cluny, Henry treated his splendid but less heroic household with a firm tact. He took advice, he respected the constitution, he carried through minor reforms but nothing radical. No believer in ruthless mortification, he allowed the monks two pittances or snacks in addition to the regular meals, on five days out of the seven. Harmonious discipline was his object, and, through that, the maximum realisable good. The good which he realised by achieving the desired harmony was more radical than any reform. A split and partially Anglo-Saxon community with a Norman head began to transform itself anew into a piece of England.

Henry's success placed him squarely in the great company of his kinsmen. He finally exorcised the hateful shadow of Thurstan; he governed without so much as a nod at the garrison. That is not to say that he did not govern. Power and privilege through all England belonged to the conquerors. But Henry de Blois was one of many who, by the process of ordering their own mastery, created an order magnificently transcending it. They made a realm and reigned; but it was a realm, not, as some had feared, an intolerably prolonged raid. William of Malmesbury could already speak of a battle won by the King at Tinchebrai as an English victory. On the other hand, in 1138, a general praised his Yorkshire levies as 'invincible Normans.' This minor confusion did not matter. The sense of interchangeability did. Before many more years had passed, there could be a Norman England – or after 1154 an Angevin England – with a common concern. A Norman or an Anglo-Saxon or even a Celt could speak of an entity called England (and sometimes Britain) without absurdity. The triumphs and traditions of all races in the kingdom could begin to be common property, or rather, to be the multiple inheritance of a new unity.

As to the unity itself, Abbot Henry lived to see a majority concur. As to the Church's status within that unity, perilous disputes might arise, and they eventually did. Henry took a Cluniac view of the matter: the Church above all. Again like many fellow-Normans, he expressed his outlook in forms more solid than controversy.

He built. It was a way the Normans had. Under the outstretched sword of St Michael, their favourite celestial patron, churches grew up as well as ramparts. Firm round arches, audacious buttresses, stalwart pillars and clenched capitals brawnily sustained the glory of God. Winchester, Ely, Lincoln, Gloucester, Durham; the list of Norman foundations reads like a roll-call of the cities. Within his own domain, Henry de Blois contributed what he could. The Abbey acquired a new chapter-house, a new cloister, a new infirmary; new sleeping and washing accommodation; a massive gateway, a brewhouse, a residence for the abbots; and many stables. The interior of the cloister was laid out in Italian style as a garden. By the addition of a bell-tower in 1150 the church took a sudden upward leap.

The funds for all these changes came partly from noble benefactors, but partly also from the proceeds of good management. One day Henry de Blois noticed a field in Brent Marsh, within Abbey territory, fenced off by a bank of earth. It was bearing a rich wheat crop, but he knew the Abbey got nothing from it. He made inquiries about this field. The monks told him that it was called No Value Field, and that Abbot Herlewin had leased it to a local knight for a very small consideration on his assurance that it had never had any value and never would have. What about all this wheat? Abbot Henry asked. Well, they replied, there must have been a miscalculation somewhere . . . but they couldn't quite see their way to interfering. . . . Rubbish, said Abbot Henry. He got rid of the knight and repossessed the land.

An auspicious event was the finding of the Great Sapphire. This was a superb ornament of precious stones in a setting of precious metal, intended to be hung over an altar. According to legend, St David had brought it from Jerusalem. During the wars of the Danish era the monks had too carefully concealed it. Their successors now discovered the treasure in a secret cupboard behind the door of the Old Church.

This lucky enrichment of the Abbey cost the Abbot nothing, but he paid munificently for others out of his own pocket. He gave tapestries, vestments, altar furniture. He gave books: the works of Origen, Jerome and Augustine; Pliny's *Natural History*; Archbishop Anselm's work on the Incarnation; seven volumes of saints' legends; histories of England and France. During the long absences which his subsequent duties forced upon him, he kept his hand on the helm through a personal representative, Robert of Lewes. Robert conducted himself with credit in his difficult position, and the Abbey prospered.

At the Norman Conquest Glastonbury had been the richest of the thirty-five English Benedictine houses, valued at £828 a year. Some of its lands had then been surrendered to Norman knights. During the greater part of the twelfth century there was a steady recovery and progress. By the end of Henry de Blois's abbacy the establishment seems to have consisted of about seventy monks and a slightly larger number of lay assistants and servants. The chief officers of the Abbot's own household were the seneschal, dispenser and cook. The Abbey steward controlled Glastonbury Fair.

In 1129 a well-satisfied King appointed Henry de Blois to the see of Winchester. With the Pope's permission he continued as Abbot, but in future Glastonbury saw him less often. Winchester became his home for most of the year. In the wealthy bishopric his spirit expanded. He indulged his interests, entertained scholars, started an art collection and a private menagerie. Chance was to draw him into statecraft, but nothing would eradicate Cluny. To his central aim, the freedom and exaltation of the Church, Henry was constant. That very steadfastness gave him a boldness in adaptation which laid him open to the charge of inconstancy. He went rather too far in supporting people; he went rather too far in opposing them; but whatever he did, it was nearly always majestically done. He entirely lacked the quick tongue and counterfeit common touch of the mere politician.

Having reigned thirty-five years the King died. The theoretical successor was his daughter Matilda. However, the barons felt no enthusiasm for a female sovereign, and Matilda was overseas with her handsome husband Geoffrey Plantagenet. Stephen de Blois, the Abbot's brother, suddenly put forward his own claim to the throne. He had sworn to recognise Matilda, but he now said that he had sworn under duress, and that the would-be queen, by a technicality, was a bastard. London saluted him as king and the counties followed. Henry de Blois organised a mission to Rome and obtained the Pope's approval.

Stephen could not rule. Believing himself to be much more weakly placed than he was, he launched his reign clumsily with concessions. Besides his less defensible deals, he made sweeping promises to his brother about the liberty of the Church, a phrase which could mean anything, and was interpreted to cover important exemptions from the King's law. For these at least there was a case, but they did not help the King. Soon Stephen was quarrelling with feudal magnates whom he could not afford to quarrel with. Little rebellions boiled up here and there, and the custom of castle-building made them hard to suppress. In the Norman domains across the Channel Matilda gained ground, and she began to find friends in England. With the Monarchy stooping into faction, its subjects looked hopefully to the other paramount power: the Church. Henry de Blois rose to represent that power. He had expected Stephen to install him as Archbishop of Canterbury. This never happened, but the Pope appointed him Legate, with an authority above the Archbishop's. At an ecclesiastical council Henry rebuked Stephen and affirmed the Church's right to decide who should be sovereign. As confusion deepened, his judgment carried more and more weight. People referred to the Abbot of Glastonbury as the real Lord of England. The status accorded him did not rest on moral suasion or even on the authority of the English bishops. Henry spoke as a Cluniac churchman openly representing Rome.

In 1139 Matilda raised her standard at Bristol and succeeded in taking Stephen prisoner. Henry de Blois determined to give the Queen a chance. He made a speech recommending her to the bishops. She entered London under the Legate's auspices. Deputations asked for Stephen's release. Henry too peremptorily repeated what he had told the clergy, and the Londoners thought they were being slighted. Matilda's reign of a few months ended in chaos. Henry gave her up and resolved to make whatever could still be made of his brother, whom she had had to set at liberty. Amid the horrors of civil war he lifted the Church's power as high as he could; and that was high. Places of sanctuary were defined, measures were taken to protect and relieve the peasants, the abbeys helped to maintain order and keep industry alive. Even ecclesiastical building went forward. Henry's work endured, but his personal share in it decreased. His last major political act was to negotiate an agreement between Stephen and Matilda's son – yet another Henry – who had come to England and was fighting in his mother's cause. Matilda gave up the crown, Stephen recognised the prince as his heir. In October 1154 Stephen died. Henry Plantagenet became King, Henry de Blois retired from king-making.

Thanks to him the English Church enjoyed an unprecedented power and prestige. He lived to impress on Thomas

Becket the duty of holding firm against royal encroachments.

Henry II had no competitors for the throne. He reigned unchallenged over the Anglo-Norman state. He also reigned over most of western France, which fell to him by inheritance and by marriage with Eleanor of Aquitaine. Anjou being the fundamental Plantagenet portion, Henry's huge realm is conveniently spoken of as the Angevin Empire. It extended into Wales. It grew to include Brittany, the overseas Wales. It overlapped regions within the orbit of Parisian culture. All these facts were to affect the fortunes of Angevin Glastonbury.

The Plantagenet monarch stands out vividly in the chronicles of his age, because he fits so well into modern categories. One well-known physiological school would call him 'somatotonic.' Arthur Koestler would pick him out as a 'commissar' type. An industrial psychologist would see in him a 'line' executive as distinguished from a 'staff' executive. Born in Detroit about 1870, he would have made a fine plant manager for the elder Ford. Squarely constructed, extroverted, forceful and profane, he turned administration into a muddled frenzy of achievement. His hair was red and his temper frightful. When angry he literally chewed mattresses. He ate heartily, but worked off any excess fat partly by hunting and partly by touring his dominions at a headlong pace, imposing law and order wherever he went, with an exasperated court trailing behind him. Of delegating authority he had only the crudest notions; he relied on his own vast energy and prodigious memory. Towards religion, at first, he was punctilious but legalistic. He banished the few avowed heretics he ever laid hands on, and he went to daily Mass, but he sat through the service drumming his heels and dictating letters. He knew French, of course, and enough Latin to read books on history and politics. But apparently he never learned English. That may have counted as a point of honour. In parts of Quebec the English-speaking managerial and professional minority still makes it a point of honour not to learn French.

In terms of tangible things the Anglo-Norman monarchy under its Angevin master was an awe-inspiring fabric. What it lacked was a mythos. Behind the King of France, ineffectual though he palpably was, there stood a long line of Frankish sovereigns descending from the mighty Clovis, champion of the Catholic Faith amid the downfall of Rome. From Clovis to Charlemagne, and through him to the twelfth century, there was a continuity which no phases of vice or failure could destroy. French kings were anointed with oil from the Holy Ampoule, brought down by a dove from heaven. The *chansons de geste* wove a web of imperishable romance round Charlemagne and his peerage. At the Battle of Hastings the minstrel-knight Taillefer had ridden before the Norman host singing of Roland's last stand at Roncevaux. The duchy of Normandy had since grown to an empire, but in 1154 its minstrels might have been hard pressed to find equivalent matter in the annals of the island kingdom that formed the nucleus.

Help, however, was on the way. The equivalent matter did exist; it was already on record; exploitation rather than exploration was the watchword. Henry's mythos came into being through the Celtic revival, which had begun a generation before, but had not attracted much attention. The prime mover, though not the principal figure, was William of Malmesbury. He himself built on foundations laid even earlier. During the eleventh and early twelfth centuries, in Wales and Cornwall and Brittany, a mass of hazy traditions had been growing more articulate. Saints' Lives had been written down. Stories about Arthur had increased in elaboration and popularity. The victor of Badon had been retroactively crowned. The prophecy of his return, originating no one knows when, had begun to impress itself on outsiders. In 1113 some French priests visited Bodmin in Cornwall with relics of Our Lady of Laon. A man with a withered arm came to be healed, and told the foreigners in all seriousness that King Arthur still lived. They laughed at him, but found to their consternation that the other Cornishmen backed him up. A fight broke out in the church and was stopped only with difficulty. (For whatever reason, the arm failed to mend.)

William of Malmesbury was aware of these fables. Yet his achievement, in the form it actually took, was not so much a discovery of Arthur as a discovery of Glastonbury. William's restrained Arthurian paragraph in the *Acts of the*

Kings has already been quoted (page 75). But his critical mind, which rejected the lore of the British hero, accepted the lore of the British monastery; a fact which speaks well for its essential credibility in the eyes of a man much closer to the events than ourselves. In a book written before his researches at the Abbey, William referred to Glastonbury with no special stress. In the *Acts of the Kings*, written after, he traced its growth in considerable detail from the earliest times down to his own. He interwove the story with general history, and showed how the English, through good King Cenwalh, had become the heirs to the Abbey and all it stood for. William enlarged on this theme in the lost genuine treatise *De Antiquitate*, dedicated to Henry de Blois. He also wrote studies of several of the relevant saints.

The *Acts of the Kings* appeared with a preface implying the patronage of the Earl of Gloucester. This was Robert, Matilda's half-brother, an enlightened nobleman of demiregal consequence in the West Country. He had a Welsh mother and a Welsh wife, and seems to have been far-sighted enough to glimpse the potentialities of a fusion of traditions. Under Earl Robert's auspices William of Malmesbury took a long stride in that direction. By his disclosure of the Celtic past, and his presentation of the English and Normans as legitimate successors to the Britons and Romans, William laid the foundation for a mature national dignity. Three other historians followed him. Henry of Huntingdon had little significance, except as a publicist for the new point of view. Caradoc of Llancarfan, Gildas's biographer, expanded the Malmesburian bridgeheads, probably doing much of his work at Glastonbury. The greatest is behind; though whether the title of historian fairly applies, opinions may differ. In the late 1130s we find the literary patronage of Robert of Gloucester extended to a further writer, one of the leading creative geniuses of the age: Geoffrey of Monmouth.

Geoffrey, at the time, was a very minor ecclesiastic, though towards the end of his life he became bishop of St Asaph. His family was at least partly Welsh, and his father's name was Arthur, a circumstance that may have imparted a certain bias to nursery story-telling. Geoffrey had the acumen to see that the Anglo-Norman monarchy would need an equivalent to the French mythos, and that the place to seek it was not in the confusions of Anglo-Saxondom but in the earlier age disinterred by William of Malmesbury, when saints and heroes walked in a tremendous twilight and the magic of the Empire survived. His *History of the Kings of Britain* professed to trace the ancestry of the British people as far as Troy, but its climax was a fantastic account of Arthur, which became the fountainhead of Arthurian romance and all it implied in the medieval consciousness.

William had dropped the hint himself, when he remarked that Arthur deserved 'not to be dreamed of in fallacious fables, but to be proclaimed in veracious histories.' Geoffrey's history was not exactly veracious. 'Oftentimes,' said the author in his preface . . .

Oftentimes in turning over in mine own mind the many themes that might be subject-matter of a book, my thoughts would fall upon the plan of writing a history of the kings of Britain; and in my musings thereupon me seemed it a marvel that, beyond such mention as Gildas and Bede have made of them in their luminous tractates, nought could I find therein as concerning the kings that dwelt in Britain before the Incarnation of Christ, nor nought even as concerning Arthur and the many others that did succeed him after the Incarnation. . . . Whilst I was thus thinking upon such matters, Walter, Archdeacon of Oxford, a man learned not only in the art of eloquence, but in the histories of foreign lands, offered me a certain most ancient book in the British language that set forth the doings of all of them in due succession.

The source-book has never been located and very likely never existed. Archdeacon Walter is also elusive. However, Geoffrey did not spin everything out of his own head. Besides using Gildas, Nennius, and the Saints' Lives, he drew on a store of ballads and folk-tales, some of which preserved fragments of mythology dating from Arthur's epoch and earlier. Occasionally Geoffrey has shocked modern historians by turning out to be right. For example, his tale of a rising against the Romans ending in a massacre on the banks of the Walbrook has been confirmed by the dredging up of a swarm of skulls. But his proper greatness is the greatness of an imaginative artist, in this case regrettably inseparable from the guilt of fraud.

Geoffrey's Arthur is a compound of the historical military leader and the enigmatic fairy prince, with amazing embellishments. There is no Round Table as yet, and no Holy Grail, but there are plenty of marvels. Arthur is the irregular son of King Uther by Igerne, whose husband, Gorlois, Uther magically impersonates with the aid of the wizard Merlin. Gorlois dies in battle and Uther makes his victim an honest woman. The boy fairly soon succeeds him as King of Britain. Arthur's war against the Saxons begins as a looting expedition during a lull, but expands into a serious campaign. He defeats the enemy chieftains in a series of battles, finally overthrowing them in the country near Bath, by means of his sword Caliburn that was forged in the Isle of Avalon. (Bath is Geoffrey's guess for Badon. What he means by Avalon in the *History* must remain doubtful.)

The King marries 'Guanhumara,' a lady of Roman family, and enlarges his empire beyond Britain. Ireland, Iceland and the Orkneys capitulate. Twelve years of peace and prosperity ensue, after which Arthur is so powerful that he can contemplate the conquest of Europe. He overruns Norway and installs his brother-in-law Lot as a satellite sovereign. Gaul and Denmark follow. Hereabouts in the story we encounter familiar names: Lot has a son called Gawain; Arthur's viceroy in Normandy is Bedevere; Anjou falls to Kay.

The victorious leader holds court at Caerleon-upon-Usk, surrounded by his knights, priests and astrologers. 'At that time Britain was exalted unto so high a pitch of dignity as that it did surpass all other kingdoms in plenty of riches, in luxury of adornment, and in the courteous wit of them that dwelt therein. Whatsoever knight in the land was of renown for his prowess did wear his clothes and his arms all of one same colour. And the ladies, no less witty, would apparel them in like manner in a single colour, nor would they deign have the love of none save he had thrice approved him in the wars. Wherefore at that time did ladies wax chaste and knights the nobler for their love.'

Arthur is provoked by Roman demands for tribute to launch a campaign against Rome herself. (But Geoffrey does not bring him into conflict with the Emperor at Constantinople. There is no definite revolt against the Imperial concept. What Geoffrey would like to do, only even he dares not go so far, is to present Arthur as a kind of Charlemagne, a rebuilder of the Western Empire round a new centre.) The Romans, led by Lucius Hiberius and supported by allies from the East, oppose him with a gigantic army. Arthur defeats them though with heavy loss to his own forces – Kay and Bedevere are among the dead – and prepares to march on the City. News from Britain recalls him. His nephew Modred, left behind there as regent, has seized the throne. Arthur returns and fights a difficult war, facing Modred at last in Cornwall. The usurper and most of the nobility fall in battle. Arthur receives a deadly wound, and is carried off to his resting-place in the Isle of Avalon. Here he resigns his crown to a kinsman and . . . is seen no more. The date is 542.

Having given the world the truth about Arthur, Geoffrey pursued the British monarchy to its final downfall, and concluded his work with a short chapter somewhat arrogantly sketching out a division of labour in the re-creation of history. William of Malmesbury and Henry of Huntingdon were welcome to the Anglo-Saxons. Caradoc of Llancarfan could deal with the later Welsh. He, Geoffrey, alone possessed the British source-book, and therefore he claimed a monopoly of the older times. He asserted this claim in practice by writing a long poem on the Life of Merlin, whose prophecies he gave to the reading public on more than one occasion.

His feats of imagination were quite generally accepted as facts. Recognition was postponed by the distractions of civil war, but after peace returned, Geoffrey's triumph was rapid. Here was the mythos, the mystique. King Henry himself encouraged the growth of the Arthurian literature, which was augmented and strengthened by fresh infusions of genuine tradition. Robert Wace made a British chronicle-epic in which the Round Table first appeared, and dedicated it to Queen Eleanor. Walter Map, a court functionary and miscellaneous author, wrote (or at any rate let his name be affixed to) several voluminous tales about the British King and his knights. The fashion spread throughout all the lands where educated people spoke French, and even beyond. The 'Matter of Britain' took its place beside the 'Matter of France' and the 'Matter of Rome' as a proper source of romantic fiction. Queen Eleanor's private court in Poitou became a meeting-place of Celtic minstrels and French versifiers. Chrétien de Troyes poured forth romance after romance, assigning the well-known roles to Tristan, Lancelot and others. A convention of make-believe prevented the drawing of any hard line between truth and fancy. By the last quarter of the twelfth century Britain was, so to speak, on the map of civilisation as the realm of King Arthur, and a strange radiance shone about the Angevin crown. The magic name was bestowed on that heir-apparent whom John murdered.

Then Glastonbury entered the scene again; and its direct

contribution was the most spectacular of all. The Arthurian Legend, from the point of view of Henry II, had one drawback. There was the doubt regarding Arthur's death. Geoffrey of Monmouth had left the topic obscure. After the last battle, Arthur had gone to that mysterious place Avalon, and there the reader lost sight of him. As long as Henry's Celtic subjects were free to maintain that their hero had never died, but would come back to lead them against the English, their final submission to overlords in London might be delayed. The value of a glorified Arthur to the monarchy might prove ambiguous. Hence the problem was to preserve the hero but lay his ghost.

Passing through Wales on one of his terrific journeys, Henry learned from a somewhat imprudent bard that the site of Arthur's grave was exactly known. It lay between the two pillars or pyramids in Glastonbury Abbey. The King discussed his news with the Abbot, Henry de Blois's successor, who tentatively offered to try excavations: proof of Arthur's death would be an acceptable gift in the royal sight. Other business interfered, so that nothing definite resulted. A catastrophe changed the whole position. On 25th May, 1184, the Abbey caught fire. The Old Church perished in the flames. The Norman Church was gutted, only Henry de Blois's bell-tower surviving. The chapels and residential buildings suffered severe damage. Little remained but ruins, with the bewildered monks camping among them and wondering how to set about restoration. The astonishing immunity of an antique image of Our Lady of Glastonbury was their sole source of comfort.

This disaster was felt as a blow to England, and indeed to Christendom. High dignitaries of the Church at once began pressing for reconstruction. The Abbot had died and no successor had been elected. Since the Abbey was a royal foundation, it devolved on King Henry to take the necessary measures. He had already granted a charter to Glastonbury town, and now he came to the rescue of the Abbey. He earmarked funds and placed his own steward, Ralph Fitz-Stephen, in charge of the job, not neglecting to issue a proclamation.

Because whatsoever a man soweth, that shall he also reap, I, in the act of laying the foundation of the church of Glastonbury (which, being in my hands, has been reduced to ashes by fire), do decree by the persuasion of

Heraclius, the patriarch of Jerusalem, Baldwin, archbishop of Canterbury, and many others, that, God willing, it shall be magnificently completed by myself or by my heirs.

So the work began, and in 1190 the ground between the pyramids surrendered its secret. A monk happened to die who had asked to be buried there himself. His request reopened the topic of Arthur's grave. It would now be necessary to dig on the spot in any case, and amid the general confusion, excavations were more in order. Moreover, the Abbey needed all the prestige it could acquire to attract the money of pilgrims and patrons for the rebuilding. The designated area was roped off and concealed by curtains. After much labour the grave-diggers discovered a stone slab, seven feet below ground level, with a leaden cross let into the underside. On the cross an inscription could be made out. Deciphering it, they read, or imagined they read: HIC JACET SEPULTUS INCLYTUS REX ARTURUS IN INSULA AVALLONIA.[1] 'Here lies buried the renowned King Arthur in the Isle of Avalon.' Buried! That was the point. Could they find him?

It was a thrilling moment. The monks converged on the pit, and many hands helped the grave-diggers. Sixteen feet down the blade of a shovel struck on wood – on a big, obstinate, curiously flat piece. Removing soil inch by inch from that stubborn surface, the monk unearthed a corner . . . an edge . . . another surface that sloped away. They all assailed the object together, and at last it lay exhumed before them: a colossal coffin, a hollowed oaken log, embedded in the ground at a slight angle.

They burst it open with axes and crowbars. One of them reached inside and picked up a bone. Human? Yes indeed, said a brother who had studied anatomy. A human shin-bone, but belonging to no ordinary man. He matched it against the leg of the tallest monk present; it projected above his knee by the breadth of three fingers. What else? A skull corresponding, with the marks of heavy blows on it. One, doubtless the death-blow, had smashed it in by the left ear.

Groping down in the recesses of the coffin, they brought out more trophies. Arthur's figure took shape. At the lower end they came to some slighter bones which did not seem to fit the heroic skeleton. Strands of yellow hair still lingered. A monk tried to lift them, but they crumbled into dust under his hand. Too late he realised, from a name scratched on the

[1] See preface, p. 8.

wood, that it had been vouchsafed him to touch the tresses of Guinevere . . .

Did this really happen? Giraldus Cambrensis, writing within four years and again later, assures us that it did. Other historians give other accounts which are manifestly not all copied from his. Giraldus himself seems to have gone to the Abbey soon after the exhumation, inspected the bones, and met the monk whose shin yielded to Arthur's. He was no gullible Arthurian. On the contrary, few contemporaries ventured as far as he did in ridiculing Geoffrey of Monmouth. He would not have given a favourable report (twice) unless he had examined the alleged finds and thought them convincing.

An inscribed cross indubitably did exist. It was preserved for a long time afterwards. Leland saw it at the Abbey in the reign of Henry VIII. Camden, about 1607, drew a picture of it. It has been traced to a Mr Chancellor Hughes of Wells in the eighteenth century, and possibly is still lying unnoticed in some family lumber-room. The lettering in Camden's picture, is said to resemble that on inscribed West Country crosses of the Dark Ages. This likeness is interesting, inasmuch as it suggests that the cross was not merely faked in 1190. On the other hand, the title Rex, the nine-foot difference in depth, and probably the name Avallonia, all tell against the idea that the object actually dated from Arthur's burial. The inscription, in any case, was much too neat as publicity. Why give a place-name? Anyone visiting the grave would presumably have known where he was. But the explicit statement of Glastonbury's identity with Avalon, clinching the inference from the presence of Arthur, was extremely convenient for the Abbey. In default of evidence I fear we must set aside the cross as an able forgery, and the story of its finding as a bit of embroidery.

The coffin itself is harder to dismiss. Burial[1] in hollowed-out tree-trunks was undoubtedly practised among the ancient Celts. The monks, however, could not have known this. If they had found nothing, but wished to pretend that they had found something, they would have invented a coffin of stone with other anachronistic details meant to prove the importance of the occupant. The description which they actually gave is so odd from their point of view, yet so plausible from ours, that one may well feel bound to believe it – substantially. They did unearth an oaken coffin with bones in it. But was the male skeleton Arthur's? We cannot say. Would a Christian have

[1] See preface, p. 8.

181

been buried in a hollowed tree-trunk? We cannot say. Dogmatism is out of order here. When the archæologists have fired their last critical shot, a wild possibility that the monks were right still survives. If we reject Arthur and postulate a pagan chief, the romance dwindles. Yet this alternative would at least confirm the conjecture in an earlier chapter, that Ynys-witrin was a pre-Christian burial site; and the conjecture has its uses. So the coffin turns out to be a highly satisfactory if ambiguous object. It should not be abandoned without a struggle.

Cross from
King Arthur's Grave[1]

No public exhibition ensued. The monks showed the bones to a favoured few, then laid them in separate chests with pictures on them, and enshrined the chests in a sepulchre in the new church. Glastonbury was now Avalon in the eyes

[1] See preface, p. 8.

of Europe, and, moreover, undisputedly Avalon. Despite the failure to expose Arthur's remains to public scrutiny, the Celts and Celtic enthusiasts raised no serious protest. The prophecy of his second coming expired, except on mythical levels. I suggested earlier that whether or not Arthur actually was buried at Glastonbury, the confidential bardic tradition affirmed that he was. The bard whom King Henry met revealed the secret, and once it was out, buttressed by archæology, denial was given up as hopeless.

By that time Henry was dead. But his son Richard Cœur-de-Lion carried Glastonbury's fame to the extremity of Europe. In March 1191, on his way to the Third Crusade, he presented Tancred of Sicily with a sword which he said was Excalibur and had been dug up in the Abbey.[1]

4

Glastonbury, therefore, had contributed largely to two historic trends: the ascent of the Church in England to a high level of privilege; and the growth of the island monarchy as a distinctive institution with a distinctive mythos. Unfortunately the two things clashed. The Church, which had risen during the civil war under the ægis of Henry de Blois as Papal Legate, was strongly Roman in loyalty. Also, the clergy had their own courts of law where the King's writ did not run. Not only were they exempt, but any civil or criminal case which could be represented as a religious matter might be taken into the ecclesiastical courts and referred, if the money held out, to the Papal Curia itself. A disputed inheritance might raise questions about legitimacy and the validity of a marriage. A breach of contract might be held to involve perjury. The possibility of dodging the royal justice by such evasions, with the right of appeal to Rome, vexed Henry II exceedingly.

[1] The date of Arthur's exhumation is hard to fix. There are sources which give 1191, others which point to 1190. One indicates that the major discovery occurred in King Henry's lifetime. However, this Sicilian affair would imply that the main find at Glastonbury Abbey, whatever it amounted to, was already celebrated enough to 'sell' subsidiary relics. The excavations, their results, and the Abbey's announcements, may have been spread over a longer period than any one document conveys.

He appointed his friend and chancellor Thomas Becket to the archbishopric of Canterbury, hoping in this way to bring the Church under his control. But Becket, incited, it is said, by Henry de Blois, conducted a stubborn defence of the very privileges he had been meant to curb. King Henry banished him and threatened the Pope with schism. All in vain. An attempted reconciliation brought him back to Canterbury. But popular demonstrations in his favour alarmed the King, and a fresh quarrel over episcopal appointments provoked Henry to the famous outburst that doomed the Archbishop.

Henry did penance for the crime, and gave up his attack on the Church. Rome, however, had upheld Becket, cautiously but unmistakably, and Henry's family continued the feud with Rome. Queen Eleanor resuscitated the threat of schism. John defied the Pope so ferociously that England was placed under an interdict. Throughout this period the Crown, and therefore its literary dependants and those under their influence, lived in an atmosphere of impotent anti-papalism. It was only to be expected that Arthurian romance would reflect this feeling – that the old British monarchy would be portrayed as in some way standing for a national Christianity, offering an example and a precedent for the Angevins.

In due course it was so portrayed, and this fresh flight of imagination was Glastonbury's third major contribution to the life of the age. As such, it was unintentional. The romancers who tried to set up *Roma Secunda* as a rival to *Roma* were not monastic propagandists. The theory of an actual Glastonbury Heresy, once put forward by Sir John Rhys, must be rejected. An outright challenge to Rome from the mighty Abbey would not have passed uncondemned. Nevertheless the will to exploit the Abbey's legends in the interests of a national Christianity did exist. And now it unfolded itself.

Chapter Seven

THE GRAIL

People who mention the Holy Grail generally think of it as a holy relic, the cup used by Christ at the Last Supper. They generally have the notion that an antique legend describes Joseph of Arimathea as bringing it to Britain. After its arrival it was buried or otherwise lost at Glastonbury.

Those who take this conventional view are wrong on all counts. The Grail makes its entry, not as a relic, but as a talisman. Its Christian guise is an afterthought, which may or may not owe something to independent Christian legends. No genuine popular or monastic tradition has a word to say about it in the religious aspect, and its connection with Glastonbury, though indissoluble, is enigmatic.

Around it, nevertheless, there grew up an odd and haunting sentiment which could almost be spoken of as Glastonbury Christianity. This was not so much a heresy as an attitude; and while the constitutional conflict which occasioned it has long since blown over, the sentiment itself has never expired. The poetry of the last hundred years includes Tennyson's Idyll on the topic, which is Christian after its fashion yet neither Catholic nor Protestant; Eliot's *Waste Land*, which is founded on Jessie Weston's interpretation of the Grail myth; and the fragmentary Arthurian epic of Charles Williams.

The word 'grail' signifies a vessel, generally a deep dish, though its application to a cup raises no difficulty. Fanciful derivations given by weavers of romance need not detain us. The conception of THE Grail, one must reiterate – the dish or bowl or goblet *par excellence* – is not originally Christian at all. Wonder-working vessels confront us in British literature long before there is any allusion to the chalice of Christ. The name Grail occurs, with its mysterious accompaniments, where the object concerned is anything but holy. Witchcraft is always present implicitly and sometimes openly. To say that the Christian Grail 'grew out of' non-Christian myths or rituals is, indeed, to fall into an anthropological trap; but the mystical romancers who told its story quite manifestly made use of such things, directly or indirectly.

At the bottom of the business lies a stratum of Celtic fable about a miraculous cauldron. In Welsh folk-lore the cauldron belongs to the Arthurian cycle as far back as we can trace it. The poem 'The Spoils of Annwn' (pages 87-8) gives a curiously multiple foretaste of later developments. Arthur and his knights go questing after the Cauldron of Annwn, the cauldron of plenty and inspiration. They seek it by way of the Glass Castle – which suggests the Glass Island. One of the characters associated with the map of the quest is Gwyn ap Nudd, King of the Fairies and lord of Glastonbury Tor. This vessel of Taliesin is already otherworldly, already Arthurian, already sought for by questing knights, and already easy to connect (though probably not connected) with Glastonbury. Nine maidens watch over it, like the maidens who tend the Grail in some of the romances.

Gwyn ap Nudd and his Welsh fairy-folk had their counterparts in Ireland, the Tuatha de Danann. These too possessed a cauldron of plenty; or perhaps the same one in Hibernian disguise. It was called the Dagda's Cauldron, and it could feed and satisfy a great company of men. The Tuatha de Danann, we learn, had three other treasures, the spear and sword of Lug Lamhfhada, and the Lia Fail or stone of fate. At this point we begin to grasp what the cauldron myth is really about. Four similar objects – a cup, a spear or wand, a sword, and a flat stone or disc – occur as a magical combination in widely separated contexts, far beyond the orbit of Celtic fable. They are found in Egypt and China, where they are thought to have a connection with the rise and fall of rivers, and they figure as the four suits in the packs of Tarot cards employed by gipsies for fortune-telling. The quadruple pattern reflects venerable rites bearing on fertility and the growth of crops, on the food-supply and therefore the fortunes of peasant peoples. What proves its relevance to the Grail is the fact that the medieval romances mention three lesser 'hallows' along with the sacred cup – namely a lance, a sword, and a dish.

In tales such as the Welsh *Peredur*, where Christian speculations have not taken control, the hero discovers one or more of the four talismans under weird circumstances. The theme has several variations, but the approximate idea is that the objects are hidden in a castle presided over by a Grail-keeper who lies wounded in the thigh and immobile. Surrounding the castle is a Waste Land. The name Avalon or Avallach occurs. The Grail itself is the cup, and it seems to be conceived as a source of food like the cauldron. When the seeker arrives everything is bewitched. The whole spellbound state of affairs is contingent on his asking or not asking a certain key question. In the most interesting version the correct question is: 'Whom does the Grail serve?' If all goes well, then the Grail manifests itself, the Grail-keeper recovers, and the Waste Land revives.

This fantasy is simply a fairy-tale transformation of primitive fertility rituals, involving mimes and incantations and riddling dialogues. In the sexually crippled Grail-keeper we recognise one of those genii of the seasonal cycle whose wounding and restoration have been the subject-matter of so much mythology; or, perhaps, one of those Sacred Kings who belong to the same realm of belief and often represent the divinity. He is a close relative of Osiris, Attis and Adonis; and these likewise had their mystical ceremonies and initiations. The clue to the confidential imaginative process probably lurks in a complicated series of Welsh legends and conundrums with which the cauldron theme is linked. So far as I know, only Mr Robert Graves has had the temerity even to begin the unravelling.[1]

During the Middle Ages there were no clear boundaries separating 'white' magic from witchcraft, witchcraft from pre-Christian cults, or the cults themselves from the darker Christian heresies. Italians frankly called witchcraft the Old Religion. Thus the Grail passed through curious transitions with remarkable ease. Chrétien de Troyes, the master of all the Arthurian romancers, composed the first part of an interminable *Conte* in which the Grail was a sinister and elusive thing under the care of a wizard. Later poets who added further instalments also added a Christian gloss, but they did not take this from Chrétien himself. The primitive Unholy Grail may be roughly defined as a miraculous source of well-being, physical and mental, the discovery or rather *achievement* of which unveiled the secret of Life itself.

Beyond this hazy notion, the early writers gave no intelligible hint as to what the Grail was or where it came from. The vision possessed the timeless and immemorial mystery of the rites which engendered it. Soon after 1190, however,

[1] It should not be assumed that I agree with Jessie Weston in regarding the Grail stories as descriptive of actual religious ceremonies; or with Mr Graves in interpreting the Taliesinic riddles as a detailed cryptogram of the god's life-cycle. But both writers, I believe, have done work of permanent value toward bringing out the nature of the ultimate sources.

a startling transformation took place. New romances in French (the first was written by Robert de Borron) began to identify the Grail with a vessel of the Last Supper, initially of course the cup, and told of its history and the strange courses by which it travelled to Britain in the custody of St Joseph of Arimathea. The Grails of previous fiction were tacitly reinterpreted as types or symbols or imperfect manifestations of the true Christian Grail. But the magical features, far from being censored out, persisted and proliferated. The miraculous vessel in the new stories was more than a holy relic. As the receptacle of the Eucharist, of the food of Eternal Life, it was the centre of a cult or mystique. Supernatural properties were ascribed to it – properties which did not replace those of the pre-Christian Grail, but instead enlarged on them.

The scriptural foundations were patent enough. The doctrine of the Real Presence, indeed, was in the forefront of theological minds. This doctrine, held with slowly increasing clarity from the first Christian centuries, affirmed that the Saviour was in some way physically present in the consecrated bread and wine of the Eucharist. (To speak of 'transubstantiation' as a Catholic dogma is inexact; the term refers to a metaphysical theory which purports to elucidate the dogma of the Real Presence. The dogma itself is an article of faith, the theory is not.) In the Gospel of St John, Jesus is portrayed as estranging his audience by a shocking affirmation which he declines to explain away as merely figurative.

Jesus said to them, Believe me when I tell you this; you can have no life in yourselves, unless you eat the flesh of the Son of Man, and drink his blood. The man who eats my flesh and drinks my blood enjoys eternal life, and I will raise him up at the last day. My flesh is real food, my blood is real drink. He who eats my flesh, and drinks my blood, lives continually in me, and I in him.

The evangelists describe the scene at the Last Supper in which the Lord, instituting the Eucharist, supplied the only tolerable interpretation for his earlier words:

While they were still at table, Jesus took bread, and blessed, and broke it, and gave it to them, saying, Take this; this is my body. Then he took *a cup*, and offered thanks, and gave

it to them, and they all drank of it. And he said, This is
my blood of the new testament, shed for many.

Thus the possibility of the Christian Grail existed from the
beginning; and the Mass, with its daily renewal of the
mystery, was always there to stimulate fancy. The idea that the
original cup, the chalice of Christ himself, might exert a high
and hidden efficacy, was a natural one in an age receptive to
marvels.

But the Grail romancers went beyond orthodoxy. Inspired
in part by the tradition of the Celtic Church, they flirted
with the conception of an esoteric element in the Catholic
heritage, a Something Else unknown or forgotten even in
Rome. This notion was fostered by the strange circumstance
that the hallowed tableware of the Last Supper had never been
traced, even by the most audacious Church fabulists. An Italian cathedral possibly claimed to possess the dish, nobody at
all claimed to possess the cup. Christ's Grail, according to the
romancers, had passed to the primitive British Church. It had
then been lost, obscurely rediscovered in Arthur's day, and lost
again, together with the spiritual fact which it mysteriously
embodied. But Angevin England had inherited Arthur; she had
inherited Glastonbury with its Celtic past; therefore she
had inherited whatever could be inherited of the Grail mystique, and in virtue of this privilege, if her kings but grasped
it, she could hold up her head in controversy with Rome.

The Quest of the Grail became, to put it prosaically, a
search in the wilderness for the headquarters of an uncanonical Christian cult. The birth of this cult was narrated at prodigious length. Literary scholars have divided the Grail material
into 'Early History' romances and romances of the 'Quest'
proper. The distinction is not very satisfactory, but it will
serve. In the Early Histories Joseph of Arimathea (meta-
morphosed into a soldier) obtains the Grail as a memento
of Christ. Afterwards he is imprisoned, and Christ appears to
him, as related in the *Acts of Pilate*. But here the narrative
breaks away from the apocryphal text. The risen Lord is
made to instruct Joseph in a secret sacrament performed with
the Grail, superior to the normal Mass. Joseph remains in
prison for forty years or more, miraculously sustained and
preserved from old age, till at last Vespasian releases him.
He leaves for foreign parts with a large body of Christians.
Adventures follow which recall the troubles of the Israelites
in the wilderness. The Grail discharges various preternatural

189

functions. Eventually the party arrives in Britain, where the Grail is entrusted to a succession of Keepers constituting a secret British priesthood set apart from the visible Church.

The Quest romances describe how Arthur's knights go to look for the Grail, which in course of time has been entirely lost sight of and practically forgotten. Finding or achieving it is an eerie process involving the magical paraphernalia of the pre-Christian stories, but with changed connotations. For example, the Lance reappears along with the Cup; it is represented, however, to be the spear of Longinus which pierced the side of Christ. The Waste Land, the wounded Grail-keeper, the crucial question, the atmosphere of initiation – all these recur in various ways, but with a suggestion of symbolism which is not always elucidated. Achieving the Grail seems to mean participating in the strange Mass performed with it. There is a constant accompaniment of visions and supernatural visitations and potent spiritual effects. Generally speaking, the knights most successful in the Quest are Percival and Galahad.

Evidently this farrago is not the fruit of orthodox piety. The ecclesiastical nationalism, and the hints at an esoteric superior sacrament, betray the hands of men anxious to set up a rival Christianity; not, of course, as serious heretics, but as opponents of the papal monopoly. The Grail saga is the compensatory daydream of nobles thwarted by a papalist clergy. It is not developed from any known holy-relic legend, and the stony silence of ecclesiastical authors is proof enough of its suspect character in clerical eyes. The most intriguing feature is the exploitation of pagan magic and its fusion with Christian motifs. Too much has been made of this; the Christianised Grail, I repeat, did not simply 'grow out of' rustic mythology as a sophisticated falsification. What confronts us is the adventurous Christianity of the twelfth century, making use of pre-Christian themes. Rivulets of myth have been swept into a deeper current of speculation, supplying its characteristic imagery. The result is best summed up as a variant of Gnosticism.

2

We have glanced at Gnosticism before, in connection with

the Celts. Its distinctive mark in the Roman Empire was the blending of Christian doctrine with magic through the conception of a Secret Wisdom. The Greco-Roman civilisation had its mystery cults – those of Attis, Adonis, Orpheus, Osiris, Mithras – the importance of which has only been appreciated in recent years. They were all based, like the fundamental Grail matter, on allegorisations of peasant fertility-ritual. The gods who figured in them, dying and being lamented over and reviving, formerly typified the seasonal cycle. But the initiate was taught to see a deeper significance. He was taught to see the world as a trap, condemning the soul to a hopeless chain of incarnations. From this evil order he was to turn away with contempt. Initiation would show him how to escape. Aided by the god, so sublimely victorious over death, he would learn the passwords needed to thread his way after his own death through the labyrinth of the upper regions, evading or mastering the demons lying in wait for him. Thus he would arrive at a safe haven, a select empyrean beyond the planets. The keynote of the Mysteries, at least in their advanced form, was this notion of spiritual distinction founded on the possession of secrets rather than the practice of virtue. Despite all allegory, the initiate was never beyond hailing-distance of ordinary magic. The passwords were akin to the formulæ which wizards recited to conjure spirits. The rites were spells for deliverance from the winter of this world.

Apostolic Christianity took a different course. No other religion had introduced the Creator of the Universe as a historical person, laying down his life for the salvation of mankind. The Church bore no real resemblance to the cliques of initiates. It was not arcane or exclusive as they were, nor did it charge the same heavy admission fees. The Christian ascetic did in a sense despise the world, but he never erred into the same absolute condemnation of the life he personally renounced. God, after all, had made the world: and behold, it was good. Yet in some restless minds the attempt to turn the Faith into another mystery cult did take place. The pioneer Gnostic, as we saw, was a wizard traditionally styled Simon Magus. The movement branched out endlessly, but its most significant product for the understanding of the Grail was the Naassene sect. Its members held that the dying-and-reviving gods of the pagan cults were simply partial manifestations of the dying-and-resurrected Christ. They were thus able to construct a scheme of initiation that absorbed all the mythologies into a Secret Wisdom compounded of pagan and Christian elements. 'We alone,' boasts a fragment of the Naassene liturgy, 'are the true Christians, accomplishing the mystery at the Third Gate.'[1]

Gnosticism in general carried over and emphasised the old mystical pessimism. It taught that the material world was the creation of a fallen and malignant being, and that for souls imprisoned in it the only proper course was to learn the esoteric technique of escape. This theory led to unbridled fancies about the relationship of spirit and matter, of God and the Devil. The Manichaean heresy, which spread from Babylon to Bulgaria during the Dark Ages and from there to western Europe, was the outgrowth of such fancies when brought in contact with the dual theology of Persia.

In England and France during the later twelfth century, the time was ripe for a renewal of the Gnostic impulse. The Celtic revival had disclosed an untapped body of pagan lore, thinly disguised or not disguised at all, and it happened to have become accessible at a moment when a vast spiritual disquiet was unsettling those territories where educated people spoke French. This showed itself on the ecclesiastical plane as anti-Romanism, and on the more strictly religious plane as a probing into the relationship of spirit and matter, the same problem which Gnosticism pushed to the forefront. The Manichaean heresy was disturbing much of Christendom under the name of Catharism. In southern France, the cultured land of the troubadours, it was even dominant: here the heretics were called Albigensians. Their religion was a mixture of amply justified anti-clericalism, psychopathic asceticism, witchcraft, and ritual suicide. Its most notorious tenets were the sinfulness of all procreation and the equality of the Devil with God. Its kinship to Gnosticism was reflected in the sharp division between the initiates or Perfecti and the more or less anarchic mob, who relied for salvation on the spiritual wizardy of the Perfecti.

Catharism, as such, made little or no impression on the Angevin Empire. Its missionaries met with lynching or exile. But its mere existence caused unease, and the uneasiness became involved with politics and literature. The court of

[1] The snob element in Gnosticism is well brought out by Mr Evelyn Waugh (that expert on snobbery) in his *Helena*. One cannot, alas, avoid a faint suspicion that if Mr Waugh had been a contemporary of Helena he would have joined a Gnostic society himself.

Toulouse had swung toward support of the Albigensians as a force making for regional opposition to Paris. Its patronage of heretics on the one hand and troubadours on the other gave the impression of a united front of literature and heresy. The actual word 'troubadour,' translated into North French as 'trouvère,' suggested a man who had 'found' some secret, achieved some quest. Queen Eleanor, the wife of Henry II, was a southerner herself with a savagely anti-clerical family background (once, when Regent, she threatened the Pope with schism). It was at her private court in Poitou that the Matter of Britain largely took shape. There the poets elaborated the code of Arthurian chivalry and the aristocratic sexual aberration called Courtly Love. Her son Richard Cœur-de-Lion belonged to the troubadour fellowship himself, and whatever his personal beliefs, the fame of his exploits helped to foster the idea of a link between literature, the knightly character, and irregular Christianity.

All this is painfully tangled, and simplification would be falsification. The essential fact is the questioning, speculative attitude, in a context of aristocratic literary culture and ecclesiastical regionalism. The notion of an exclusive quasi-Arthurian cult for the Angevin knighthood could easily take root. The rich military order of the Knights Templars, a body very much under Angevin patronage, was already practising secret rituals and initiations. The Templar institution probably gave a strong impetus to Grail romance. There is ground for thinking that the Templars toyed with Gnosticism. When a King of France, aided by a captive pope, eventually suppressed and despoiled the order, the alleged crime which he employed as his main excuse (and brutally extorted 'confessions' to) was the celebration of blasphemous rites. What the Templars really did in the twelfth century we do not know, but at any rate they had an aura of mystery.

The official Church, for its part, did nothing to reduce controversy. By laying more and more stress on the doctrine of the Real Presence, it prevented the hot debates over spirit and matter and the nature of life from dying down. Men within the Church itself, even men held in high reverence, contributed actively to the broad unrest. Indeed, the first positive link between Arthurian literature and Christian speculation was forged by the disciples of Joachim of Flora. That saintly Sicilian, influenced perhaps by Greek or Arab ideas, had proclaimed that human history was divided into three phases corresponding to the three Persons of the Trinity. The Age of the Father was, roughly, the period up to the Incarnation. The Age of the Son was the period of the Church Militant. The Age of the Holy Ghost would attain fruition when the Church's battle was won. This third age would see the Church transformed. Hierarchical authority would wither away; the typical Christian would be the monk, the contemplative; and all mankind would enjoy undreamt-of enlightenments. Joachim expounded his theory from the Apocalypse, and from other portions of Scripture which he chose to read as prophetic. He picked out symbols and types and foreshadowings. A favourite device was to detect the triadic pattern in a group of three characters. It was said to be prefigured, for instance, by Peter, Paul, and John. As we should expect, the third era was that of John.

Joachim himself remained an orthodox Catholic, and there was talk of his canonisation. Heretical agitators were afterwards to twist his doctrine into a forecast of a new dispensation superseding the Christian. In his lifetime this did not happen. His writings, however, awoke a fresh interest in prophecies generally, and among those current during the twelfth century were the so-called prophecies of Merlin circulated by Geoffrey of Monmouth. Alain de Lisle, a scholar and theologian of enormous repute, composed a commentary on them about 1180. In the light of Alain's general outlook, there is not much doubt that Arthur's court-wizard was enlisted in the service of Joachism.[1] Into this realm of imagination, in fact, the dreams of Celtic enthusiasts could very readily find a way. Especially relevant were the Lives of the Welsh Saints. Quite apart from Merlin, the Joachite theory must have seemed to accord rather neatly with the Sense of Something Else lurking in Celtic Christianity. Whether or not the religion of the Celts actually had a Johannine streak, its monastic bias looked like an anticipation of Joachim's third era. Conceivably the British Church was the church of the future, destined to return and transfigure the world.

Thus, from a convergence of causes, we get this massive body of Grail romance representing Arthurian Britain as

[1] A character called Alain occurs in the Grail stories, but if his name has any special significance, the clue has been lost. Sebastian Evans made it the jumping-off point for his theory of a *roman à clef* identifying Sir Perceval with (of all people) St Dominic, but few readers took him seriously.

enshrining a mighty mystery of the Faith; as preserving the possibility of an unthinkable insight. And, at least in some versions, the insight is regarded in Gnostic terms as the opening of a gate. It is a means of transition from the hopeless Waste Land of the visible universe into a hidden and superior mode of being. When Galahad achieves the Quest he does not come back.

Much argument has raged round the problem of origins – of the exact way in which the Grail became Christian or pseudo-Christian. If, however, we keep our eyes fixed on Glastonbury, the sequence of events is plain and straightforward. In 1190 the monks announced the exhumation of Arthur. Ynys-witrin was placed in the limelight and publicly equated with Avalon. Thus the visionary themes of romance acquired, for the first time, a local habitation. Also for the first time, they came squarely into contact with Christian tradition. Geoffrey of Monmouth's bogus ecclesiastical details had no vitality; Glastonbury Abbey, with its immense past, was a solid and unassailable fact. At this juncture, then, the Grail's imaginative associations – Arthurian, Avalonian, and generally otherworldly – converged all of a sudden to connect it with Glastonbury, and to foster the notion that it could really have been a Christian object imported by those disciples of Christ to whom tradition ascribed the building of the Old Church. Robert de Borron's conception followed in short order.

Suggestive also is William of Malmesbury's *arcanum sacrum* or holy secret concealed in the floor design of the church. A possible relevance of this phrase to speculations about the chalice and the Real Presence would have been patent to anyone who could read a missal. At the consecration of the wine in the Latin Mass, the priest takes the chalice and recites the following formula:

Simili modo postquam coenatum est, accipiens et hunc præclarum calicem in sanctas ac venerabiles manus suas, item tibi gratias agens, benedixit, deditque discipulis suis, dicens: Accipite et bibite ex eo omnes; hic est enim calix sanguinis mei, novi et æterni testamenti; *mysterium fidei*; qui pro vobis et pro multis effundetur in remissionem peccatorum.

In like manner, after he had supped, taking also this excellent chalice into his holy and venerable hands, and giving thee thanks, he blessed, and gave it to his disciples, saying: Take, and drink ye all of this; for this is the chalice of my blood, of the new and eternal testament; *the mystery of faith*; which shall be shed for you, and for many, to the remission of sins.

The speech of Christ is paraphrased from the Gospels, but the actual words *mysterium fidei* are not in any evangelic account of the Last Supper. They are a gloss added (not later than the seventh century) by a liturgical author wishing to underline the 'mysterious' aspect. The words are not William's, yet the phrase means very much the same as his, and the associative step is easy. Whatever William's intention, Glastonbury Abbey was the one place in England where a twelfth-century man could find anything even remotely susceptible of interpretation as a great secret connected with the chalice of Christ.

And now, what about St Joseph of Arimathea? If he was already named in monastic legend as the founder of Christian Glastonbury, we need look no further to see how de Borron's imagination worked. But if we exclude Glastonbury as an influence, or reject the idea of a ready-made Joseph legend attaching to it, the old question 'Why?' recurs and ramifies. Why did the poet Christianise the Grail just then . . . or at all? Why did he hit on St Joseph as the object's keeper, or as a potential missionary to Britain? The only documents concerning the saint, the short Gospel texts and the apocryphal *Acts of Pilate,* could not have suggested either phase of his attributed activities. From some modern authors you would get the impression that Joseph had been thrust into prominence by a sudden discovery of the *Acts of Pilate* in the twelfth century. Yet Gregory of Tours used this book in the sixth, and a paraphrase of the Joseph passage, embedded in his *History of the Franks,* remained constantly accessible. If there was no Glastonbury legend, nothing at all had happened in the twelfth century to make Joseph a celebrity. Without such a legend he is inexplicable.

Nevertheless, notable sceptics like Jessie Weston and Armitage Robinson have declined to admit the difficulty. An Anti-Glastonbury case does exist, and we can no longer postpone its examination. The next section is the only part of this book entailing a head-on clash with specific opponents. I deeply regret the necessity of writing it.

Miss Weston's elucidation of the Grail, as far as it goes, is an immortal feat of scholarship. Her account of the way the story grew is perhaps less convincing. As a matter of fact neither she nor those who agree with her have made themselves entirely clear. But, piecing together several theories, I arrive at the following as the most cogent statement I can devise in the role of devil's advocate.

'From 1171 onward, the Benedictine monks of Fécamp in Normandy used to show people a relic of the Holy Blood, with an accompanying tale tracing it back to Nicodemus, the ruler who came to Jesus by night (*John* iii. 1-21). Robert de Borron, mystically Christianising the Grail in ignorance of Glastonbury and casting about for a Grail-bearer, noticed Fécamp and assigned the Nicodemus-like part to the disciple whom Nicodemus assisted in the burial of the Lord (*John* xix. 39). The *Acts of Pilate* also brought them together. In the romances of de Borron and his successors there was never any clear mention of Glastonbury. No legend associated St Joseph with it. The Abbey, through William of Malmesbury's interpolator, simply annexed him from the romancers with an eye on the rival house at Fécamp.'

Such is the opposition's case. The first and most manifest objection is that the Grail is not primarily a relic of the Holy Blood. As Miss Weston proves – and her whole theory of the Grail turns on this – the pervading stress is on the Divine Presence, on the Sacramental Meal, on the Bread of Life; on the happenings of Maundy Thursday, not on those of Good Friday. The Christian Grail is essentially a vessel connected with those happenings. De Borron makes it the cup, and between his archetypal version and the story told at Fécamp there is no significant overlap at all. He and his successors do make St Joseph use the Grail to receive drops of Jesus's blood, but the doubling of themes is infelicitous, and the emphasis is certainly not on the blood itself but on the receptacle – and, at that, not as a holy relic but as something much more peculiar.

By the way, what was the Fécamp legend? If you glance through the scholars you will readily find statements about the 'close connection' or 'imitation.' You will not so readily find what the object of the supposed imitation actually was. Here is the story which they told at the French abbey.

When Nicodemus helped to bury the Lord, he took a knife and scraped off some of the dried blood. He gave this to his nephew Isaac. Isaac's wife, observing his reverence for the relic, accused him of idolatry. Isaac left her and went to Sidon. Learning in a vision that Jerusalem would be destroyed, he put the blood and the knife in two tubes of lead, and hid both inside the trunk of a fig-tree. Then, at God's bidding, he cast the trunk into the Mediterranean. It drifted through the Straits of Gibraltar and ran aground near Fécamp. Three saplings sprouted from it. A holy man removed these, but the trunk stayed immovable where it was, till an angel transported it a little way from the shore. Early in the sixth century some hunters discovered that the trunk exerted a force, keeping them at a distance. A chapel was built over the marvellous object. At last it came open and disclosed its contents. The tube with the blood in it was placed in various parts of the abbey church, ending on the altar.

And this is the fable which the sceptics hold up as the original of the Grail's early history! It is hard to know where to begin pointing out its inadequacies. In the first place, as we noted, the French holy article is a relic of a different kind. In the second place, it is a relic only, with no mystical properties beyond the minor thaumaturgical powers ascribed to all relics. In the third place, Nicodemus – the character who is alleged, by association, to have suggested Joseph of Arimathea – is not conspicuous at all. He is not, as Miss Weston calls him, the protagonist, but a mere contrivance. The question 'Why Nicodemus?' has an obvious and trivial answer. Given the relic of Christ's blood, Nicodemus was a natural person to think of. He was one of the very few in a position to obtain such a relic, and the fabulists put him in for that reason. They did not bring him to France. For that matter they did not even bring Isaac to France. The Grail romancers, on any showing, added the enormously important theme of the voyage. Their hero and his actions present a problem which the appeal to Fécamp only confuses. Given the miraculous vessel, there was indeed no earthly reason to think of Joseph.

De Borron could have asked himself primarily, 'Who would have been likeliest to get hold of this thing?' The answer then would have been, 'One of the Apostles who sat at the Last Supper.' Or he could have asked himself, 'Who first evangelised Britain?' The answer then would have been 'St Philip' or 'St Paul' or 'Aristobulus' or 'Faganus and Deruvianus,' according to the legend he happened to hear. Or he could have asked himself, 'Who was the arch-mystic among the Apostles, the theologian of the Incarnation and the Real Presence, the patron of Celtic Christianity?' The answer then would have been 'St John.' Even if he did take a hint from Fécamp (though I do not see why he should have hit on this particular Holy Blood relic when there were dozens), why did he replace Nicodemus himself – a known recipient of Jesus's mystical teaching, and a purely Johannine character unmentioned by the other Evangelists – with the far less significantly distinguished Joseph? The *Acts of Pilate* text gives the story of Joseph's release from custody by the risen Christ, thus enhancing his stature somewhat. But there is nothing about the vessel, or about instruction of any kind, or about a missionary voyage. The blood episode, awkwardly foisted in, may show the influence of Fécamp. But if so, surely it is enough to say that the author added it to the story so that Joseph should not seem to be outdone by his colleague in the Interment. This hypothesis is quite enough to dispose of the sceptics' only positive evidence, a reference in one of the romances to a book at Fécamp.

To sum up: if de Borron really started with pagan Celtic talismans (unlocalised) on the one hand, and a French relic of the Holy Blood (one among many) on the other, with no intervening terms, he would never have brought them into relationship. Nor even if juxtaposed, would they have generated the Christian Grail or suggested Joseph as its bearer. The contortions and falsifications of Scripture which de Borron goes through in order to get the Grail into Joseph's hands simply do not make sense, if there was no tradition dictating the choice of hero. Fécamp explains nothing. A prior legend of St Joseph explains everything.

The other part of the Anti-Glastonbury case concerns the alleged piratical appropriation of Joseph by the Abbey itself, several decades after the romances first introduce him. The chief exhibit is the interpolated text of William of Malmesbury's book *De Antiquitate Glastoniensis Ecclesiæ.* Comparison with William's draft does show that the chapter about St Joseph is an addition by another hand. The manuscript probably belongs to the mid-thirteenth century; hence, it is argued, Joseph's journey to Glastonbury was fabricated then for the greater glory of the Abbey, as an attempt to cash in on the romances or as a direct retort to Fécamp. We have already surveyed this famous chapter. The tale which it tells is plainly at variance with the sceptical view. For the saint does not bring the Grail with him. He does not bring anything with him. He settles on Ynys-witrin with his companions, builds the Old Church, and dies.

If St Joseph's whole raison-d'être in the first place was to bring the Grail, why did the interpolator not mention it? The utmost anybody can urge in reply is that from a clerical point of view the Grail was subversive, so that the monastic writer fought shy of it. But if the fundamental motif at Glastonbury was a retort to Fécamp in the form of a rival relic, which would, in itself, be ecclesiastically safe – again, why not mention the relic? Conversely, if the Grail was conceived otherwise, surely the writer would still have needed virtually no imagination to strip away the dubious trappings and leave a sacred and creditable object? All the ingredients had been provided. This clerical re-editing is exactly what does happen when the story comes to be handled by the fourteenth-century chronicler John of Glastonbury. John makes Joseph bring two vials or cruets containing the blood and sweat of the Lord. But in *De Antiquitate* we do not hear of any relic at all.

The bias of the sceptics appears in their unequal treatment of William of Malmesbury's interpolator and William himself. Their usual starting-point in the deflation of Glastonbury is the paragraph quoted in Chapter Two, where William discusses the tradition about the Old Church's apostolic foundation. From this they argue: 'William of Malmesbury does not mention St Joseph. Therefore nobody can have mentioned him up to the time when William wrote. He is a late invention.' Very well; but now let us imagine a scholar doing research on this topic without benefit of text-books. He unearths *De Antiquitate,* and John of Glastonbury's Chronicle with its Holy Blood relic, and a later piece of Grail fiction such as Tennyson's. That, for the moment, is all. 'I perceive,' he says, 'that after 1300 or thereabouts immense emphasis is laid on a sacred object supposed to have been brought by St Joseph. But the *De Antiquitate* writer does not mention this object. Therefore nobody can have mentioned it up to the time when he wrote.' Thus our scholar elegantly disproves the existence of earlier Christian Grail romance. This absurdity brings out the looseness in the argument about William of Malmesbury. The proper inference is as follows. 'William does not mention St Joseph; therefore, probably, St Joseph did not figure in the sources he used.' Having phrased the inference accurately, let us apply it to *De Antiquitate*. 'William's interpolator does not mention a sacred object; therefore, probably, no such object figured in the sources he used.' We are now treating William and his interpolator in the same way, and the notion of a theft from the romances or Fécamp has evaporated. Any sceptic who rejects the inference from the words of the interpolator must also give up his own inference from the words of William himself, and thereby remove the cornerstone of his case against a Joseph tradition.

Actually I do not believe for an instant that the *De Antiquitate* writer is trying to cash in on the romances. Quite possibly he has never heard of these trifles. He is a pious man. It seems to me that he is doing just what he purports to be doing – preparing a second edition of William's book, with new material brought to light since the first appeared. In the same spirit he puts in paragraphs about Arthur. His new material concerning St Joseph is a legend preserved among the Celts, probably in Wales, and brought back to Glastonbury during the latter half of the twelfth century. This is the common source used by himself and by the romancers.

There are three arguments against the existence of this original. First is the obvious one, the fact that no document demonstrably embodying it has so far turned up. That is not too serious. Every theory of the Grail involves postulating a good deal of lost matter. But, not long after de Borron, we do discover a Grail romancer citing a Glastonbury record as his main source. The anonymous *Perlesvaus*[1] was written about 1225. It ends with an epilogue containing the following passage.

> The Latin from whence this history was drawn into Romance was taken in the Isle of Avalon, in a holy house of religion that standeth at the head of the Moors Adventurous, there where King Arthur and Queen Guenievre lie, according to the witness of the good men religious that are therein, that have the whole history thereof.

This would seem to prove the presence of a relevant document in the Abbey before 1225, and it certainly refutes the contention that the borrowing was all *from* the romances. In the course of the narrative, 'Avalon' receives visits from Lancelot and Arthur. The place is portrayed as lying in a fertile valley surrounded by woodlands. There is a steep isolated hill with a stream running down it past a chapel of the Virgin. Close to the chapel are three monastic buildings, each with its own orchard. A graveyard is adjacent.

This topography is romanticised, but probably the romancer did stay at the Abbey. One wonders, however, what he read there. When alluding to his authority, to the person responsible for the Latin source-document, he names 'Josephus.' It has been suggested that he means Flavius Josephus, the great Jewish historian. William of Malmesbury, in his chapter on the foundation of the Old Church, cites Freculfus regarding St Philip's mission to western Europe, in which the church's founders were thought to have participated. Freculfus in his turn cites Josephus. An Abbey book-list dated 1247 shows that the Glastonbury library had two manuscripts of Freculfus: a remarkable duplication of an obscure author. One of these manuscripts may have been copied from the other, with interpolated material about Joseph of Arimathea and his successors, as an expansion of the passage on Philip. Freculfus's reference to Josephus could then have led to the whole story being fathered on the unfortunate Jew.

(Ferdinand Lot, a Frenchman with an anti-monastic animus, argued that the Freculfus passage was behind the Joseph story originally. He thought that in the mind of some unscrupulous Benedictine forger the historian Joseph suggested the disciple. The next step was to urge that the romancers attributed St Joseph's release from prison to Vespasian because Vespasian actually did release Josephus, and the two Josephs were now hopelessly confused. I find this view far-fetched. Even if it were accepted, it would tend to prove my main point, that the Arimathean was connected with Glastonbury before the romancers got hold of him. A Glastonbury fabulist, inspired by William, might have delved into Freculfus and hit on the ambiguous name; the romancers certainly never did. By the way, there is no trace of a confusion in *Perlesvaus*. Its author knows that his authority 'Josephus' is not the Grail-bearer Joseph.)

[1] Known to English readers through Sebastian Evans's translation, entitled *The High History of the Holy Grail*, and published in the Everyman Library.

The second argument against the common original is the fact that the monks did not give out the legend as soon as it presumably reached them – that is, at some date between 1125 and 1190. But their silence is easily explained by the long strife between the Holy See and the Angevin sovereigns. If the tale of Joseph came back to Glastonbury after 1165, the abbots up till the death of King John would have preferred not to annoy Rome by publicising extreme claims for the British Church which rebellious royalty could turn to account. Rumours might leak out, but they had to remain strictly unofficial. King John died in 1216. The publication of *Perlesvaus* with its Glastonbury acknowledgment followed within a decade.

The third argument is the fact (supposing it to be a fact) that the earliest Christian Grail romances do not bring Joseph or the Grail to Glastonbury, do not so much as mention Glastonbury. This is the opposition's trump card. What is it worth?

The only romance for which the problem is at all pressing is de Borron's *Joseph,* the pioneer Early History. If de Borron drew on a Glastonbury legend, we should certainly expect to see traces of it in his poem. A lack of such traces in romancers who followed him could fairly be attributed to a lack of interest in British geographical detail. But if it were shown that de Borron, in a complete and rounded text, failed to introduce Glastonbury, the theory of a fundamental monastic legend would indeed look dubious.

Here is a summary of his poem.

Joseph of Arimathea, seeking a keepsake of the Lord, obtains possession of the vessel used at the Last Supper. The Jews imprison him. Christ appears to him in prison and teaches him the secret words of consecration which no one can rightly utter unless he has learnt the mystery of the Great Sacrament performed with the Grail. Joseph is miraculously sustained in the prison for forty-two years. Meanwhile Vespasian has been cured of leprosy by St Veronica's kerchief. Becoming interested in the Christians, he releases Joseph and accepts baptism himself. Joseph joins his sister and her husband Brons, and together with a large party of fellow-Christians they leave for another country, taking the Grail. In this ill-defined country various tribulations assail them. Joseph prays before the Grail and learns that God is offended at his companions' sins. Instructed by the Holy Spirit, he makes a square table as a symbol of the table at which the Apostles sat, with a place for the Grail opposite the chair corresponding to Christ's. Brons is to catch a fish and lay it nearby. Next to the place of Christ there is an empty chair for Judas. This (it is revealed) will only be safely occupied by a certain mysterious descendant of Brons. Joseph causes his companions to sit at the table in the remaining chairs, and the more virtuous ones feel the blessed influence which proceeds from the Grail. The Holy Spirit also informs Joseph that a grandson of Brons will occupy the vacant seat at another table resembling this.

Time passes. Brons and his wife have had twelve sons. All are married except Alain le Gros, whom Joseph consecrates to God's service. Again the Holy Spirit communicates the divine will. Alain himself is to have a son who will inherit the Grail, far away in the west. Petrus, one of Joseph's companions, is to go at once to the place appointed and wait. Brons meanwhile must assume custody of the Grail and learn the secret words. Because of the fish, he will be called the Rich Fisher. After his initiation he is to go westward with the remainder of the party, to the place appointed, and wait there for his promised grandson to whom he will entrust the Grail. Thus there are three Keepers: Joseph, Brons, and the son of Alain. They symbolise the Trinity (an idea very strongly recalling Joachim of Flora). Joseph delivers the Grail to Brons. . . . Now, however, the poem peters out, and Joseph's own final destination is not made clear.

De Borron planned a trilogy, but he never finished it. In its oblique arrangement it anticipated Priestley's play *Time and the Conways*. The second part was to deal with Merlin and the Arthurian age, the third was to revert to Alain le Gros and the adventures of the Grail-Keepers in Britain. A portion at least of *Merlin* was written, but there is no convincing trace of Part Three.

The archetype, therefore, is incomplete. No adventures in Britain ever materialise. The map cannot be drawn. We can only investigate the poet's intention by looking for clues among his fragments. These fortunately contain a clue; a single one, but all-sufficient. When God commands Petrus to sail westward and prepare a place for the Grail and its Keepers, the designated spot is the 'Vale of Avaron.' I do not think even the hardiest sceptic would deny that this name is a garbled version of Avalon, and in any case there are two puns which prove it. Whatever the case may have been before, whatever it may have become later, in those precise years when de Borron wrote his poem the identification of Avalon with Glastonbury was inescapable. It is most unlikely that any literary man would have spoken of Avalon just after the exhumation of Arthur if he meant any other place. In *Perlesvaus* there is still not the slightest doubt. Moreover, as if to clinch the matter, de Borron uses the word 'Vale.' If he had said 'Isle,' he might still conceivably have meant the unlocalised Never-Never-Land of the Celts. But the 'Vale' of Avalon is, quite unambiguously, the stretch of low country between the Mendips and Poldens. Somerset's Vale is a by-product of Somerset's Isle. The name is still current, and it has never stood for anything else. Celtic mythology had an Isle of Avalon but never a Vale. Petrus's destination, the British rendezvous of the whole mission, is therefore Glastonbury. No alternative exists. The supposed silence of the romances is a mare's-nest.

Notice, however, that we only reach this conclusion because of an artificial emphasis. In order to fathom de Borron's overall scheme it is necessary to underline a single couplet and pause on it. His followers and embroiderers may well have missed it altogether, and certainly they need not have felt that the geographic touch possessed crucial importance. They were concerned with Britain rather than particular localities there. Thus the undeniable fading-out of Glastonbury, and the substitution, in one romance, of nonsense about Northumberland, can be readily accounted for. De Borron based his conception on the Abbey's legend of St Joseph; but since he failed to carry it through, all he transmitted to his successors was the identity of the hero. *Perlesvaus* may give us a second instalment of monastic material. However, it is so heavily overlaid with fantasy that the nucleus is hardly worth seeking, and again Glastonbury is lost sight of.

In the upshot I see no reason to doubt that by 1190 a Celtic Joseph legend, preserved in Wales, had returned to the Abbey, and that this was the common source for Robert de Borron and the *De Antiquitate* interpolator. Perhaps its actual language hardly ventured beyond the bare statement that Joseph came. It may have been embalmed in a triad, in which case nobody could have made much of it. But there is a last point in favour of its existence which has hitherto escaped notice. Joseph of Arimathea is generally conceived as by no means young at the time of the Crucifixion. Yet *De Anti-*

quitate brings him to Britain only in A.D. 63, and the romances only after the fall of Jerusalem, i.e. in the 70s. These notions at any rate it is no use hunting for in the New Testament Apocrypha or anywhere else. But a perfectly simple explanation lies ready to hand. The substratum of the oddity is an attempt by conscientious if credulous monks to discipline intractable matter. About 1165, let us say, the Joseph legend returned to the Abbey from its Welsh hiding-place. It was too glorious to reject, yet it had to be reconciled with what William of Malmesbury had written about St Philip, for whose mission to Gaul other legends already assigned a date. The monks therefore drew out the saint's life into the 60s and 70s, and made their much-travelled founder a centenarian.

If the first writers to mention Joseph were simply inventing, why did they not choose a younger man . . . or else assign an earlier date?

4

We are under no obligation here to thread all the labyrinthine intricacies of Grail romance. It will be enough to note a few relevant themes and passages. The chief development after de Borron is the working out of the counter-papal notion in the person of a new character, Josephes or Joseph II, the son of the Arimathean saint. He receives the Grail and the title of 'First Bishop of Christendom.' Josephes makes his début in the *Grand Saint Graal* (c. 1200), a long Early History based on de Borron. The author conveys the party as far as Britain, but his geography is disappointing, except for a reference to the 'Abbey of Glays.' He presents his story as a revelation vouchsafed to someone else in the year 717 after the Passion, that is, between 745 and 750. The fact in itself would scarcely deserve attention; but it so happens that a chronicler named Helinandus, who does not seem to have this particular book in mind, speaks of a British hermit as receiving divine communications about the Grail in 720. We may perceive hints in these two authors at a much earlier version of the myth, now unhappily lost.

The *Grand Saint Graal* has perplexing visionary sections that foreshadow a branching out and diversification of the central image. Characters in the romances henceforth begin to see a variety of sights and to undergo a variety of experiences which cannot be entirely referred to a relic, however wonderful. The *Queste* (1200-10), Sir Thomas Malory's sourcebook, describes the adventures of several of Arthur's knights who ride out Grail-seeking. From the point of view of the Round Table their attempt is disturbing rather than beneficial. The greater knights, such as Lancelot, fail. Those who achieve the Quest are minor ones such as Galahad. Galahad succeeds in occupying the Siege Perilous, the Round Table equivalent of the Grail-keeper's chair. The Grail is phantasmal and elusive, appearing and vanishing in different places without human agency, usually under a covering of samite. It is the vessel transfigured, glorified, made emblematic. Sir Galahad, the personification of chastity, is admitted to the Great Sacrament, together with Sir Bors and Sir Perceval. He sees Joseph II preserved in a preternatural timelessness with the provocative title on his forehead. He also sees one of those strange visions of Christ which the heroes of romance constantly discern in the Grail. The Saviour steps out of the frame, as it were, and gives communion with his own hand, telling Galahad to remove the Grail to 'Sarras, the spiritual city.' In Sarras, Galahad and Perceval die. Bors returns to Britain.

Besides the Glastonbury paragraphs, *Perlesvaus* 1225 has a scene of intense interest, because of the way in which it drives home the idea of an initiation. Arthur himself sees the Grail in a chapel.

The Grail appeared at the sacring of the Mass, in five several manners that none ought not to tell, for the secret things of the sacrament ought none to tell openly but he unto whom God hath given it. King Arthur beheld the changes, the last whereof was the change into a chalice.

If the Grail was a chalice in its fifth avatar only, what was it in the other four? And what did the changes signify? Plainly the author wishes to have it understood that he is keeping something essential back.

Parzival (1210), a German Quest-epic composed by Wolfram von Eschenbach, brings us nearer to the probable truth, though in some respects it is baffling. Its hero Parzival is Sir Perceval. Its Grail is not a cup but a stone or jewel, the Lapis Exilis. This was formerly in the custody of a group of angels who remained neutral during Lucifer's rebellion, and therefore fell, though not to so deep a depth. They wafted the Grail to earth. Its descent and later vicissitudes, we are told, were committed to writing by 'a heathen, Flegetanis.' No heathen, however, could fully understand it. A Christian poet named Kiot deciphered Flegetanis's treatise in an Arabic manuscript at Toledo. He then hunted through Britain, France and Ireland for the Grail-keepers, eventually finding them at Monsalväch, a castle in a forest not very remote from Nantes.

Wolfram takes up the tale of the Quest. He strays far from the other romancers, his contemporaries, yet he speaks more openly of some of the themes that are in their minds. For instance, he works out genealogical links between Parzival, Arthur and the Angevins, naming these last by name and introducing bits of their family history. He portrays the Grail-Keepers as a mystical knighthood rather than a priesthood, and he calls them Templars. This word is particularly striking in view of the Angevins' patronage of the real Templars. Henry II founded a Templar community in 1170, at Vaubourg in the Roumare forest, which may well have supplied the model for Monsalväch. Wolfram's knights live by the Grail, which is a source of nourishment and a restorer of youth. It is the secret of the Phœnix's rebirth. It is an oracle. It bears markings which form themselves into letters designating the persons whom God summons to its presence. Every Good Friday a dove flutters down from heaven and leaves a Host on it, renewing its powers: the connection with the Eucharist is still vital, though obscure.

In this extraordinary version St Joseph and Britain are thrust aside, but on certain points von Eschenbach is refreshingly frank. He admits a non-Christian source, and it may be more than coincidence that the cauldron of Welsh legend was made according to the prescription of a sorcerer in Toledo. He stresses the Templars and the House of Anjou. And, by breaking free from de Borron's bondage to a physical relic, he makes clear what the *Perlesvaus* passage only implies – that the mystical romancers came to conceive the Grail as something ineffable, the source of a stream of visionary enlightenment and mysterious life. Christ's chalice was a medium through which the senses could apprehend a deeper reality, which might, however, be apprehended through other media.

There are several more romances which do not add much.

During the thirteenth century, the youth of the Inquisition, the tide set towards Catholic orthodoxy. The later Grail authors left out the radical elements – the secret words, the primacy of the Josephite priesthood – and slipped into a dull strain of semi-allegory. In trying to grasp what the Grail meant in its heyday, we must keep mainly to the earlier books and ask two questions. First, what was the imaginative process that produced such different results in writers professedly dealing with the same topic? Second, were the romances purely fantastic; or did they reflect anything that actually happened or could happen? Some of them assert that the Grail finally vanished in Arthur's day and that no man has seen it since. On the other hand the passages describing its apparitions are often so curt, so cryptic, so allusive, that they have the air of being hints at matters known to the author and to some of his readers but not described. As Sebastian Evans said: 'We feel as we read that the words employed are intended to convey some deeper meaning than the fiction bears on the face of it. The romance is more than a romance. It is also a secret written in cipher. Its mysticism is as marked as its mystery. Throughout, there is a continual suggestion of hidden meanings, a recurrent insistence on things seen as types and symbols of things unseen.' *The Magic Flute*, it is stated, only becomes intelligible in the light of the doctrines of an esoteric society to which Mozart belonged. Could the same have been true of Grail romance? Are we getting glimpses here (as Jessie Weston believed) of a practising school of Gnostic initiation, with political overtones?

The Grail is basically the source or secret of Life. But how do its literary exponents develop this idea? We can perhaps trace a sort of coherence in its properties: let us run over them. To begin with, even in the most highly spiritualised texts, the Grail retains its primitive ritual function. It is a cauldron of plenty, a producer of food. This feature has often struck fastidious readers as absurd or repellent, but there is no getting past it. When the Grail hovers over the Round Table in the *Queste,* the knights experience the effects of a banquet. The stone in *Parzival* seems to provide the Templars with all the nourishment they need. Scholars have professed to see signs that von Eschenbach was unhappy about including this detail. He may have been. But after all, nobody compelled him to put it in. If it was a mere vestigial remnant of a transcended fairy-tale, he could have dropped it. This food-producing magic was clearly conceived as essential to the theme.

The Grail is associated also with apparitions of Christ. They take two forms. Sometimes it is the Holy Child that appears. The stress then is presumably on the Incarnation, the human birth of God. Sometimes it is the mature man, crucified or bearing the wounds of crucifixion. Then the Atonement predominates. The apparitions are beheld in the Grail, or round about it, or emerging from it.

Sometimes, again, the Grail-seer is represented as seeing a chalice. That sounds simple and obvious, yet it is not so simple or obvious as it would be if the fully developed Grail actually *were* a chalice in the prosaic sense. One author speaks of it as taking the form of a chalice, another speaks of it as containing a chalice. The meaning is obscure, doubtless intentionally so. Here, at all events, we indubitably encounter the doctrine of the Real Presence, the eucharistic food of the soul. It is with this aspect of the Grail that we should probably connect its oracular powers. The vessel is still a cauldron of inspiration, even though the enlightenment proceeds from the Holy Spirit. St Joseph kneels before it to pray for guidance, and when he places it on the table, it attracts those who are worthy of its company and repels others. These are the same properties which Parzival is permitted to learn.

Behind all these modes of the Grail there is a single thought which all the romancers are variously driving at. The dream which haunts their imagination is that somewhere on earth there was once a certain Object. It was the Ark of the New Covenant; de Borron says so explicitly. It was a visible pledge, *the* visible pledge, of God's friendship toward mankind. More is meant here than a vague benevolence or goodwill. Friendship, particularly the friendship of the great, can be tragically demanding and disruptive. The Grail atmosphere sometimes recalls the peremptory invitations in the parable of the Supper (*Luke* xiv. 16-24). A knight who achieves the Quest may wreck his life doing it. But the Grail rewards him with the priceless assurance: God is there, God's hand reaches towards us through the cruelty and indifference of the world, God wills that human beings shall enter into the ranks of the blest. Whatever the sacrifice, that assurance is worth it.

Such a meaning is easily abstracted from the life-giving talismans and relics belonging to various levels of the myth. A special symbolic value belongs to the chalice in which the

God-Man perpetually offers himself. The other aspects of the Grail are apposite also. It contains (so to speak) the daily bread by which God sustains Man on his earthly pilgrimage toward heaven. It contains the Incarnation and the Atonement, by which God draws Man to himself. It contains the sacraments by which God sanctifies and enlightens him. Yet, after all, this exegesis does not take us much farther. If the Grail is only an allegory or confirmation of Christian commonplaces, there is nothing to explain the aura of mystery, the violent effects of the Quest, the insistence that knowledge of the Grail is a tremendous and extraordinary thing. When the romances were composed the Real Presence was one of the most familiar theological themes. Apparitions at Mass had already been reported widely enough to prevent the Grail visions as described from commanding any unparalleled awe. However literally taken, they offered nothing unique or even particularly novel – in themselves. We have seen how magic supplied some of the imagery, but there seems to be a profounder magic that still escapes us.

Let us revert for a moment to that business of visions. A surprising number of scenes can be accounted for by the supposition that the Grail is an instrument for *scrying* . . . loosely called crystal-gazing.[1]

The rapacious gipsy with her glass globe has become a hackneyed joke. However, there really are many people who can see images in a crystal if they fix their eyes on it for a few minutes undisturbed. Divination by this method is familiar throughout the world. While no well-attested cases indicate prophecy, and very few indicate telepathy, the phenomena need not be written off as faked. Watching the crystal induces a sort of partial hypnosis in which visions project themselves from subconscious sources. They have been compared to the hypnagogic images which dart into the mind on the verge of sleep. Occasionally the crystal vanishes and the seer perceives the image as substantial, like the images of Christ in the *Grand Saint Graal* and the *Queste*. As it happens, though, the 'speculum' does not have to be a crystal. For a person with the gift the potentialities are endless. North American Indians gaze into water; South American Indians use a polished slab of black stone; Australian medicine-men stare at a flame; Egyptians contemplate ink; Roman soothsayers examined the blades of swords. Anything bright or shiny will do.

A Catholic with the 'scrying' gift, who recited prayers or

texts over and over while gazing at a shiny surface, might easily undergo the kind of experience recounted of Grail-seers. His meditations could conjure up visions of Christ; his prayers could elicit visible answers; his semi-hypnosis could make him insensible to hunger; and the end of a prolonged session might well be a marvellous sense of illumination and revelation. Roman theologians to-day would regard such an exercise with suspicion, but in the twelfth century there was more latitude. The Inquisitors themselves afterwards discussed crystal-gazing at length before condemning it, and even then they only condemned it as a technique of divination. If a scrying session evoked visions of sacred matters, or induced ecstasy, it might have appealed to honest Catholics as an innocent and exciting aid to devotion.

I have no idea whether anybody actually tried. If the Inquisition had flourished in England, its records might be helpful; but it only crossed the Channel for a short time and for a particular purpose, the suppression of the Templars many years later. A twelfth-century treatise by John of Salisbury gives an account of the *specularii* who divined by means of crystals. This at least shows that the technique was known in England.

To conceive a God-given speculum would not have required an immense feat of imagination. Certainly the Christianised Grail, however the author of the moment may picture it, and whatever fertility-magic and so forth may have gone into it, does behave as if it were such a speculum. Hence its selectivity, so notable in de Borron and von Eschenbach. To those without the scrying gift, here considered as a mark of divine favour, the Grail is blank.

Gawain in *Perlesvaus* is entertained at the Castle and sees the Grail. The episode is most interesting, both because of the apparitions themselves and because Gawain's failure to ask the crucial question seems to be due to a species of hypnosis or trance.

> Thereupon Messire Gawain was led into the hall and findeth twelve ancient knights. . . . They have set Messire Gawain to eat at a right rich table of ivory and seat themselves all round about him. . . . Thereon, lo you, two damsels that issue forth of a chapel, whereof the one holdeth in her hands the most Holy Graal, and the other

[1] See preface, p. 9.

the Lance whereof the point bleedeth thereinto. And the one goeth beside the other in the midst of the hall where the knights and Messire Gawain sat at meat, and so sweet a smell and so holy came to them therefrom that they forgat to eat. Messire Gawain looketh at the Graal, and it seemed him that a chalice was therein, albeit none there was as at this time, and he seeth the point of the lance whence the red blood ran thereinto, and it seemeth him he seeth two angels that bear two candlesticks of gold filled with candles. And the damsels pass before Messire Gawain, and go into another chapel. And Messire Gawain is thoughtful, and so great a joy cometh to him that nought remembereth he in his thinking save of God only. The knights are all daunted and sorrowful in their hearts, and look at Messire Gawain. Thereupon behold you the damsels that issue forth of the chamber and come again before Messire Gawain, and him seemeth that he seeth three there where before he had seen but two, and seemeth him that in the midst of the Graal he seeth the figure of a child. The Master of the Knights beckoneth to Messire Gawain. Messire Gawain looketh before him and seeth three drops of blood fall upon the table. He was all abashed to look at them and spake no word.

Therewith the damsels pass forth and the knights are all adread and look one at the other. Howbeit Messire Gawain may not withdraw his eyes from the three drops of blood, and when he would fain kiss them they vanish away, whereof he is right sorrowful, for he may not set his hand nor aught that of him is to touch thereof. Therewithal behold you the two damsels that come again before the table and seemeth to Messire Gawain that there are three, and he looketh up and it seemeth him to be the Graal all in flesh, and he seeth above, as him thinketh, a King crowned, nailed upon a rood, and the spear was still fast in his side. Messire Gawain seeth it and hath great pity thereof, and of nought doth he remember him save of the pain that this King suffereth. And the Master of the Knights summoneth him again by word of mouth, and telleth him that if he delayeth longer, never more will he recover it. Messire Gawain is silent, as he that heareth not the knight speak, and looketh upward. But the damsels go back into the chapel and carry back the most Holy Graal and the Lance, and the knights make the tablecloths be taken away and rise from meat and go into another hall and leave Messire Gawain all alone.

5

Having progressed so far, we must take stock. The myth of the Grail concerns a life-giving, vision-inducing, oracular object of divine antecedents, the presence of which confers a special status on the Arthurian part of Christendom. To experience it, though tremendous and troubling, is essentially joyous. (De Borron and others spell the word 'greal,' deriving it from *gré*.) Very well. But any attempt to define the thing more exactly, or to reconstruct the Grail Book which has been looked for behind the literature, is probably a waste of time, unless reason can be shown to believe that the literature reflects the imaginings of an actual cult: perhaps only a dilettante cult, an intellectual Catholic parlour-game, but at all events a real human practice or spiritual system transcending the romances themselves.

One point in favour of such a cult is the theme of the Great Sacrament or uncanonical Mass. This is an idea which does recur among Christian experimenters with magic. The priest-magician in Huysmans's *Là-bas* performs a 'sacrifice of glory' that purports to be the Mass of the future, of the Johannine epoch. It is doubtless a variant of the Gnostic Mass which glimmers faintly through the vapours of occultism. Jessie Weston, after decades of research, declared in her best-known book that the Grail romances are factual and that the Quest is still possible; she must, I think, have been referring to some secret society with an initiatory rite culminating in such a Mass. If any modern man of unquestioned repute could have told the secret, his name was probably W. B. Yeats. In the presence of these daydreams one recalls more sinister topics – the antics of charlatans like Yeats's friend Aleister Crowley[1]; the scatology of religious perverts like Canon Docre; the blasphemies of Madame de Montespan. A Gnostic or Manichee form of devil-worship seems to have existed among the heretics of the twelfth century. The alleged Arthurian writer Walter Map has much to say about it. To that unhealthy region of thought the Grail evidently

[1] See preface, p. 9.

214

does not belong. The stress on moral ideals (chastity in the *Queste*, charity in *Parzival*) is enough to prove the distinction. But white magic is still magic. De Borron's secret words of consecration may be beneficent, but they are still secret. The forbidden realm is not so far off. Historically considered, the romancers' hints do have an air of hinting at a reality which it is not advisable to discuss in public.

Several of the pre-Weston generation of scholars tried very hard to show that the Quest of the Grail represented a Templar ritual. This is plausible, though von Eschenbach's poem is the only direct evidence. When the Templars were suppressed, the chief excuse was an accusation of satanism. Dubious confessions extracted under torture were read in court. Mention was then made of an uncanonical Mass. The precise charge, however, was that the Templar chaplains turned the ritual into a mockery by omitting the words of consecration, an irregularity just opposite to the one connected with the Grail. Though it is natural to suspect that the Templars of the Grail period were involved somehow, the Templar Mass theory seems to be a dead end. In any case the discovery of an abnormal Mass, whoever performed it, would not solve the problem. We would still want to know what happened at this Mass, why it was so terrific, and what was supposed to be learnt by participation. We would still have to search for the profounder truth.

Suppose we were to unearth the records of an actual Grail cult, exposing the symbolism and unravelling the whole tangle. What might they be likely to reveal?

We could expect to find four things. First, that for Latin Christendom in that age the cult had novelty. Though perhaps not new, it meant an elaboration and revaluation of old ideas, opening up fresh imaginative springs. Possibly some version of it had long been familiar in the East, in the lands within the Byzantine purview which the crusaders had rediscovered. Several of the romances contain curious allusions to Egypt and India. A cult arising from pre-existing western beliefs, developed in flamboyant style by crusaders' importations from Asia, would be the most reasonable expectation.

Secondly, the cult would certainly turn out to be bound up with the chivalric ideal, with the knightly character, with the literary and musical fashions of the day. It would spread out against a background of Queen Eleanor and King Richard and Templars and troubadours and court ladies suddenly raised to poetic pedestals. The spirit of that society breathes in all the romances.

Thirdly, the cult would be such that people in the Angevin era had grounds for thinking that disciples of Christ had introduced it into first-century Britain; that Arthur had known it, that about his time it had been rather lost sight of amid the migrations and changes of Celtic Christianity; but that for these historical reasons Britain enjoyed a senior claim to it.

Fourthly, in view of the implied nationalism, we might expect to find that the cult bore some sort of causal or antecedent relationship to the special growth of English religion in later years. Given the characteristic flavour of Catholicism in medieval England, it is a fair guess that the Grail cult, if delineated, would be such as to help us to account for it.

And now the full paradox emerges. All these requirements are met by a phenomenon that stares every historian in the face. It is the cult of Mary.[1] What did the Glastonbury missionaries do in William of Malmesbury? They built the Old Church, which Christ dedicated in person to his mother, making Britain the first country to honour her. What did Nennius draw attention to in Arthur's religion? His devotion to the Virgin, whose likeness he affixed to his armour. What happened to her cult in the Dark Ages? It was powerful in the Byzantine world, comparatively weak and perfunctory in the Roman. What happened to it in the twelfth century? The crusaders rediscovered it in the East, St Bernard preached it, the Oriental impulse promoted it. What effects did it have on western culture? It transfigured the arts; it inspired all that was good in the chivalric code and the troubadours' idealisation of women. What was the peculiar mark of English Catholicism during the high Middle Ages? The extreme popular love of Mary; the attitude which made this country 'Our Lady's Dowry.'

Every test answers. What the Christianised Grail cult ought to be is an esoteric mode of devotion to Mary. The conclusion looks baffling. Given the standard summaries of the romances, you would suppose that they scarcely mentioned her. With the fresh clue, however, we may now re-examine them to see whether and under what circumstances she does occur.

In *Perlesvaus,* the book with a Glastonbury source, the knights and ladies invoke her, though usually in conventional

[1] See preface, p. 9.

216

terms. Near the beginning there is a scene introductory to the Grail theme. King Arthur comes to a chapel in the woods. Owing to his sins, a supernatural force debars him from entering, but he catches glimpses of what is passing inside.

He looketh at the holy hermit that was robed to sing Mass and said his *Confiteor*, and seeth at his right hand the fairest Child that ever he had seen, and he was clad in an alb and had a golden crown on his head loaded with precious stones that gave out a full great brightness of light. On the left hand side, was a Lady so fair that all the beauties of the world might not compare them with her beauty. When the holy hermit had said his *Confiteor* and went to the altar, the Lady also took her Son and went to sit on the right hand side towards the altar upon a right rich chair and set her Son upon her knees and began to kiss him full sweetly and saith: 'Sir,' saith she, 'you are my Father and my Son and my Lord, and guardian of me and of all the world.' King Arthur heareth the words and seeth the beauty of the Lady and of her Child, and marvelleth much of this that she should call him her Father and her Son. He looketh at a window behind the altar and seeth a flame come through at the very instant that Mass was begun, clearer than any ray of sun nor moon nor star, and evermore it threw forth a brightness of light such that an all the lights in the world had been together it would not have been the like. King Arthur seeth it who marvelleth him much thereof. But sore it irketh him of this that he may not enter therewithin, and he heareth, there where the holy hermit was singing the Mass, right fair responses, and they seem him to be the responses of angels. And when the Holy Gospel was read, King Arthur looked toward the altar and saw that the Lady took her Child and offered him into the hands of the holy hermit . . . and when the Child was offered him, he set him upon the altar and thereafter began his sacrament. And King Arthur set him on his knees before the chapel and began to pray to God and to beat his breast. And he looked toward the altar after the preface, and it seemed him that the holy hermit held between his hands a man bleeding from his side and in his palms and in his feet, and crowned with thorns, and he seeth him in his own figure. And when he had looked on him so long and knoweth not what is become of him, the King hath pity of him in his heart of this that he had seen, and the tears of his heart came into his eyes. And he looketh toward the altar and thinketh to see the figure of the man, and seeth that it is changed into the shape of the Child that he had seen tofore.

When the Mass was sung, the voice of a holy angel said *Ite, missa est.* The Son took the Mother by the hand, and they vanished forth of the chapel with the greatest company and the fairest that might ever be seen. The flame that was come down through the window went away with this company.

It is doubtful whether this half-seen rite is the Great Sacrament itself. The author of *Perlesvaus* never states in so many words that the Grail can appear outside the Grail Castle. Also, the apparitions begin before the ceremony and do not seem to result from the consecratory formula. At the very least, however, the scene in the chapel points the way towards the crowning experience. Farther on is confirmation. Enemies have captured the Castle and slain the Grail-keeper (called 'King Fisherman' as successor to the 'Rich Fisher' Brons). A voice is heard at midnight lamenting:

'The good King Fisherman is dead that made every day our service be done in the most holy chapel there where the most Holy Grail every day appeared, and where the Mother of God abode from the Saturday until the Monday that the service was finished.'

And now, the *Queste.* This is the tale in which the supreme vision is most unequivocally achieved. When Christ appears to Galahad and his two companions, he tells them they have not yet beheld everything. At his commandment they take the Grail out of an unworthy Britain to Sarras. There, in the spiritual city, Galahad is made king. He keeps the Grail in a temple on a silver table, and covers it with an ark of gold and jewels.

When the end of the year came round, on the anniversary of the day when he had first won the crown, he and his companions arose early in the morning. And when they came into the temple, they looked at the sacred Vessel; and there they saw a handsome man garbed like a bishop

(Josephes), and he was on his knees before the table. . . .
He rose up and began *the Mass of the glorious Mother of
God*. And when he came to the mystery of the Mass and
had removed the platter from the sacred Vessel, he called
Galahad, and said to him: 'Come forward, servant of
Jesus Christ, and thou shalt behold what thou has so
desired to see.' Then Galahad stepped forward and looked
within the sacred Vessel. And when he had looked in, he
began to tremble violently, as soon as mortal flesh began
to gaze on the things of the spirit. Then Galahad stretched
forth his hands toward heaven, and said: 'Lord, I adore
thee and thank thee that thou hast brought my desire to
pass, for now I see clearly what tongue could not tell nor
heart conceive. Here I behold the motive of courage and
the inspiration of prowess; here I see the marvel of marvels.'

'The Mass of the Mother of God.' That is decisive.

To grasp how Mary could have been, as it were, assimilated
to the Grail scheme, we must glance again at the cloudy
pagan background. In the Celtic fertility-ritual behind the
Grail imagery, the spear and cup were sexual symbols, the
cup being female. That cauldron of plenty and inspiration,
which was the cup in its most primitive guise, belonged to the
mother of a semi-divine son. She was named Ceridwen and
her son was Gwion. It is not definitely known whether these
two were related in any clear way to the protagonists of
the ancient Mysteries; but in the cults of Osiris, Attis, Adonis
and Orpheus the hero's mother was always prominent. She
was regarded as Earth or Nature, the source of plenty, or
as the Muse, source of inspiration. Probably she was always the
same goddess under different masks? Isis, the feminine cosmic
principle. She invaded Gnosticism and imposed curious con-
structions on Mary. Ceridwen with her son Gwion may or
may not have been a debased Occidental counterpart. Indubitably the mother-and-son pattern was there, and the
mother was in some sense a female supernatural power,
manifesting herself as, or through, the cauldron.

Conjectures in this ill-defined field will bear no stress. But
the fate of the *ewig-weibliche* vessel at the hands of medieval
Christians is not a matter of conjecture at all. They did turn
it into an emblem of the Mother of Christ. D. W. Nash, in
his *Taliesin*, has this to say: 'The Christian bards of the
thirteenth and fourteenth centuries repeatedly refer to the

Virgin Mary herself as the cauldron or source of inspiration, to which they were led, as it seems, partly by a play on the word 'pair,' a cauldron, and the secondary form of that word, on assuming the soft form of its initial 'Mair' which also means Mary. Mary was 'Mair,' the Mother of Christ, the mystical receptacle of the Holy Spirit, and 'Pair,' the cauldron or receptacle or fountain of Christian inspiration.' Thus the poet Daffid Benfras, whose lifetime overlaps those of the Grail romancers, has the line:

> Crist mab Mair am Pair pur vonhedd.
> Christ, son of Mary, my cauldron of pure descent.

To return to the point in the 1190s when the Grail became Christian. The mystic responsible, Robert de Borron or another, had formed the notion that the life-giving vessel was a Christian object brought to Britain by the founders of the Old Church at Glastonbury. But his bardic mentors, we may suppose, had apprised him of Ceridwen and Gwion, and the essential female symbolism. The Mair-Pair conceit was perhaps in his mind also. He meditated like this: 'The Welsh fables and the Glastonbury traditions converge. I cannot ignore the Old Church's dedication. The Grail must be thought of as a vessel associated with the Mother of Christ, through tradition or symbolism or in some other way. Its life-giving properties suggest the Eucharist, and, of course, the cup or bowl containing the body of the Lord is an apt image of his mother. We already salute her as the chosen vessel of honour and reverence, as *vas honorabile*, as *vas insigne devotionis*. That idea gives me a starting-point.'

Thus he may have pondered. Thus, probably, he did ponder. We might almost leave the topic there. But we can pierce deeper.

6

De Borron makes no notable allusion to Mary. He insists, however (as does the *Grand Saint Graal* author), that he is keeping something essential back. The full revelation belongs to the Arthurian part of the story; and there in effect we have already found it. He does not explain what this ultimate secret of the Grail is about. The nearest he comes is to say that when the revelation occurs, 'then will the significance of the Blessed Trinity, which we have conceived to be in three parts, be fulfilled and made manifest.' The preface to the *Grand Saint Graal* represents its message in similar fashion as dispelling doubts about the Trinity. From the nature of the visions, and from the history of the Grail itself, it is plain on which aspect of the Trinity's operation the emphasis lies. It lies on the manner in which the Second Person descended into the material world, inhabiting that world in a human body and in the sacrament, so as to draw men to himself. Carrying the thought further with the aid of *Perlesvaus* and the *Queste,* we can infer a little more. The secret of the Grail is an insight into the mystery of the Word made Flesh, communicated by her in whose womb it happened.

When a priest celebrated the special Mass with the Grail, the elements gained an extra power of producing effects perceptible to the senses. These were repetitive, in some way, of the process by which the Second Person became incarnate in Mary. What was re-enacted thereby under her auspices was not simply the Last Supper but the life-giving Incarnation itself, with all its consequences implicit: Christ's ministry and death, his resurrection, his mystical body the Church, the sacramental system.

In the *Queste,* we should not overlook a certain gesture of Josephes. When he has consecrated the host, he elevates it as usual. The radiant image of a child comes down from heaven and vanishes into it, making it glow red. Josephes puts it back in the Grail. From this, after his departure, the figure of the crucified Christ emerges. What exactly has happened? Josephes has presumably spoken the secret words, giving the host extra properties. The Incarnation has recapitulated itself visibly. But when he replaces the transformed bread in the Grail, surely something further takes place, in keeping with the imagery of the Welsh poets like Daffid Benfras. A kind of secondary Real Presence results. The vessel that receives the host into itself becomes, for a space of time, the Mother of God. Only thus can we interpret that cry of lamentation in *Perlesvaus* about the chapel where the Grail appeared and Mary 'abode' from Saturday till Monday.

This change in the Grail, this mysterious indwelling, is the justification for its complexities. Once allowed to be capable of identification with Mary, the Grail acquired any attribute of hers which the romancers cared to ascribe. It was surprising how well she fitted the existing myth, it was surprising with how much ease and enrichment her attributes could be assigned to the Grail. For example, the pre-Christian cup was a source of physical nourishment. But so was Mary: she physically nourished her Son, in the womb and at the breast, and through him the whole mystical body of believers incorporated with him. Thus the apparently crude magical property was still apt. Then again, after the Annunciation, Mary was the receptacle of the Holy Spirit. Therefore the Grail could be so regarded, and could be made the medium of the Spirit's communications to Joseph. This principle could be taken further. To some extent, Grail romance looks like a fantasia on the terms applied to Mary by poets and mystics – a fantasia which turns metaphors into concrete facts.

The Holy Grail is a vessel venerated as no other. Mary, in her Litany, is *vas spirituale, vas honorabile, vas insigne devotionis*. The Grail belongs to man's joy, to his *gré*. Mary is *causa nostræ lætitiæ*. The Grail is the Ark of the New Covenant. Mary is *foederis arca*. The Grail is associated with a castle. Mary is *turris Davidica, turris eburnea, domus aurea*. The Grail is associated, most cryptically, with a chair or seat. Mary is *sedes sapientiæ*. The Grail is, or acts as if it were, a speculum in the medieval magician's sense. Mary is *speculum justitiæ*. This last epithet is startling. The partial Marian equation will explain all the Grail's extraordinary shifting and changing. The point of departure is the word 'speculum' applied to the Blessed Virgin.

Parzival remains puzzling, but less puzzling than before. Von Eschenbach is a foreign poet who understands what the Grail is about in an external, academic way, but revalues it for his own ends. On the social and political side he is more nearly frank than his contemporaries. The Grail, moreover, keeps its properties of nourishment, healing, revivification, and so forth. But it is frozen in its specular aspect; it is a kind of crystal ball; and its history has become confused. I cannot help suspecting that von Eschenbach may be trying to portray a later phase of the adventures, when the truth is generally forgotten and almost everyone has long since given up the Grail as an illusion. The Grail has therefore withdrawn into inscrutability. However that may be, we can now appreciate that the German is closer to the other romancers than he seems. The annual earthward flight of the divine dove, which renews the Grail by placing a host on it, repeats the action of Josephes.

While von Eschenbach is in some ways reticent, other Germans are less so. Three vernacular poets, writing in Mary's honour, give away a large part of the secret in plain words: *Thou art the Grail*.[1]

7

There was no popular or monastic tradition about the Holy Grail. Was there a subterranean one?

An old form of Marian devotion, involving a cup and a legend and a peculiar Mass, could have lingered on in the East till the Crusades. It is certainly strange that nobody publicly pretended to have the vessel of the Last Supper. The obvious parallel is the silence regarding the body of the Virgin herself, due to the widespread belief in her Assumption. Perhaps there was a corresponding conviction that the cup was . . . elsewhere. If so, the mystery surrounding it must be very ancient indeed, and no mere medieval invention.

While every investigator must keep on his guard against the temptation to postulate occult schools, the hypothesis of an esoteric cult should be taken seriously. It would complete the picture of Christian Grail romance by resolving it into three ingredients:

(1) The Celtic fairy-tale;
(2) The legend about the Old Church at Glastonbury;
(3) The cult itself, rediscovered by crusaders, then elaborately disguised, and blended with the Celtic matter as developed by Chrétien de Troyes and his continuators.

This theory is not simple. But no theory of the Grail is simple. An alternative is that the cult was a literary concoction of the twelfth century, put together from apocryphal writings and Celtic Christian traditions, given a bogus history, and embodied in a lost manual which was the key to the romances. Parallels are not wanting in the affairs of post-Reformation secret societies.

To inquire whether any subjects of the Angevin kings

[1] See further Appendix A.

actually tried to reproduce the Great Sacrament would lead to a mere exercise in guesswork. It is unlikely. To begin with, the practice would have required priests. That obstacle might have been surmounted, but the rumour of bizarre Masses, unless they were very carefully concealed, would have provoked disciplinary action by the priests' superiors. Of such action directed to such an end there is no trace. Moreover, the romancers insist that the true Grail has vanished. It has been caught up to heaven. It has been removed to the kingdom of Prester John or somewhere equally inaccessible. Whatever its resting-place, no man has seen it since the days of King Arthur. Unless this insistence is a deliberate blind, it rules out belief in a complete attempt to renew the mystery in England. The likelihood of a partial attempt remains open to debate, though not very profitable debate. Templar chaplains or other secluded clerics may have tried, say, to bring about the scrying of images in a brightly-lit chalice by an incantatory muttering of the secret words. Glastonbury knew something; but the political bedevilment and the Abbey's own troubles (to be spoken of shortly) were enough to impose silence.

More interesting than any such conjectures is the reality with which the romances very possibly place us in contact. The Grail cult may well have been only the most complex codification of a bold strain of mysticism, persisting through the centuries but never openly unfolded. The essential theme was always the same, that through some technique of communion with God's Mother one could obtain the grace of a higher insight into the Incarnation. Twelfth-century Arthurians fastened on a tradition of this technique and used British mythology to give it a gorgeous context. The daring notion of the Real Presence of Our Lady – if only as a creative fiction – produced a Grail-image of astonishing elasticity. This imaginative tempest blew over. But the old tradition went on in severer terms. Charles Williams has observed that the climax of the *Divine Comedy* is, in effect, the achievement of the Grail. Just as Dante diverted courtly love to the ends of orthodoxy in the character of Beatrice, so he purified the dreams of the Arthurians in this other respect.

The poet stands beside St Bernard at the summit of Paradise, in the Rose of Light formed by the blessed souls; and Bernard prays to Our Lady to vouchsafe Dante a glimpse of the unveiled Trinity – the goal of de Borron's mysticism. (I quote the Fletcher translation.)

'Thou Maid and Mother, daughter of thy Son,
  Thou humble and high over every creature,
  Bourn by eternal counsels fixed upon,
Verily thou art she who, by partaking,
  Didst even so ennoble human nature,
  Its Maker scorned not to be of its making.
Within thy womb rekindled was the love
  Under whose warmth in the eternal peace
  This flower had its burgeoning. Here above
Unto ourselves meridian torch thou art
  Of charity, and thou art there below
  The living spring of hope in mortal heart. . . .
And now this man, who from the nethermost
  Pit of the world to here hath seen the lives,
  One after one, of all the spirit-host,
Beseecheth thee, of grace, for such largess
  Of power that he may lift him with his eyes
  Yet higher towards the final blessedness. . . .'

She grants the prayer.

The eyes which God in loving doth revere,
  Fixed on the one there praying, proved for us
  How unto her the prayer devout is dear,
Then turned they unto the eternal Ray,
  Whereinto, as we must believe, no eye
  Of creatures else findeth so clear a way.
And I, who to the end of all desires
  Was now approaching, quenched, as I needs must,
  Even of my desire the inner fires.
Smilingly, Bernard beckoned unto me
  To look on high; but I of mine own self
  Already was as he would have me be;
Because my sight, that pure and purer grew,
  Deeper and deeper entered through the ray
  Of the high Light which in itself is true. . . .
Within the deep and luminous extension
  Of the high Light three circles showed themselves,
  Of threefold colour and of one dimension;
One by the other, as Iris by Iris wreathed,
  Appeared reflected, and the third seemed fire
  Which equally the one and other breathed.

Yet as the poet faces God, he falters in the midst of his joy.

He sees an enigma in the depths. It is the Incarnation:

> That circle which as radiance reflected
>> Appeared to be conceived within Thyself,
>> When for some little by mine eyes inspected,
> Within itself, with colour of its own
>> Was painted with our image, as it seemed;
>> Wherefore I gave mine eyes to it alone.
> As the geometer who fain would tax
>> His wits to square the circle, and finds not,
>> By taking thought, the principle he lacks,
> Such at that wondrous sight was I; for trace
>> I would how to the circle was conformed
>> The image, and how there it found a place.
> But wings had not been mine for the high aim . . .

Suddenly knowledge seizes him. The insight, though incommunicable, is granted:

> Save that my mind was smitten suddenly
> As by a lightning-flash – and its will came.

Whereupon the vision closes. But Dante, like Galahad, is irrevocably committed by what he has seen.

Whether it is worth seeking clues in Dante's sympathy for the Templars, or in William of Malmesbury's geometrical *arcanum,* are questions beyond our present scope.

Dante's vision introduces the final problem. His own orthodoxy is incontestable. Are we dealing, then, with a heresy; or are we dealing with a devotional practice as purely Catholic as the Rosary, but one that went astray through secretiveness and church politics and an unwise alliance with magic?

The vague atmospheric thing which I have called Glastonbury Christianity cannot be defined. It has been Catholic or schismatic or Protestant in an off-centre way according to the mode of the moment. The cult behind the Grail is far more exact. It seems to have puzzled contemporaries. There was no ecclesiastical recognition; yet there was no ecclesiastical condemnation. The chronicler Helinandus, a gentleman by birth ordained rather late in life, is the only clerical author who even mentions the Grail. He simply transmits without positive comment the story told him in his youth as a fashionable layman. The Church plainly could not countenance a hole-and-corner mystification implying the spiritual aristocracy of the Angevin knighthood. Nor could Josephes be admitted as the First Bishop of Christendom. With the accidentals out of the way, however, could a Catholic abide by the residue?

The Great Sacrament could perhaps be accommodated to orthodoxy. The real question about the cult is whether it is truly Gnostic; whether it tends to supplant Christian principles with a cliquish idea of initiation on pagan lines.

It is Gnostic in that it employs quasi-magical devices and culminates in learning a secret. But its Gnosticism does not follow the ancient anathematised model. The *Queste*, almost throughout, is solemnly and even boringly orthodox. The Gnostic theme of escape or deliverance is indubitably present: Galahad voluntarily dies after looking into the Grail. On the other hand, he does not dismiss the world and the world's values with the contemptuous gesture of the Gnostic initiate. He exclaims, 'I behold the motive of courage and the inspiration of prowess.' That is the thought of a crusader, and in *Perlesvaus* the knights do crusade against heathen princes. The hint of something tremendous, of a spiritual lightning-bolt, may seem to carry a connotation of magic. It may suggest a straining after forbidden experience. The Marian clue, however, dispels this impression. The Virgin of Catholic devotion is so much more than the lowly dedicated maiden of Nazareth. She is Queen of Heaven and Our Lady of Victories: the woman clothed with the sun, the moon under her feet, and about her head a crown of twelve stars; terrible as an army in battle array. Her apparitions and interventions are often portrayed in the very colours of Grail phenomena. 'If you had seen her,' said Bernadette of Lourdes, 'you would have no thought or purpose which was not hers.' I forbear to discuss the validity of all this. The point is that the conception exists and that it matches.

This Grail initiation breaks through the Gnostic trap and returns on itself. The doctrine of the Great Secret has historically gone with a certain unchristian attitude – superiority, contempt, dismissal of Creation as mean and hopeless and profitless. But if God thought Creation worth entering in humility as a human being, if he perpetuates that hallowing by his sacramental presence, then the Gnostic attitude to Creation is false. If the Great Secret is a special insight into the Incarnation, which enables the initiate to understand it more deeply and believe it more firmly, then the initiate automatically abandons the Gnostic point of view. He confesses, after all, that God's world must be good because he loves it, that God has taught us by example not to turn our backs on it or retreat to a metaphysical tower. While the gate of illumination may lead to ecstasy, there is a path back to ordinary life.

The cult, in a phrase, was Esoteric Orthodoxy. But contemporary trends were too much for it. The Grail was doomed by the pontificate of Innocent III. The Lateran Council redefined the Real Presence. The Albigensian War, an orgy of murder and destruction, broke the back of heresy and discouraged the more extreme sort of speculation. Political changes ended the anti-papalism of English royalty. New religious orders infused new life into Catholicism. The flaunting romantic imagery withered. But the afterglow of the vision endured.

Chapter Eight

A GOLDEN AGE

In entering the high Middle Ages we enter a period where completeness is no longer even approachable. A mountain of miscellaneous documentation defies any attempt to tell the full story connectedly and readably. All that a single chapter can do is to depict the Abbey's golden age in its broadest outlines, with the lame assurance that those who wish to delve deeper can find ample material. Any possible book about Glastonbury suggests dozens of unwritten ones.[1] This is not an abstract of documents or an architectural guide. All the antiquarian details have been fully and capably described elsewhere. Nor, incidentally, is it a record of great men or spectacular achievements. No Glastonbury name occurs frequently in other contexts. For three centuries there were no canonised saints, no celebrated scholars, no ecclesiastical statesmen of the calibre of Henry de Blois. The Abbey which Dunstan had made the parent of all other English abbeys remained the largest in the land and by universal consent the most venerable. Yet its enormous eminence lay not so much in *doing* anything particular, as in *being* something very particular indeed. It was the site of St Joseph's chapel and Arthur's grave; and even when the footfalls of the Grail's partisans had died away, the Abbey continued to exist as a national shrine with an altogether distinctive aura. It was loyal to the Papacy. If there had been the feeblest flirtation in such a quarter with the dream of a Josephan episcopate, we would assuredly have heard the thunders of denunciation. But Glastonbury had its own glamour none the less.

Above all it was far and away the oldest English dwelling-place of devotion to the Blessed Virgin. The rise of Walsingham and of other shrines in the Norman period gave the community a strong motive to stress this aspect of their tradition. When Ralph FitzStephen took charge of the re-

[1] As a matter of fact, any account of the medieval abbey must be strictly provisional till the documentary labours of Dom Aelred Watkin have received all the analytic attention due to them.

construction after the fire, his first care was to build a Lady Chapel on the exact site of the Old Church. He swept away the charred remains of wattle-work (necessarily depriving posterity of a priceless relic) and raised the chapel with astonishing speed. The ruin stands to-day. The evidences of its past beauty and exquisite proportions are still plain. Its most interesting features are the two doorways. The north doorway has four bands of carving, two representing leafage and animals, two representing scenes from the Gospels. We can make out the Annunciation, the Nativity, the journey of the Magi, and the flight into Egypt. On the south doorway are similar carvings of scenes from Genesis, but for some reason they break off. Only a close inspection of the doorway will reveal that the Lady Chapel was never quite finished. It was finished for practical purposes within two years: the date of consecration was 11th June, 1186.

Besides creating this chapel, FitzStephen restored part of the living quarters. He also laid the foundations of a church on a grand scale, extending eastward and altogether effacing the remains of the Norman Church. To quote the chronicler Adam of Domerham: 'He carried the foundations to the length of four hundred feet, and to the width of eighty-five feet. Passing on rapidly with the work he spared no expense. What he could not obtain from Glastonbury, that the royal bounty supplied. Into the foundations of the church were put the stones of that great palace which Abbot Henry built, as well as those of the walls of the courtyard. Thus having built a good part of the church he would have completed the rest if God had prolonged the King's life.' But no. A phase of catastrophe now began. 'Death, covetous and too watchful, snatched him away and thus inflicted another wound upon the monks, who were only just recovering from their last misfortune.'

When King Henry died there was no one to foot the bill. The exhumation of Arthur may or may not have been undertaken with an eye to the attraction of new patronage; if so the publicity campaign was almost unbelievably languid. Certainly no patron stepped forward. Speaking tours by the monks proved no more successful. The whole work slowed to a standstill, and this uncomfortable pause appeared likely to drag on for years, until something could be saved out of the Abbey revenues.

Nor was impecuniosity the only affliction. Henry was succeeded by his son Richard I, Cœur-de-Lion. Richard was engrossed in the Third Crusade, and cared little for England except as a source of funds. It is a notorious item of 'Believe-it-or-not' general knowledge that his queen never saw the country which she was queen of. The regencies of Eleanor and Prince John were adverse to the Church. Altogether Glastonbury had nothing to hope for from royalty. But as it turned out, what Glastonbury got was far worse than nothing.

On his way back from the crusade Richard fell into the hands of the German Emperor, who demanded 100,000 marks ransom. One shudders to compute this in modern money. The ransom being promised, the Emperor agreed to release his prisoner. Negotiations were necessary, and in this capacity a certain Savary appeared at his court, inaugurating a tragi-comedy that was to last for a generation.

Savary was Bishop of Bath and Wells. He had acquired his see by influence. Formerly archdeacon of Northampton, and then treasurer of Salisbury, he had gone to his diocese because the previous bishop had been translated elsewhere and had insisted, with due prompting, that Savary should succeed him. Savary got the Emperor's ear (they were related) and managed to use him as an agent in the blackmail of Richard. The Emperor summoned the captive King and set before him, incongruously enough, a document authorising a local administrative change in the English Church. Glastonbury Abbey was to be annexed to the See of Bath, and the bishop, namely Savary, was to be abbot as well and draw the income. The fact that Abbot Henry de Sully, appointed by Richard himself, was already in possession signified nothing. They could shift him away. Richard hesitated, perhaps, but Savary offered to cede him the revenues from the city of Bath, and he approved. A vacancy existed for Abbot Henry in Worcester; he was bundled off to be bishop there. Pope Celestine, who may have been growing slightly uneasy about the queer stories clustering round the British abbey, consented to its abasement.

The monks rose in a fury and refused to recognise Savary. For years Archbishop Hubert of Canterbury supported them, while Savary pulled wires in Rome. Eventually Savary prevailed. Then the community scraped together a large bribe, placed it in the hands of their shadow-abbot William de Pica, and sent him to King Richard in France. Richard withdrew his gift to Savary as given under duress, and nominated William. The Archbishop of Canterbury, a difficult man to deal with, refused William too. Richard exploited the deadlock as an excuse to keep the Abbey in his own hands and skim off the monetary cream. In 1199 he died. King John was no less accessible to bribes, but now the bribes came from Savary, and opened a path for him. The indefatigable Bishop, who had hovered so long across the marshland ready to pounce, descended on Glastonbury armed with a royal warrant and demanded to be installed. The warrant was not his only means of persuasion. He came attended by an armed mob of citizens and cathedral canons from Wells.

Finding the gates bolted, Savary's retinue battered their way through by force. Most of the monks fled to the refectory. The canons locked them in, grabbed the vestments, and performed the ceremony of installation. That being safely concluded, Abbot Savary and his followers ate their dinner and went to bed, taking no notice of the yells and thumps from the refectory. The next day, after a leisurely breakfast, they unlocked the door and brought the monks into the chapter-house, where the Abbot gave them their first taste of his paternal care in the form of a flogging.

For a short while a hush descended. Then Savary learned that the monks were preparing a clandestine appeal to Rome. His corps of canons burst in on their deliberations and ordered a halt. They barricaded themselves in the Lady Chapel. The canons and lay assistants forced the door. After a brief scrimmage with crucifixes and other ecclesiastical furniture, the stronger party prevailed. The monks were dragged out by the hair, herded into carts and removed to Wells. Savary banished them to other monasteries and closed the Abbey gates. A number of stragglers got away; most were retaken; one was thrashed to death. But a certain Martin de Summis managed to make off with a considerable amount of money. Accompanied by William de Pica, he went to Rome and obtained an audience with Innocent III. Martin wept. William wept. At last the redoubtable Innocent wept himself and promised redress. His letter summoning Savary to Rome reached the Abbot-Bishop in Flanders. Savary tried to pretend it was a forgery, but in the end he capitulated and set off for the Eternal City armed with a munificent bribe. After discussion Innocent decided that Celestine's grant must be permitted to stand. Savary, however, was to pay the costs of the whole affair and leave off persecuting the monks.

What the ultimate result would have been we cannot tell.

Savary died in 1205. His successor, Bishop Jocelin, maintained himself as Abbot of Glastonbury more or less innocuously till 1218. Then the arrangement was abandoned. Jocelin withdrew from the Abbey, contenting himself with the cession of a few benefices. The monks elected William Vigor, of whom, however, nothing is known except that he took steps – appropriately – to strengthen the beer.

2

During these troubles the rebuilding had continued to languish, not only because of the monks' dismal preoccupations, but also because the interloper had diverted so much of the revenue to his own pocket. A portion of the great church's eastern end was completed in 1213, and on Christmas Day of that year the community began to make use of it. However, no serious progress followed here or anywhere till the election of Michael of Ambresbury as Abbot in 1235. Michael possessed a sound business head. He restored solvency and invested in a programme of secular building. Thanks to him, a hundred new houses began to draw in rents for the Abbey.

The church which got fairly under way during his reign was the largest England has ever seen, except old St Paul's. When the last touches had been added (though they were not added till the eve of the Reformation) the total length of the building with its attendant chapels was 594 feet. The architectural style, so far as we can now judge, was conservative. Zigzag ornamentations round the windows looked back to the twelfth century. Even the work done in Tudor times had Norman reminiscences. There was a vast decorative opulence with an aristocratic tinge. Heraldic bars and chevrons and chequers crowded the stone. Heraldic lions and leopards ramped. Eagles soared. Stone birds picked at stone fruit-trees. Foliated designs ramified.

Abbot Michael carried the choir much farther and put the transepts in recognisable shape. On his death in 1253 he made various personal legacies to the Lady Chapel, including two silver cups with matching basins. Under Roger Forde (1253-60) a side altar dedicated to St Thomas of Canterbury – that is, Becket – was erected in the north transept. John of

Taunton (1274-90) completed the high altar. His abbacy, however, witnessed another cruel setback. An earthquake damaged the chapter-house, and ruined the chapel of St Michael which had stood on the Tor since at least Norman times. There was a longish lull. Then Geoffrey Fromond (1303-22), one of the Abbey's great builders, resumed the advance. He partly restored the chapter-house, put up a central tower in the church, and started work on a magnificent hall. Judging the church adequately finished, after more than a century, he caused it to be consecrated. Fromond spent £1000 on his building activities. He has an accidental interest as being mainly responsible for the only part of the Abbey still intact, the Abbot's Kitchen. The name is misleading: strictly speaking this kitchen was meant for guests and pilgrims, as distinct from the community, and served a separate dining hall. To-day it is a museum, and the exhibits divert attention from the architecture, which, however, repays study. The fireplaces cut off the corners, making the inside octagonal. Overhead rises a ribbed and ventilated dome, built of stone with no timbers at all, as a precaution against fire.

Abbot Walter of Taunton (1322-3) set up the choir screen and contributed many statues. Adam of Sodbury (1323-34) placed the image of Our Lady St Mary of Glastonbury over the high altar, and vaulted the nave. An enthusiast for the arts, he provided his church with an organ, eleven bells and a series of paintings. He also gave St Michael a new chapel on the Tor. The tower stands to-day, fenced in with a railing, and overpeering the Vale of Avalon. John of Breynton (1334-41) was another lavish spender. The £1000 which he laid out enlarged the guest accommodation and administrative offices, completed the Abbot's Kitchen, embellished St Dunstan's shrine, raised an altar to St Andrew, and enriched the wardrobe with splendid vestments. Walter Monington (1342-75) extended the vaulting and improved the reredos of the high altar. He gave twenty-two statues. Somewhere aloft, he suspended the Great Sapphire of St David. John Chinnock (1375-1420) had, on the whole, a utilitarian turn of mind. He improved the chapter-house, built a new cloister and dormitory, and finished Fromond's hall. However, he did not neglect the beauty of his additions. They contained window-tracery with striking floral motifs. In 1382 Chinnock restored a small ruined chapel in the ancient cemetery, dedicated to St Michael. The chief ornament of the new chapel was a triptych with a life-size figure of Christ 'according to

GLASTONBURY ABBEY

[as it probably was]

1. Lady Chapel, 1184–1187. 2. Galilee Porch, 1274–1291. 3. North Porch. 4. Body of Church and Transepts, 1184–1255. 5. Choir, 1184–1374. 6. Edgar Chapel, 1495–1539.
[from Abbot Horne's 'Guide to Glastonbury Abbey', published by the Catholic Truth Society]

the tradition of the Fathers,' and the scenes of his taking down from the cross and burial, with Joseph of Arimathea given prominence. The Abbot's regard for the legends of the place inspired his sponsorship of John of Glastonbury's Chronicle, which appeared during his reign and superseded all earlier versions.

Nicholas Frome, elected in 1420, finished the chapter-house. The principal monument of John Selwood (1459-93) was the church of St John the Baptist, outside the Abbey entirely. It remains in excellent condition, a very lovely fabric with a tall tower. Visitors are shown dubious relics of Richard Whiting, the last abbot, and a much more interesting crucifix carved out of bog-oak.

Other surviving buildings due to the monks are the Tribunal, where the abbots tried cases in their judicial capacity; the Pilgrims' Inn, now called the George and Pilgrims; and the barn, which the visitor passes on his way to the Tor.

3

Even before the Norman Conquest, Glastonbury Abbey was more than a religious house. It was a bolt in the constitutional frame. Under Ethelred, the Abbot was *ex-officio* one of the King's three chancellors, holding that position in rotation with the Abbots of Ely and Augustine of Canterbury. The arrangement lapsed, but Glastonbury's abbots continued to sit in the House of Lords, inclining, on the whole, toward the Crown rather than the baronage. In the latter part of the Middle Ages the Abbot of Glastonbury was the most important man in the West Country. He wore a mitre like a bishop; his revenue exceeded a bishop's, and for that matter an archbishop's; he ruled over an establishment of fifty to eighty monks, larger than any other in England except Westminster – and even Westminster only stood very slightly ahead in size and wealth. The Abbot's seal with which he ratified all major pronouncements was eloquent of his high claims to celestial patronage and historical dignity. On the obverse it bore the Blessed Virgin, St Catherine and St Margaret. On the reverse it bore St Dunstan, St Patrick and St Benignus. Popular belief about the Abbot's earthly immensity was summed up in an irreverent saying: 'If the

Abbot of Glastonbury married the Abbess of Shaftesbury, they would have more land than the King of England.'

The monastic domain was composed largely of fields and manors and villages throughout Somerset, mile upon mile upon mile: Not wholly so. Rich donors added pieces of territory outside – the island of St Michael of Lamman in Cornwall, for instance, and a surprising amount of property in Wales. Much of the land was occupied by small tenants. Yet the Abbot, in his economic aspect, was more than a mere landlord. For the year 1252 we have a census of the livestock owned by the Abbey itself. This included '892 oxen, 60 bullocks, 23 colts, 223 cows, 19 bulls, 153 heifers and young oxen, 26 steers, 126 yearlings, 6717 sheep, and 327 pigs.'

In feudal terms the Abbot's rights were considerable. He could sit as judge on any case that arose in the tract of country called Glastonbury Twelve Hides. The legendary grant to St Joseph reflected an awareness that in some form or other this privilege did go back a long way. The inflated Twelve Hides covered 24,610 acres and took in Baltonsborough, West Bradley, Meare, Nyland, West Pennard, North Wootton and the two parishes of the town itself. Within that area the Abbot was practically king, if he chose to be. At Easter 1278 Edward I, perhaps the most able and successful of all English sovereigns, came to Glastonbury as the guest of Abbot John of Taunton. He assumed that his seneschal would make all the arrangements for the royal party. The Abbot, courteously but firmly, refused to allow this, and saw to it that his own marshal Richard Pyke had the honour (and the control over expenditure). A second crisis ensued. Edward had proclaimed that he would hold assizes on Easter Monday wherever he might happen to be – and here he was in the Twelve Hides. Abbot John asserted his rights again; the King moved beyond the boundary. Worse yet. A quarrel broke out between a certain Philip de Cogan and members of the King's bodyguard. Philip drew a knife. The bodyguard seized him and locked him up in jail – yes, but in the Twelve Hides! Again John of Taunton intervened. Again the King conceded his rights. Philip was released, tried in the Abbot's court, and fined by the Abbot's bailiff.

While monarchs treated Glastonbury with consistent respect, bishops were not always so reverent. Strained relations with Wells endured long after the death of Savary, to the scandal of the countryside. Bishop Drokensford made a visitation in

1312 and accused the monks of a conspiracy of silence. A satirical wood-carver in a church at South Brent decorated the ends of the benches with cartoon-animals dressed up as monks and cathedral canons. There can be little doubt which monks and canons he had in mind. The abbots successfully asserted their jurisdiction over the small monasteries of Athelney and Muchelney, and over a number of parishes. Seven in the Poldens, for instance, were supplied by Glastonbury monks: Chilton, Catcott, Edington, Greinton, Sutton, Stawell, Moorlinch. Concerning these an amusing story is told. A set of bells having been made available, the parishes disagreed as to which should get them. The Abbot adjudicated, saying the bells should go to the first parish to record three births and three deaths. Before long Stawell announced three births and *two* deaths, and started work on a belfry. In the excitement, however, no one wanted to die. While the oldest and frailest people in Stawell persisted in thriving under the most exact scrutiny, Moorlinch quietly crept up: two babies; three babies; and then . . . three sudden corpses in a row. The prize went to Moorlinch. Stawell left its belfry unfinished.

The Abbot's functions as a judge and ecclesiastical arbiter by no means exhausted his importance. He was a kind of admiral, in the early sense of that word. He was the doge of an English Venice. He claimed 'wreck of sea' along the coast from Barrow to Brean Down. He imposed his own tolls and duties on the waterways, and toured his estates by boat seeing that the regulations were kept. In the reign of Henry III fishermen lodged a complaint about the damage done by the monastic flotilla; it is not known whether they got satisfaction. Later, when Richard II was still precariously upholding the Plantagenet title, Abbot John Chinnock found himself challenged over a purchase of salt. A merchant named Roger Brymmore had brought his ship the *Mary de Dertemuth* up the Axe and sold four quarters of salt to the Abbey at the price obtaining in those parts, which was not the King's price. On 31st July, 1401, Thomas Barton, the Abbot's procurator, finally appeared in court to explain. The Abbot's rights on Axwater were immemorial; he could levy his own excise and fix his own prices; could the King's lawyers prove otherwise? They could not. The prosecution collapsed. John Chinnock (that sternly practical builder of dormitories) seems to have followed up his triumph with a display of authority. We hear of a priest of Street crying to high heaven that the Abbot has taken away his plough and imprisoned his labourers, all because of a trifle, a disagreement about the tithes.

Mention of events on the lowland waterways directs notice to the waterways themselves. These counted for a great deal in the Abbey's affairs as a temporal institution, and their gradual taming was one of its principal achievements. During the early Middle Ages the lake known as Meare Pool still covered several thousand acres. Domesday refers to three fisheries there. To approach Meare dryshod you walked along a causeway said to have been thrown up originally by Beon. Everywhere the river courses were unreliable, the ground was swampy. Thirty-five-foot tides in the Bristol Channel menaced the coast and the hinterland up to Avalon and beyond. Sea-walls were an elementary need; these the monks built and maintained, apparently with success, though after the dissolution their works decayed, and the Stuart period witnessed three huge inundations. In the fourteenth century they embanked the River Parret. In the fifteenth they cut a channel from the Brue towards Mark to join the Axe. This canal was called the Mark Yeo or Pillrow River. It drained the moors south of the Mark-Wedmore ridge, and improved Glastonbury's access to the sea. All the local tenants contributed to its upkeep.

Glastonbury, indeed, became a far from negligible seafaring centre, with the mouth of the Axe as its port of entry. Water transport was economical in an age of poor roads and animal traction. About 1500, when Abbot Bere's masons were finishing the Church of St John the Baptist, they had the problem of fetching the seats from Bristol. The distance was twenty-five miles, with a really difficult pass over the Mendips. It was resolved to outflank the hills entirely. Two large boats conveyed the seats down the Avon, along the coast, and up the Axe to Rooks Mill. There they met barges sent from Meare. Some completed the journey by water, others were carted without much effort along the track to Glastonbury.

A medieval monastery was not, of course, an industrial centre, but other economic activities besides pure agriculture were carried on. A charter of the Archbishop of Canterbury dated 1281 refers to the Abbey's official mead-maker, who drew a pension from the income of various churches belonging to the Abbey — forty-three and fourpence a year from Shapwick, half a mark from St Peter's, Ilchester, and so forth. Mead may later have given place to wine. In the reign of

Edward III there were eight acres of vineyards.

More lasting monuments than wineskins were left by Peter Lightfoot, the only member of the community to attain permanent fame as an artist-craftsman. He flourished about 1325, under Abbot Adam of Sodbury, a music-lover and connoisseur of beautiful objects; and he made clocks. We cannot tell how many, because his pupils carried on the workshop and put together 'Lightfoot clocks' till at least the turn of the century. Lightfoot himself constructed one for his own Abbey, which perished at the dissolution. Others that may have been his are associated with Wimborne and Exeter. The surviving Lightfoot in Wells Cathedral is almost certainly the work of a pupil, but it gives an insight into the master's methods and imagination. It recalls speculations of Roger Bacon and others about the Ptolemaic astronomy and the theory of the microcosm, or human nature as the image of the visible universe. To quote the descriptive leaflet:

The clock is mentioned in the account-roll of the Communar of the Dean and Chapter for the year 1392-3. . . . The dial plate is 6 ft 4½ ins in diameter, contained in a square frame in the corners of which are angels holding the Four Winds. The outer circle is divided into 24 parts, intended to represent the 24 hours of the day. . . . A large gilt star, representing the Sun as it moves round the Earth, points to the hour. An inner or second circle shows the minutes, and a small star moves round the circle every hour. A third circle gives the days of the lunar month: a crescent with a pointer shows the Moon's age. . . .

Above the dial plate is a panelled tower, around which knights on horseback revolve in opposite directions every hour on the striking of the clock; which revolution is meant to represent a Tournament. A figure known as Jack Blandifer, seated at some distance from the clock, and higher up, strikes with its heels against bells.

Throughout the Middle Ages the regular Benedictine life of Glastonbury went on. Prayer in its fullest sense, a lifting up of the mind and heart to God, continued incessantly. Education and charity and hospitality pursued their orderly round. Until the general decline of the fifteenth century, the moral tone, if seldom heroic, was habitually high. Conservative in atmosphere as in architecture, the Abbey produced no extraordinary thinkers or scholars. But it stored up the achievement of the past in a library that excited every scholar who saw it.

For this library, one of the finest in England at the dissolution, we possess nothing like a full catalogue later than 1247. That of 1247 gives several hundred titles, some corresponding to Blois's donation, but many additional to it. Books of Scripture account for the first page or two. The Latin Fathers are chiefly represented by Athanasius, Jerome, Augustine and Gregory, more or less complete. Origen puts in an appearance for the Greeks. Bede, Anselm and Bernard are the principal exponents of Catholic thought after the Fathers. Gildas, Isidore, Freculfus and William of Malmesbury supply material for the Abbey's history. Other historians are Livy, Sallust, Orosius. For philosophy and science the library has books by Plato (*Timæus*), Aristotle, Pliny, Porphyry and Boethius, with works on astronomy and astrology. The last is marked *inutilis*. It would be agreeable to think that the librarian saw through the astrologers' claims, but probably he only meant that the manuscript was in bad condition – doubtless, alas, through being handled too often. There are commentaries on Scripture and the Benedictine Rule; compilations of sermons, decretals, saints' lives (mostly English), and miracles of the Virgin. Priscian and Donatus are the grammar-books. Cato and Virgil speak weightily for pagan Rome, and the obscene satires of Persius bring up the rear to set us wondering.

4

The growth of the Glastonbury mythos was inevitable. From about 1250 onwards Avalon was the pre-eminent shrine of knighthood, the holy place of the monarchy, and the accredited apostolic fountain-head of the British Church. On 13th April, 1278, when Edward I came to the Abbey with Queen Eleanor, the visit was ceremonious in the last degree. The Archbishop of Canterbury arrived by the Abbot's leave to sing Mass, despite angry diocesan protests. Edward had just returned from a campaign in Wales, and it occurred to him to ask for an exhibition of the remains of Arthur, which would remind the Welsh once again that their avenging *rex futurus* was dead. The monks brought out the two painted chests in which the bones of Arthur and Guinevere had been placed. Everything was exactly as Giraldus described – the long legs, the dinted skull, the death-wound over the ear. Edward and Eleanor treated their predecessors with reverence. The skulls were briefly set up outside the gate for the public to see. Then all the bones were enwrapped in precious cloths, replaced in their chests and buried before the high altar at a spot still marked by a notice. Edward himself carried the remains of the King, Eleanor carried Guinevere.

Having reaffirmed Arthur's death and asserted his authority as Arthur's true heir, Edward proceeded to stamp out what was left of Welsh independence. Because of his success and undoubted statesmanship, the spiritual aspect of his conduct is too easily overlooked. The act of homage at Glastonbury shows that the Ruthless King of Gray's poem did see himself as the rightful inheritor of the British tradition. Minor actions confirm this view of him. When in Italy he lent Rusticiano of Pisa a book of romances which inspired the Italian Arthur cycle; and in 1284 he gratefully accepted an ancient circlet of metal which somebody said was Arthur's crown. Being lawful successor to the British monarch, he of course had every right to proclaim his son Prince of Wales, as, in fact, he did.

That son, the androgynous Edward II, is historically perplexing. The Battle of Bannockburn deprived his reign of any Arthurian glory, and his love-affair with Piers Gaveston led to personal disgrace and a revolting death. But a secret rests hidden. There is an arguable case for the theory that Edward carried on certain practices connected with the old magical religion. It is said that the record of his relation with Gaveston betrays something deeper than a vulgar sodomitical partnership. It is certainly true that a local cult of Edward, like the cult of a saint, arose after his murder. This cannot be accounted for by a delusion of saintliness, for his vices were well known. A note of interrogation hangs over him to this day. The possibility that he kept a flicker of private mysticism alive in the Plantagenet family should not be ignored.

We are on safer ground with Edward III, who talked openly of reviving the Round Table, and did institute the Order of the Garter. Behind his attempt to conquer France it is not too fanciful to see conscious imitation of the imaginary wars in Geoffrey of Monmouth. In 1331 he paid a visit to Glastonbury with Queen Philippa. Abbot Adam of Sodbury entertained them with almost unbelievable lavishness: a chronicle mentions expenses amounting to £800. Edward moved on to Wells to observe his birthday, giving the Bishop occasion for an uncharitable envy of his neighbour's prosperity.

The monastic historians who concern us most are Adam of Domerham and John of Glastonbury. The first takes his name from his Wiltshire birthplace, a village that belonged to the Abbey. He was a Glastonbury monk till 1291 or later, holding the offices of cellarer and sacristan. Adam's chronicle is not much more than a continuation of *De Antiquitate*. John of Glastonbury belongs to the last decade of the fourteenth century, and his book gives us the authorised legendary synthesis arrived at by then.

One hardly knows what to make of John. To a large extent he simply copies earlier writers, and needs no comment. But the most remarkable parts of his work present a problem. What precisely is he doing? He may be using his own imagination. He may be recording stories elaborated by others, such as the monks who acted as guides for pilgrims. He may be trying more or less honestly to interpret the fables of romancers, and dig historical truth out of them. He may even be transmitting genuinely ancient material, unearthed in Wales after the final English conquest. Perhaps he is doing all these things. Whatever the underlying process, however, the exploitation of literary resources is very deft. John combines Celtic lore, Arthurian fantasy and Catholic tradition in such a way as to keep hold of everything with prestige value yet get rid of everything ecclesiastically suspect. He does more: he re-creates.

John's account of St Joseph and his voyage is pretty well the definitive text, as summarised in Chapter One. Only the Thorn has yet to make its appearance. The authority cited is a Grail Book which may have been an adaptation of the *Grand Saint Graal*. John's handling of the clerically frowned-upon Grail theme is ingenious. He knows that it is too famous to drop, but he knows also that its queer paraphernalia, with the secret sacrament and the rival pope, is impossible from the Abbey's point of view. Therefore he breaks the conception up. He tells, first, how St Joseph brought the two cruets or vials containing the blood and sweat of the Lord. No marvellous properties are attached to these. They are simply relics, though transcendently precious, and they are said to be buried with him.

John also tells a story about King Arthur, in which the idea of apparitions at Mass is introduced but altered. He adapts his tale from a passage in *Perlesvaus* already quoted (page 217). He says there used to be a convent by Wearyall Hill which Arthur paid visits to. Once an angel appeared to him there and told him to go at dawn to the oratory of St Mary Magdalene at Beckery. Obediently he did so, and entered the chapel, this time having a clear view. The Blessed Virgin appeared with the Holy Child. By a gracious gesture of her hand she seemed to flick the priest's vestments on to his shoulders. After the offertory she gave him the child, whom he placed on the altar by the chalice and elevated at consecration. Then the vision turned macabre. The priest slew the child and summoned Arthur to eat a piece of his flesh. At the end of the Mass the child was seen to be whole and living as before, and returned to Mary's arms. Arthur owned himself convinced as to the dogma of the Real Presence, and vowed to comply with every request made him for the honour of Mary and her Son.

Thus in John's chronicle the visionary wonder surrounding the Grail is gracefully transferred to Our Lady of Glastonbury, and she is made to instruct no less a personage than Arthur himself. The damage done to the myth may be interpreted as proving that John does not understand it. But he manages very well. The convent and chapel are interesting innovations. Archæological work near Wearyall might repay the effort.

To revert to St Joseph, John raises some intriguing issues by his citation of Melkin's Prophecy (pages 45-46). If John or one of his brethren really concocted this, why concoct it in just this form? Who is Abbadarè? Why the apparent allusion to a pre-Christian burial ground – plausible enough, but never hinted at in the literature before John? Why Melkin; presumably Maelgwn, but not traceable in Welsh legend? And what is the two-forked line or *linea bifurcata*?

I confess to a strong impression that further bardic and hagiographic odds and ends did reach Glastonbury after the conquest of Wales, and that Melkin's Prophecy is not totally fraudulent. The strange, compressed, cryptic Latin could be explained by the supposition that it is translated or at least imitated from a Welsh original. John certainly wants his readers to think that he has studied Welsh records. He includes British heroes like Caradoc and Coel among Glastonbury's illustrious dead. The two-forked line remains a puzzle. In 1345 a man named John Blome, who said he had had a revelation, obtained a licence from Edward III to search for

Joseph's body. He failed to find it. The fact that the monks were too honest to fabricate Joseph's grave is an incidental argument for the genuineness of Arthur's.

Despite John's undeniable shortcomings as a purveyor of literal truth, his treatise has an imaginative truth which extorts respect. This edifice of marvels is not jerry-built or faultily founded. It overtops all but the highest towers in the Troys and Camelots of the spirit. Medieval Glastonbury's far-spreading fascination finds proof in the list of relics which John describes as included among the Abbey's treasures. Unlikely as many of them are, they imply, even as fakes, a majestic distribution of origins. Two of St Illtyd's teeth represented Wales. Part of the 'crown' of St Cunoglass represented Cornwall. There were fragments of the Irish and Scottish saints – Patrick, Bridget, Benignus, Columba – and of the famous Gauls, Martin of Tours and Germanus of Auxerre. St Helena's relics must have come from Italy, St Basil's and St George's from Asia. Nobody now can declare the provenance of the sample of manna, the sliver from Aaron's rod, the chip off the stone on which Jacob dreamed, the piece of Isaiah's tomb, the paving-tile from the Temple, the Magian gold, the stone which Jesus refused to turn to bread, the splinter from the table of the Last Supper, the thread from the Virgin's robe. John's list is prolix and fanciful. But it shows that the Abbey where pilgrims left such gifts enjoyed contact with most of the accessible world.

That world, for its part, could not help hearing about Glastonbury. The legend of Joseph was impressive, and it grew more so. It grew, in fact, utterly incredible. Several of the late medieval writers pushed the British mission backward in time to a date immediately after the Crucifixion. A Vatican manuscript mentioned by Baronius is most interesting, not only as embodying a stage in the process, but as embalming scraps of what seems to be an alternative tradition. It narrates how Joseph was expelled from Jerusalem in the dispersion of the disciples after the death of Stephen. The persecutors drove him into an unseaworthy boat with a party of fellow-Christians, including Lazarus, Mary Magdalene and Martha. The boat was towed out into the Mediterranean and set adrift. A miraculous wind caught it, however, and bore it over the waves like the Fécamp tree-trunk, only not quite so far. The party landed at Marseilles. Joseph proceeded into Britain.

This tale probably resulted from an attempt to combine

the Joseph theme, popularised by Arthurian romance, with the southern French legend of Mary Magdalene. It implied an earlier date than A.D. 63 for the arrival in Britain. The absurd choice which some imaginative people at length concluded on, A.D. 31, arose from a careless reading of phrases such as 'in the XXXI year after the Passion of Christ.' The Passion, not the Birth. The Abbey itself never budged from its first position, but a bronze commemorative tablet which was fixed to a column of the great church contained an unfortunate ambiguity.

In the year XXXI after the Lord's Passion, twelve holy men, of whom Joseph of Arimathea was the chief, came hither and built the first church of this kingdom, in this place which Christ at this time dedicated to the honour of his Mother and as a place for their burial.

Observe the effect of interpolating a comma after 'XXXI.' The early date was most vehemently insisted on at the Church Councils of Pisa, in 1409, and Constance, in 1417. Disputes had broken out over precedence. The French bishops claimed seniority in western Europe on the ground that St Denys (Dionysius the Areopagite) had planted the Faith in Paris shortly after his conversion by Paul. The English bishops retorted with St Joseph, who had come to Glastonbury, they said, immediately after the Passion of Christ. There was another council in 1424 at Siena, where Richard Fleming, Bishop of Lincoln and founder of Lincoln College, upheld Joseph single-handed against the French, Scots and Spaniards. At yet another council – Basle, 1434 – the dispute occurred on the diplomatic level, between the ambassadors of England and Castile. This time the English reverted to the more plausible date, A.D. 63. Alphonso Garcia de Sancta Maria, doctor of laws and Dean of the Churches of Compostella and Segovia, stood up to reply. In the first place, he questioned whether Joseph had ever gone to Britain. In the second place, while not conceding that the onus of proof lay on himself, he begged leave to remind his audience of a report that Joseph had been found imprisoned in Jerusalem in A.D. 70. (Thus, by citing a story indirectly derived from the Grail books, he *dis*proved the mission.) In the third place, even if Joseph did go, there was no evidence that the British Church amounted to anything. In the fourth place, everybody knew that St James had founded the

Spanish Church well within the lifetime of Peter, and before Joseph's ostensible embarkation.

It was not to be expected that these mulish foreigners would yield. The point is that they took Glastonbury seriously.

5

Last of the strictly medieval abbots was John Selwood, elected in 1459. Within the house his rule was lax and inglorious, but not absolutely disgraceful. An inquiry by Bishop Stillington led to no drastic action. He died in 1493. The monks chose a successor without consulting the Bishop of Bath and Wells. That offended dignitary applied to the King for permission to cancel the election and nominate an abbot himself. Henry VII, absolutist by policy and temperament, granted the request, and the Bishop proceeded to install Richard Bere.

Before the turn of the century Abbot Bere had a crisis to contend with. The King to whom he owed his office taxed the West Country beyond endurance, and in the summer of 1497 a horde of poverty-stricken Cornish rebels poured through Somerset on their way, as they supposed, to London. There were fully six thousand. The Vale of Avalon twinkled with their camp-fires. They behaved very correctly, taking care not to pillage, but their leaders came begging to the monastic houses, and a certain amount of food and assistance could not well be refused. This expensive demonstration collapsed almost immediately. A few weeks later, however, the more dangerous army of the pretender Warbeck arrived at Taunton. Luckily it never reached Glastonbury. The royal advance-guard got there first, and quartered itself, as a matter of course, on the Abbey. Henry appeared in Bath with thirty thousand men; Warbeck scuttled to sanctuary; on 1st October all was over, and the King attended *Te Deum* in Wells Cathedral, later visiting Glastonbury himself at the Abbot's expense.

The county had shown an inclination to side with Warbeck, and in the ensuing months the King's agent Sir Amyas Paulet exacted retribution. He dealt out fines right and left, and bore especially hard on the abbots of Ford, Cleeve, Muchelney and Athelney, who had so far forgotten their duty as

247

to give food to the hungry peasants in Warbeck's train. Glastonbury itself escaped. Bere's hospitality to Henry proved a sound investment. But Somerset generally had suffered. Throughout that reign and the reign which followed, the Abbot of Glastonbury had more reason than most men to feel a horror of civil strife and a desire to avert it at almost any cost.

Bere himself, now entering on a quarter-century of peace and construction, was a curious figure. He governed well. The Abbey prospered, and adjectives like 'grave,' 'wise,' and 'discreet' were applied to its head. Glastonbury stood as far off as might be from the evil atmosphere of the Borgia-Medici papacy. But Bere was no Savonarola, no narrow puritan reactionary making war on the Renaissance as such. He moved easily in cultured and scholarly circles. King Henry employed him on a diplomatic mission to Italy. He took an intelligent interest in the New Learning: Erasmus himself asked for Bere's criticism of a translation he had made from the Greek Testament. Bere advised against publication. Erasmus deferred to his advice, and admitted afterwards that the Abbot had been right.

Yet Richard Bere's permanent contributions to the Abbey were amazingly inappropriate to a friend of Erasmus. While the Dutch scholar was mobilising European opinion against improbable legends and superstitious devotions, his English adviser was encouraging both. Near the eastern end of the church, on the north side, he built a chapel to . . . Our Lady of Loretto. Now the Loretto legend is not precisely one of the most reputable of Catholic traditions. It concerns a cottage, the Holy House, supposed to be that of the Holy Family, miraculously borne through the sky from Nazareth. Newman was prepared to believe in this, and St Thérèse of Lisieux, with her habitual joyous acceptance, carried forward credulity into recent times. But the authenticity of the Holy House is not *de fide*, and the papal designation of Our Lady of Loretto as patroness of aviators constitutes an endorsement on the poetic rather than the literal level. To an early Tudor abbot such fine distinctions would not have been conceivable. Bere's chapel implied Bere's belief. The dedication at such a moment was a direct challenge to the iconoclasm and scepticism unleashed by Erasmus and his set.

Bere also maintained the genuineness of his relics of Dunstan against the Canterbury Cathedral Chapter, which had had the Canterbury tomb opened with results satisfactory to itself. More remarkable still was his ardent sponsorship of Joseph of Arimathea as a saint. All through the Middle Ages Joseph had remained a literary hero and little more. He was the Founder, of course, and he had died at Glastonbury, but nobody pretended to know where his grave was. He had no shrine, and the pilgrims made no offering to him. Suddenly – when a new enlightenment and a new incredulity were already sweeping over Europe – Abbot Bere chose to place the almost mythical missionary on the same historical plane as Dunstan or Patrick. His motive possibly lay in a reawakening of popular interest due to Malory's *Morte d'Arthur*, printed by Caxton, which introduced Glastonbury and included an adaptation of the *Queste*. He delved out a crypt under the Lady Chapel, put an altar at the end, and dedicated the place to St Joseph. In order to make room for a high ceiling he raised the floor of the Lady Chapel, blocking two of its doors and considerably spoiling its former beauty. The crypt-chapel was floored with hexagonal tiles, and roofed, for no clear reason, partly in imitation Norman. It is still there, mutilated and reinforced, and most people regard it as deplorable. A short passage on the south side leads to a well fed by a spring, probably dug in Bere's day to supply water for the many Masses regularly said in the chapels and church.

Pilgrims were now encouraged for the first time to pay their respects to St Joseph, and a popular cult sprang up that flourished unabated till the fall of the Abbey. An Arimathean coat-of-arms was devised, with the two cruets and drops of blood. Visitors point it out on a window of St John's Church. In 1520 Richard Pynson, the royal printer, brought out an anonymous blackletter pamphlet on the *Lyfe of Joseph of Armathia* evidently meant as publicity. The Life consisted of fifty doggerel eight-line stanzas, some of them barely recognisable as verse. Part of it retold the developed legend, more or less as in John of Glastonbury. The rest described various alleged relics and supernatural cures. Here are two specimens:

> So Joseph did as the angel him bad
> And wrought there an image of Our Lady
> For to serve his great devotion he had,
> And that same image is yet at Glastonbury
> In the same church there ye may it see
> For it was the first as I understand

That ever was seen in this country
For Joseph it made with his own hand.

.   .   .

John Gyldon, gentleman, of Port Melborne,
The side of his mouth was drawn to his ear,
His left side and his arm was benumb,
That he of his life stood in great fear.
Speak could he not, nor himself steer:
He prayed to Joseph promising his offering;
So of his sickness he was delivered clear,
Save only of an hurt in his left arm.

The pamphlet is notable for an early allusion to the Thorn.
It says very little:

The hawthorns also that groweth in Werall
Do burge and bear green leaves at Christmas,
As fresh as other in May when the nightingale
Wrests out her notes musical as pure as glass . . .

Joseph's staff had not thus far taken root.

It should not be thought that Abbot Bere's building efforts
were confined to these dubious exercises in piety. He was, in
fact, among the most active of the abbots. He strengthened
the steeple, arched the aisles, and added a magnificent altar
of silver gilt. He put up the Tribunal; the Church of St
Benen – that is, Benignus – now known as St Benedict's; a
row of women's almshouses near the Abbey gate, named after
St Mary Magdalene and long-enduring, with the Arimathean
arms on the wall; and a suite of rooms called the King's
Lodgings. He also began a chapel of Edgar at the eastern
end of the great church, extending it to the almost unrivalled
length visible to-day.

Half-way through Richard Bere's abbacy the King died,
and the community paid its homage to a new sovereign, who,
beyond reasonable doubt, was destined to continue the
favour shown by his predecessors. He was young, brilliant,
cultivated, a model Catholic. Before he became heir-apparent
there had been talk of his taking holy orders. Long live King
Henry the Eighth!

Chapter Nine

DISSOLUTION

Bere survived his royal patron by sixteen years. Early in February 1525 his death brought his long and variegated reign to a close. On the 11th of that month the forty-seven monks eligible to vote for a new abbot assembled in the chapter-house. Henry Coliner, the Prior, presided over the meeting. No vote was taken; five days were allotted for discussion and canvassing. The general sense appears to have been that there was no obvious choice, or, at least, no candidate who could be elected without causing acrimony. On the 16th they met again. After a Mass *de Spiritu Sancto* and the singing of the *Veni Creator* to invite the enlightenment of the Holy Ghost, the Sacristan read the roll-call, and passed round a volume of the Gospels on which every monk swore to vote according to conscience. William Benet, the monastery's expert on canon law, explained the various procedures which they could follow. But all that the meeting did was to register a decision already made informally. The monks adopted the method called Compromise, which meant entrusting the choice to a responsible outsider, and they unanimously asked Cardinal Wolsey to appoint their new head.

The Cardinal, who always showed to the best advantage in matters of Church government, wasted no time. Within a week or so he had made up his mind. On 3rd March he received a deputation from Glastonbury led by the Cellarer and the Sub-Prior, and to them he handed a document setting forth his choice. It had fallen on Richard Whiting, whom Wolsey referred to as 'an upright and religious monk, a provident and discreet man, and a priest commendable for his life, virtues, and learning.' The document bore the signatures of three witnesses. One was Sir Thomas More.

A few days later the deputation returned to Glastonbury and announced Wolsey's decision. The Precentor intoned *Te Deum* and the monks filed into the church, where a crowd of citizens had gathered. Here a notary public read the letter over again from the steps of the altar. Whiting himself was diffident. He walked over to the guest-house and sat down trying to collect his thoughts. Two colleagues, William Walter and John Winchcombe, followed him there and urged him strongly to accept. He asked a respite for prayer, left them for a while, and came back at last saying that he consented. The machinery of installation began thereupon to move. Wolsey sent two commissioners to verify Whiting's fitness for office. They summoned anyone with a reasonable objection to speak up within three days. When the days had safely passed, the Procurator produced witnesses as to age and character. Among them was Sir Amyas Paulet, who had made Whiting's acquaintance during his pacification of Somerset, and kept in touch ever since. All spoke highly of the Abbot-elect. Whiting took a formal oath of obedience to the bishop of the diocese, and was blessed by Dr William Gilbert, a suffragan. The process was now complete.

Richard Whiting, the last Abbot of Glastonbury, belonged to a junior branch of a distinguished West Country family. Several other members figure in ecclesiastical records. An earlier Richard was chamberlain in the monastery of Bath during the 1450s. There was a nun named Jane Whiting in the reign of Henry VIII. Two nieces of the Abbot went abroad after the Reformation and became postulants in the exiled English Franciscan convent at Bruges. The Abbot himself was getting on in years at the time of his appointment. 1459 has been mentioned as the most likely date for his birth. Not much is known about his life before Wolsey's action. He probably went to school at the Abbey and entered directly into the novitiate. It is certain that they sent him to Cambridge University, where he took his MA in 1483, but he seems to have served a long term at the Abbey as a teacher or secretary before the reception of holy orders. He was ordained acolyte in September 1498 by Thomas Cornish, a suffragan of Bath and Wells. The other minor orders followed. On 6th March, 1501, Whiting knelt before Thomas Cornish again in the Chapel of the Blessed Virgin at Wells, and was finally a priest. Returning to Cambridge, he graduated as Doctor of Theology in 1505. Like his namesake at Bath, he became Chamberlain of his Abbey, in charge of the wardrobe, dormitory and wash-rooms. It was in keeping with monastic tradition that a scholar should not enjoy a life of undisturbed scholarship.

In accepting the post of Abbot, Chamberlain Whiting assumed responsibility for what was still the greatest religious house in England. Westminster alone was larger, though not much so, and even Westminster fell far short of Glastonbury in point of prestige. We happen to possess a valuable piece of writing about the Abbey during this last phase, from the pen of William Good. William was born at Glastonbury in 1527 and grew up there. Afterwards he was a clergyman in the Church of England, but when Elizabeth I committed the country to Protestantism he went abroad and became a Jesuit. His manuscript was discovered in the English College at Rome. It shows how devotion to St Joseph of Arimathea had increased during the Abbacy of Bere.

At Glastonbury there were bronze plates as a perpetual memorial, chapels, crypts, crosses, arms, the keeping of St Joseph's feast on July 27th, as long as the monks enjoyed the protection of kings by their charters. . . . The monks never knew for certain the place of this saint's burying, or pointed it out. They said the body was hidden most carefully, either there or on a hill near Montacute, called Hamdon Hill, and that when his body should be found the whole world would wend their way thither on account of the miracles worked there. Among other things, I remember having seen at Glastonbury, on a stone cross overthrown during this Queen's reign, a bronze plate, on which was carved an inscription relating that Joseph of Arimathea came to Britain thirty years after Christ's Passion, with eleven or twelve companions, that he was allowed by Arviragus the King to dwell at Glastonbury, which was then an island called Avalon, in a simple and solitary life: that he had brought with him two small silver vessels in which was some of the most holy blood and water which flowed from the side of Christ. This cross, moreover, had been set up many years before to mark the length of the chapel of the Blessed Virgin, made by Joseph with hurdles. The length was measured by a straight line from the centre of the cross to the side of the chancel afterwards built of hewn stone, under which also there was of old, in a subterranean crypt, the Chapel of St Joseph. Outside, in the wall of this Chapel of the Blessed Virgin, there was a stone with the words *Jesus, Maria*, carved in very ancient letters.

We may pause to remark that the inscription is still there, in an excellent state of preservation. Father Good goes on:

> There was likewise at Glastonbury, in a long subter-
> ranean chapel, a most famous place of pilgrimage, which
> was made to a stone image of St Joseph there, and many
> miracles were wrought at it. When I was a boy of eight,
> for I was born there, I have served Mass in this chapel.

So much for externals. But as to the way things were conducted, as to the way the monks lived and the standards they
observed, we are not so lucidly informed. The only major
clue, though important, is negative – that despite ruthless
inquiry by scandal-seeking visitors, there was never any
specific scandal. Probably the best mode of approach is to
form a composite picture of English monasticism at this time,
and then infer that Glastonbury was somewhat above the
average, but not sharply so. Great saintliness or great
scholarship or remarkable artistic achievement would have
excited comment. With a few incidental exceptions to be
noted, comment is lacking.

Much nonsense has been talked about the religious communities on the eve of their dissolution. The former Protestant stress on sexual vice and riotous living is now generally
dropped. Vows of chastity were broken, but not so widely
as to bring the whole system into disrepute. Apologists for
the cloister, on the other hand, have relied unduly on a few
favourable reports and on the tainted character of the adverse
evidence. Monasteries and convents in the reign of Henry
VIII were most certainly decadent. A downward trend had
been manifest for a hundred years. The prevailing disease,
however, was not so much downright and definable sin as
mediocrity.

Religious houses had three principal functions: prayer and
charity – both broadly interpreted – and hospitality. It should
be borne in mind that these functions continued to be discharged. For instance, despite some bad lapses, no catastrophic
break had occurred in the sacramental and liturgical round.
The trouble was that the life had gone out of it. Divine
service perfunctorily performed by monks with their minds
on food or sport cannot have been very convincing in the
sight of men, or very acceptable in the sight of God. Again,
alms were regularly dispensed, but dispensed in a mechanical
routine; and the accumulation of wealth in lay hands, the
growth of capitalistic ideas, had begun to alter un-'enter-

prising' habits of thought which kept religious charity vital. The new maxim 'Poor man means idle man' was probably in the minds of the religious themselves, making them grudging and censorious in their almsgiving.

Under the heading of hospitality we find an active awareness of obligations, but also an increasingly commercial spirit. During the Middle Ages the traveller who stayed at a monastery was expected to pay, or leave a gift, if he seemed well off. His payment, however, was only a glorified tip, and generally speaking he was not pressed for it. By Henry's reign the larger abbeys were becoming more and more like hotels. They spent considerable sums providing good entertainment, including minstrels, comedians and play-actors, and they expected a return. Some of them had already taken the logical step of building separate inns for travellers, run on business lines. Here Glastonbury led the way. The George and Pilgrims Inn dates from the fifteenth century.

Monastic scholarship had undoubtedly declined. All monks were supposed to reach qualifying standards in grammar, philosophy and logic. But in the Tudor world, with its new secular opportunities, the number of postulants for admission decreased, and boys of low intellectual attainments had to be accepted to keep the numbers up. A statute of Benedict XII required every abbey to send about one monk in twenty to a university. This was very imperfectly complied with. The lowered educational level among the monks reduced the amount of monastic teaching. Large houses took the sons of rich parents as paying boarders. They also took a certain number of poorer boys on a charitable basis. Throughout England, however, there were probably not more than 2000 of these charity scholars.

Monastic study and literary activity were almost dead. The writing of chronicles had petered out in the fifteenth century. The libraries were intact but neglected. Here we get a direct shaft of light on Glastonbury in the notes of John Leland, who visited the Abbey in Whiting's time. His tone is rapturous; the library must have been beautiful and well cared for; but we do not know how many monks actually read the books.

The same slackness appeared in arts and crafts. Because of a few exceptional convents, notably Ulverscroft, it is sometimes imagined that these still flourished among the monks and nuns. On the whole they did not. If an abbot wanted a vestment made or a book copied, a picture painted or a rug woven or a building decorated, he hired an outsider to do the job. The record on public works is more creditable. In particular the Somerset sea-walls were kept in good repair, the drainage of the marshlands went on.

All in all, we must not conceive Richard Whiting in terms of Cluny or Clairvaux. He took office as head of a large, wealthy, respected corporation, which still paid lip-service to sanctity and scholarship, but produced neither. Barring miracles, the most he could hope to do was to administer his charge well and keep sound discipline. There is indeed no sign that he ever seriously envisaged anything more. The few glimpses we have show him as a great gentleman rather than a saint or reformer. Though simple in his private life, he seems to have been especially concerned with maintaining a tradition of splendour and open-handedness. He finished the Edgar Chapel, rounding off the vast fabric entrusted to him, but he did not start any new building which might have led to financial difficulties. The Abbey's wealth was devoted to human beings. Whiting entertained as many as five hundred guests at a sitting, and paid people compliments in stained glass.

One of his letters is particularly revealing. Lord Lisle had complained of the Abbot's lack of cordiality toward Stephen Pike, a retainer. Whiting answered that a servant of Pike's had several times broken into the Abbey and stolen his poultry. He had lost five cygnets in this way, and was therefore unable to present them to the executors at the funeral of Sir John FitzJames: a loss, he said, which meant more to him than twenty times the price of the birds. Here is the true country gentleman speaking. We catch another glimpse of him in the legal testimony relating to a debt. Just after New Year's Day a Mr John Lyte came to pay £10 out of £40 which he owed to the Abbey. Whiting received it in person, says the witness, in 'the little parlour on the right of the great hall.' On a Sunday in midsummer Lyte arrived to pay off the remainder. He came to the Abbot in his garden, on the south side of the church, while High Mass was singing. The Abbot had Lord Stourton with him, but he tactfully drew the debtor aside into an arbour of bay and took the money there, remarking pleasantly that he was glad it was gold and could be counted quickly. He asked if Lyte would put up his own abbatial coat of arms on a new house he was building. Lyte agreed, and Whiting gave him eight angels to pay for the job.

It is not surprising to learn that this Abbot bestowed special attention on the more gentlemanly aspects of education. Despite Bere's example, the New Learning had made no serious inroads at the Abbey. A single monk was reported 'infected' in 1528, that was all. But the Abbey gave schooling to three hundred boys of good family; one suspects that they were learning aristocratic accomplishments rather than logic or mathematics. On 16th August, 1534, Whiting engaged a certain James Renynger as music-master and organist. The Abbot was to pay Renynger ten pounds a year in quarterly instalments, and provide a rent-free house or thirteen guineas a year in lieu. He was also to provide a gown annually or 13s. 4d. instead. What is striking is the size of the cash equivalents. There is no need to discuss whether we should multiply by thirty, forty, fifty, or x to compute Renynger's income in modern money; the essential point is that Whiting valued the musician's accommodation at more than the total of his other living expenses. It is as if a modern headmaster were to propose maintaining an assistant in a luxury flat of the type agencies handle. The Abbot probably felt that any failure on his part to provide a house would mean, in effect, letting the music-master down and causing him serious inconvenience, so that there was a moral obligation to compensate him generously in such a case.

Renynger's duties were quite extensive. He had to sing and play the organ at services in the Lady Chapel and in the high choir, and he had to arrange special programmes for Christmas and other holidays. Six boys chosen by the Abbot were to be given tuition – all six of them in prick-song and descant, and two also in organ-playing, the Abbot providing 'clavyngcordes' for the purpose. Renynger apparently gave satisfaction. After the dissolution the Government continued to pay him, it is not clear exactly for what duties. In 1569 he was still drawing his £10 a year.

The picture of Richard Whiting which emerges from the casual fragments is that of a very capable, very honest, very magnanimous administrator. He must have been like the best type of pre-1914 public-school headmaster or colonial governor. (His splendid watch, happily preserved in a museum, somehow strengthens that impression.) He had the knack of imposing strict discipline without making himself unpopular, and, to judge from various odd references and local traditions, he won the respect of all classes and the love of the poor. On Wednesdays and Fridays he personally dispensed charity. He attended the House of Lords, but cared little for politics. Thomas More had a 'corrody' or pension for acting as the Abbot's parliamentary proxy. Whiting preferred his role of paternal autocrat in the country. There he chose to live, and there, horribly, he died.

2

I have taken the liberty of picturing Abbot Whiting musing over public affairs, any time during the first five years of his reign.

'What strikes me most,' he reflects, 'is that England is so peaceful. How well I remember the alarms and excursions in my youth – Richard of Gloucester seizing the crown, Henry killing him at Bosworth, and the mobs quartering themselves on the Abbey's land. You never knew where you were in those days. People were afraid to build, afraid to invest, afraid even to farm properly. All their work could so easily go for nothing when the next army passed by. Things have changed since then, and we know where to give the credit, too. The King is strong enough to keep order at last. It's natural for old men like me to say how much better it was to live fifty years ago. In some ways it was. But in one way to-day is better, far better. We have a real monarchy, and that has given the country peace and prosperity.

'Of course there are fools who go too far on this monarchy question. Fawning courtiers and fashionable wiseacres who read Machiavelli and claim the King can do practically anything. That's nonsense. But I would agree to this extent. We ought to endure practically anything at the King's hands rather than start a fresh civil war.

'What *would* justify resistance? If Henry turned heretic, perhaps. . . . But he won't. Why, he actually took the trouble to write a book against Luther. Quite a competent piece of work for a layman. And even if he breaks faith himself, there are limits to the harm he can do. No earthly prince could cause a real breach between England and the Holy See. The idea's absurd. I know there were Emperors in the past who quarrelled with Rome and put up anti-popes for a year or so, but they got rid of them as soon as the argument was over. The Greeks and the Lutherans – yes, they do seem to have broken away for the moment, but strictly on ecclesiastical points. These schisms and heresies are the business of churchmen. Kings meddle in them sometimes, but they never start them and they never control them. Henry is theologian enough to understand his position.

'Bad advisers? Yes; I suppose he has a few really dangerous characters at his court. So many mad notions are in the air these days. Go up to London and you never can tell who will buttonhole you next – a fat Hanseatic merchant jabbering about justification, or a New Learning crank who says we can't be Christians unless we memorise the Greek alphabet, or a lord of the manor who has evicted his peasants to put sheep on the land and swears he's done it entirely in the public interest. There never was such a time for innovators. The King's Peace doesn't extend to that. . . .

'It's sheer indiscipline, of course. The Church has failed in her duties. That's another thing that a deal of rubbish is talked about. Some of these agitators pretend we clergy are falsifying the Faith. We aren't. Our doctrine is the same as it has been from time immemorial, and I defy anyone to point out where and when the Church first deviated from the Apostles' teaching. One heretic says it happened in the first century, another says the seventh, another says only yesterday. I leave them to fight it out among themselves. Then there are these super-holy individuals who call us too worldly. I suppose Wolsey has overdone it, with his robes and his retinue and his mansion. But the Church has uses for wealth. Not to mention charity and good works in general, I find from experience that display itself is not to be sneezed at. Only these envious malcontents are really against it. The ordinary man respects you if you make a fine show, and feels disappointed if you don't. The same sort of argument applies to relics and pilgrimages. Nobody can teach me a thing on that score, I know Glastonbury too well. Pilgrimages suit ordinary people. They travel, they make friends, they get a holiday, and however short of genuine piety they may be, the pilgrimage keeps them out of mischief and makes them remember their Creator for a minute or two. As for relics, the pilgrims expect them, and our collection would stand up to examination as well as any.

'No, the Church's failure isn't there. I could put it in a word: Muddle. No authority, no respect. A crazy tangle of jurisdictions. Endless jobbery and litigation. Plenty of money about, but never enough in the right places. Take only one example, the training of priests. It seems to be nobody's business. I never saw such a scurvy crop as we have these days. They bring religion into contempt. And that contempt shows itself in a way which affects me very closely. The monasteries are emptying for want of new blood, and the quality of the lads who do come in is lower, because we've had to ease our requirements to get them at all. The same slackness everywhere, the same conniving! I sicken to think what goes on nowadays in the name of religion.

'Fundamentally there's still plenty of soundness in the Church. The gates of hell shall not prevail. The crisis will pass. But at present the sounder elements don't get support at the top level. The state of Rome is deplorable. The Holy Father has neither power nor prestige. What can you expect when Europe's in a permanent uproar and he can only pay his way by winking at every kind of shady practice? . . .

'Peace. I keep coming back to that. Peace and order, a general council of the Church, and a common front against the Turks. King Henry has a wonderful opportunity there. With our home troubles disposed of, he can set the example to Europe. In fact he can go beyond that, he can set the example to Rome itself. With his theological training he'd be the ideal man to start putting the Church in order, on the administrative side, that is. He'd know enough not to let the hotheads push him too far. Personally I think he could go a long way and still be within his rights. The Pope is supreme, yes, but what does his supremacy really amount to? How much do we have to believe about him as an article of faith? No one seems to have settled that. Certainly the events of the last few years haven't encouraged us to take a very exalted view of him. Perhaps God only intended that Rome should be a High Court of Appeal for difficult cases in faith and morals. We must straighten it all out as soon as we get the chance.

'Peace and order and a general council. That's the key to the situation. As God is my witness, I would dearly love to take steps toward a reformation myself. But the monastic climate is altogether too hostile to heroic virtue. No! The King is keeping the peace in the realm, and I will keep what order I can in my own territory. That is my proper contribution, and it's enough of a job for anyone.'

Thus we may imagine the Abbot soliloquising, on one of

those summer afternoons when he rode out to inspect his canals and manor-houses: turning his horse at last, and letting his eye rove back to the Tor; unaware that the path he had chosen led to that eerie summit and did not come down again.

3

In July 1530 a curious document was laid on the Abbot's desk. It was a letter addressed to the Pope, Clement VII, urging him to dissolve King Henry's marriage, and threatening dire consequences if the petition were not granted. Somebody at court had drawn the thing up, and it was now being passed round for the Lords Spiritual and the Lords Temporal to sign.

Whiting did not approve. Like most of his fellow-subjects he sympathised with Queen Catherine. The King, indeed, had made out a sort of case for the invalidity of the marriage. His conscience (that active but unpredictable organ) discerned a sign of celestial displeasure in her failure to produce a male heir. But the real crux, as everyone knew, was that Anne Boleyn insisted on the status of queen, so that her royal lover had to get his wife out of the way. Henry was now relying on the subtle counsels of Thomas Cromwell. Apart from his amatory problems, lavish expenditure was causing anxiety about money, and Cromwell promised to make him the richest prince in Christendom.

The Abbot of Glastonbury did finally set his name to the letter, in common with twenty-one other abbots. Rome still refused to grant the divorce. The political pressure of Catherine's Spanish relatives, who did not want her disgraced, prevented Clement from giving the favourable answer he was inclined to give. At last Henry's theological training came to his aid. On top of the discovery that his own marriage was invalid, he superimposed the further discovery that the Pope's claims were invalid too. The Catholic Faith did not depend on allegiance to the Bishop of Rome. The proper course in the circumstances was to set up a National Catholic Church, a Church of England, with himself at the head. Such a body could restore the Faith to its apostolic purity, and, incidentally, grant its head a divorce.

The ecclesiastical changes which now began were far from simple. There were four principal factors: Henry's scheme of a National Church; Cromwell's policy, inaugurated about the same time, of dissolving the religious houses and confiscating their wealth; heretical Protestantism, imported mainly from Germany; and the New Learning. The inter-relationships were exceedingly complex. Most Protestants supported Henry, but Henry had no use for Protestantism. The chief advocates of the New Learning opposed Protestantism and were divided about Henry. Cromwell served Henry but flirted with foreign Protestants. Many abbots who opposed the dissolution raised no objection to royal supremacy in the Church. And so forth. But the original decisive step, on which every later development depended, was Henry's demand that all his subjects acknowledge him as head of the Church of England.

Proposals were put forward, oaths were administered, bills were rushed through Parliament. All the bishops but one consented. The National Church started on its career, with Thomas Cranmer, a Boleyn family chaplain, as Archbishop of Canterbury. Anne yielded. The nation had to yield too. The King's programme was published and expounded. A few Catholics knew it for what it was, namely a breach with Catholicism, and a tiny handful suffered exile or martyrdom accordingly. A few Protestants welcomed it for exactly the same reason. Some of these also were to suffer when the King's policy took a further twist. Others again sincerely accepted the royal theory of a National Church. But the vast majority failed to see the truth, because the truth was incredible. Those who thought at all interpreted Henry's measure as a personal whim which would blow over; as a political move which would be withdrawn; or as an assertion of control over the Church's temporalities which left the Pope supreme as a spiritual arbiter. Those who did none of these things simply did as they were told. The issues were beyond them, and if the bishops assented, who were they to resist the King?

In the summer of 1534 Richard Whiting and fifty-one Glastonbury monks signed a paper renouncing obedience to the Pope – with whatever mental reservations their private thoughts may or may not have suggested. Soon after they signed another paper recognising the royal supremacy. The monks used the names which they had adopted in religion, and thus furnished evidence of Glastonbury's mighty *esprit de corps*. Most were taken from the history and legends of

262

the Abbey itself. The list includes Joseph, 'Abaramathea' (i.e. ab Arimathea), Gildas, Aidan, Dunstan, and even Arthur.

Meanwhile Cromwell was busy making the King richer. The dissolution of abbeys and convents was nothing novel. During the Hundred Years' War the Crown had seized and sold French monastic possessions in England. In Henry's own reign Wolsey had closed a number of small priories, transferring the monks to other houses. But on all previous occasions the proceeds of the sale had been used for charitable or educational purposes. Apart from the minor embezzlements which doubtless occurred, neither public treasury nor private cash-box had ever benefited. It was in February 1532 that Henry and Cromwell set the new precedent. The house of Augustinian canons at Aldgate was dissolved under royal auspices, and the proceeds were not used for either education or charity. The prior and canons signed a deed of gift to the King with no such provisions. A monastic property, for the first time in English history, was simply secularised.

In this transaction Cromwell saw the solution to the King's money problems. With the divorce question settled and the Pope out of the way, the road was open. Hitherto a wholesale nationalisation of abbeys would not have been practicable. The religious orders, always more international than the hierarchy, would have worked through Rome to make the King's position untenable. Excommunication and interdict would have beaten him down. But after the breach the abbeys were atomised. They had nothing to lean on, and the abbots could be defeated in detail.

Cromwell began by announcing a programme of inspection. The object, he said, was not to abolish monasticism but to purify it. Royal commissioners toured the religious houses and submitted reports. As a result many of the smaller ones were declared useless or corrupt and seized by the Crown. The larger ones were at first given a clean bill of health, and ostentatiously spared. But the falsity of the 'purification' pretence was soon manifest. Even when the commissioners reported favourably, and advised in explicit terms that a given religious house should be left alone, suppression was liable to follow.

To strengthen his hand as much as possible, Cromwell employed agents with talents for muck-raking, who could be trusted to smell out the slightest discreditable rumour. He relied especially on a person named Richard Layton. Layton would have found his natural milieu in modern Sunday journalism. At that time, however, the King's service offered the brightest prospects. On 21st August, 1535, having gathered anecdotes of concubinage and sodomy at various abbeys in the West, Layton arrived at Glastonbury. He retired baffled. Even rumour failed him. 'At Glastonbury,' he wrote to Cromwell, 'there is nothing notable; the brethren be so strait kept that they cannot offend: but fain they would if they might, as they confess, and so the fault is not with them.' On his return to London he seems actually to have spoken in Whiting's favour, since we later catch him apologising to Cromwell for having done so.

Cromwell's campaign was moving into a fresh phase. In the name of reform he was imposing stringent regulations on the religious houses, which made life so awkward for their inmates that many were glad to anticipate dissolution by surrender. Layton dictated a set of rules of this kind at Glastonbury. Shortly after his first visit Nicholas FitzJames, a friend of the Abbot's, wrote to Cromwell asking for a relaxation. Under one rule anybody who cared to inform about a breach of discipline, real or supposed, could go and report it to the King at the Abbot's expense. FitzJames pointed out that scandal-mongers would willingly invent stories for the sake of the trip. His plea was ineffectual. A few weeks later, Whiting himself had a more urgent request. The royal decrees had taken away his jurisdiction over Glastonbury town. Cases were pending in the court. What should he do?

It was, of course, Cromwell's intention that the Abbot's life should be made unbearable. He had already begun to persecute him with outright blackmail, demanding one gift after another for himself or his friends, with the unspoken threat that refusal would hasten dissolution. On 26th August, 1535, Whiting gave him the advowson of Monkton church. On 9th September he assigned Thomas More's corrody to him, sending £10 of unpaid arrears. At subsequent dates he made over the rents from his farm at Northwode Park, the mastership of game in the same park, and the advowson of another church. His surviving letters give the impression that this form of harrying was pressed further than the documents show. Certainly an idea got about that Glastonbury Abbey was scheduled for expropriation. Cromwell's helpers were obliged to deny it, and in 1538 Cromwell repeated the assurance himself. Abbeys and convents, even the larger ones, were now vanishing so fast that his promise had a hollow ring, and he stultified it in any case by making it conditional on loyal behaviour, he himself being the sole judge of what constituted disloyalty.

Nevertheless he may have meant what he said, in so far as he ever did. But the tide of events was bearing him on toward a crisis. His own acts were provoking counter-measures, and conjuring up unexpected demons.

As early as 1536 a rising had broken out in Lincolnshire. From the Midlands northward, the dissolution inflicted a deeper wound than it did in the south. The religious houses were economically much more important, their role in public service was much more conspicuous, and their disappearance, therefore, caused a more serious dislocation. Lincolnshire's protest was only a headless tumult stirred up by rumours, but it greatly alarmed the uneasy capital. Cromwell dispatched letters to the major landlords of England, both lay and ecclesiastical, ordering them to raise military levies among their tenants. Such was his anxiety that he even sent as far as the West Country. From Richard Whiting he demanded a hundred men, the largest contingent required from any abbot. The revolt soon failed and the order was countermanded, so that Whiting was spared the necessity of taking sides. This false alarm, however, was only a foretaste of the tribulations to come.

Soon after the Lincolnshire fiasco a more ominous portent appeared in Yorkshire. It was the Pilgrimage of Grace, almost the last truly popular uprising of English people. At York, under the banner of St Cuthbert with the Five Wounds of Christ, vast numbers of commoners assembled in arms. The benevolent neutrality of the northern peerage enabled the rebels to outmanoeuvre King Henry's officers. Royal authority momentarily collapsed north of the Humber. But no nobleman came forward to take command. The leadership was thrust on a lawyer, Robert Aske, who drew up a proclamation protesting at the suppression of monasteries. Cromwell agreed to negotiate. Aske, trusting in a safe-conduct, came to London and was arrested and executed. A series of hangings in the north brought the Pilgrimage to a close. Its effects were lasting. It dispelled all illusions as to the tendency of the King's proceedings – including those cherished by the King himself. Henry had been turning over the idea of a reconciliation with Rome, but now he saw that he was committed too far. Any reversal would be a fatal capitulation to an opposition whose existence he had not hitherto acknowledged. That opposition, meanwhile, had itself grown more conscious and coherent.

Many prominent Catholics understood at last that the schism was real and that Henry was drifting toward alliance with Protestantism.

Richard Whiting was one of these Catholics. In 1538 a group of aristocratic conspirators devised measures to restrain the King. Their leader in England was the Marquis of Exeter, the most influential nobleman in the West Country. Abroad, but maintaining a very poor liaison, Exeter's cousin Reginald Pole tried to enlist foreign support. A blind musician named William Moore acted as courier for the domestic anti-royalists, and carried letters from person to person. His physical handicap diverted suspicion, his simple baggage consisted of a harp and a bundle of correspondence. Moore's itinerary included the surviving abbeys of Reading, Colchester, and Glastonbury. It is not likely that the three abbots either took or contemplated political action themselves. Their conduct seems to have been entirely proper. But they sympathised. When the Exeter conspiracy failed, it left them in a confirmed though unobtrusive alignment against the Crown. On 7th April, 1539, Whiting wrote to Cromwell excusing himself from attending the House of Lords. His plea of ill-health was probably justified, but it must have struck the chief minister as unconvincing.

Exeter's wandering kinsman Reginald Pole was a clumsy diplomat who did no good to his own cause. Foreign courts gave him a cold reception. He had powerful friends in the Church, however (later he nearly became pope), and his close blood relationship to the Tudors made him look more dangerous than he was. The English Government, fearful that he might inspire a sort of crusade, felt impelled to spend heavily on war preparations. All the monetary gains of the past seven years were wiped out. The King's hangers-on were richer, the King was not. In the spring of 1539 Cromwell's agents made the round of the bigger churches extorting what was described as superfluous plate. The list of the proceeds includes 'a superaltar garnished with silver gilt and part gold, called the Great Sapphire of Glastonbury.' And still the slide toward bankruptcy continued. In August Sir Brian Tuke, Treasurer of the Chamber, admitted that the treasury was virtually empty.

What was there left to seize? The unhappy Council scanned the horizon, while bills accumulated and the King's personal extravagance flourished unchecked. There remained those three rich abbeys, Colchester, Reading and Glastonbury

– more especially Glastonbury, the most splendid of all the English houses. Charges of treason could now surely be pressed home. The financial crisis acknowledged by Tuke was not more than a few days old when Cromwell made a note in his memorandum-book to 'proceed against the abbots of Reading, Glaston and the other, in their own countries.'

4

Glastonbury itself was feeling the economic pinch, though not in quite the same way. Richard Whiting and his subordinates had no foreigners to contend with, but they had a more insidious and implacable foe, namely inflation. Throughout the 1530s prices were rising, while the Abbey's income was largely fixed. The main source of revenue was a rigid mass of copy-hold tenants, paying rents fixed in the fifteenth century, and protected by agreements which no lawyers could shake. Avaricious courtiers supported by Cromwell's blackmail had stripped away some of the rents entirely; and among the tenants from whom the Abbey could still collect, many were enterprising farmers who maintained the inflation by pushing up their own prices while paying relatively smaller and smaller annual amounts for the use of the land. Glastonbury's monastic ship was gradually foundering in a sea of parvenu wealth.

Each Abbey official had his own problems, yet most of the problems were reducible to the same one – how to discharge heavy responsibilities with decreasing resources. The Pittancer, for example, had the task of providing light refreshments as a supplement to the main menu. On a Monday shortly before Christmas 1538 we find him offering pea soup and snacks of fish. On Tuesday it is vegetable soup and fritters. On Wednesday it is fish soup with pepper, cinnamon and raisins. Manifestly a certain standard is expected. Liquids are mentioned as well as the more nutritive items, and here the shadow falls darkest. A pipe of wine which cost 17s. in 1534 costs £1 in 1538. Sack bought at Bristol has gone up from £3 4s. 4d. to £3 16s. 8d. in a single year. Even more alarming, the cost of cartage has risen from 6s. 4d. to 9s. 7d.

The Sacristan's difficulties must have been at least equally complex. He was allotted the rents paid by various house-holders in Glastonbury, the money taken up in collections at one or two churches, and the profits of a monastic water-mill. Out of that income, the larger part of which stayed immovable while prices climbed ever higher, he supported a wide variety of more or less religious activities. His expenses for the year 1538-9 included the replacement of broken glass in the chapel windows, the mending and laundering of priests' vestments, and the provision of myriads of altar-breads and eleven hundred pounds of wax and whole hogsheads of wine and oil. Water conduits had to be overhauled and paving-stones laid. A chest in St John's Church needed repairs. And so on and so forth. Most irritating of all, perhaps, were the gifts. The Sacristan, at Christmas, felt that he could not decently present the Abbot with anything less than a complete pig. At other times eels were more seasonable. He was even called upon to hand out gratuities to undergraduates at Oxford.

The Prior and the Almoner had the delicate duty of administering charity. The demands of the needy were only vaguely predictable. A poor man might die and his family arrive at the Abbey gate asking for a shroud. A sick horse might require medicine which its owner could not afford. An ill-fed mob might assemble in the street and have to be satisfied with a distribution of beans. Then there were the more regular obligations. Robert Clerke, the Prior, managed an almshouse for ten poor widows. On top of the complications of management (none of the widows could practise as a midwife or use private funds, and all had to be shepherded punctually to Divine Service in the Abbey), the Prior's almshouse budget provided for meals eaten at the common table throughout the year, Sunday uniforms of black broadcloth with the arms of St Joseph, and winter fuel.

Another harassed official was the Infirmarian. For him the year 1538-9 was extraordinarily vexatious. A radical plumbing job proved necessary, and four stills used in preparing cordials for the patients kept breaking down and needing repairs. Since the Abbot insisted on the sick being properly fed, luxuries such as ginger and geese added to the inevitable cost of staples, such as butter and porridge. Not unnaturally, the monks tended to regard the infirmary as a place to rest in. The Infirmarian had elderly brethren on his hands for six or eight weeks together.

Thus, in a cloud of expenses increasingly hard to meet, Glastonbury's last year rolled on. The community and its dependants consumed 176 oxen, 634 sheep, 2183 shellfish, 8532 herrings, and 27,000 bundles of firewood. Everything was stretched to keep up the unretrenched grandeur and munificence which the Abbot required. The settled policy was not to reduce expenditure but to increase income. Several unfortunate results followed from this. When a tenancy agreement expired, the monks raised the rent for the new tenant; and since the chance did not often occur, the temptation to raise it unduly high was not always resisted. The Abbey joined in the general enclosure movement denounced by Thomas More, taking possession of open fields and waste spaces, and letting them profitably. Experiments were made with new business ventures, notably fulling-mills. But a conscientiously-run abbey could not have the singleness of purpose of the new capitalists. The monks, for example, recognised and honoured a duty to cut the rent for the widows of deceased tenants, and they provided free quarters for superannuated servants.

A different abbot might have pursued solvency with more ruthlessness. But Abbot Whiting was not the man to skimp. He may, of course, have foreseen the end and let matters drift accordingly, but in any case it is fairly clear that he believed in a mode of living and giving conformable to the dignity of his household. In the early autumn of 1539 he paid a call on his niece, Mrs Burgess, who lived at Wells. Her husband Robert had just embarked on some rather ambitious building operations. Repairs and structural changes to his mills and farmhouses threatened to involve him in heavy expense, amounting perhaps to a hundred pounds, the equivalent of several thousand in modern money. The Abbot inspected the property and offered to contribute to the cost of the work. Burgess even alleged afterwards that he promised, before completion, to pay the whole bill. I do not think any man as familiar with builders and their ways as a great abbot could possibly have made such a reckless pledge. But there is no reason to doubt that Whiting promised financial help of some kind, whether given or lent. The seemingly irresponsible gesture was simply part of his duty as he conceived it. Magnificence was expected of him.

And with this flourish of generosity Abbot Whiting the magnate fades from our sight. Blessed Richard Whiting the

5

On 19th September, 1539, at about ten in the morning, Henry's commissioners arrived without notice at the Abbey. One was Layton, ready after four years to avenge his former discomfiture. The others' names were Pollard and Moyle. Whiting was at his grange at Sharpham, two miles away, and there the party followed him. After some hostile questioning they brought him back to Glastonbury and searched his rooms, where they found nothing incriminating except a manuscript of arguments against the royal divorce and a printed life of St Thomas Becket. Properly convinced of his treason, they placed the Abbot under arrest, and with a certain show of politeness – he being now 'a very weak man and sickly,' and, it would seem, an octogenarian – packed him off to the Tower to be examined by Cromwell. The Abbey, they reported, was the finest house they had ever seen, meet for the King and for no man else. Among its unworthy occupants there was not a single monk with a Doctorate, and only three Bachelors, 'meanly learned.' (Their prisoner, as a matter of fact, was a Doctor himself.)

As soon as Whiting had left they searched more thoroughly, and discovered a gold chalice and other handsome objects hidden away, no doubt to thwart Cromwell's collectors of superfluous plate. Their first impulse was to blame the treasurers and sacristy clerks. Afterwards they hit on the ingenious notion of charging the Abbot with robbing his own church. But there were numerous other matters to attend to. Glastonbury excited them. 'The house,' they reported on the 28th, 'is great, goodly, and so princely as we have not seen the like, with four parks adjoining, the farthest but four miles from the house; a great mere of five miles compass being a mile and half from the house, well replenished with great pikes, breams, perch, and roach.' Anxious to secure this estate for its destined master, the commissioners dismissed the servants and evicted the monks, although, as yet, the Abbot had not even been formally accused.

The terms of the eviction were not so cruel as some have imagined. It was no part of Cromwell's programme to flood the countryside with destitute and desperate men capable of fomenting unrest. In earlier suppressions, the monks had been given the choice of moving to another house or going out into the world with a royal pension. Those who did the latter generally found a niche in the parish clergy. When Glastonbury's turn came there were no other houses to move to, and the inmates inevitably scattered. But not as paupers. Each received approximately £5 a year, enough to pay about half the living expenses of an economical bachelor. Successive governments honoured Cromwell's pledge; twenty-five Glastonbury monks were still drawing their pensions in Mary's reign. King Henry and his advisers, in short, were only too eager to harness the monastic priesthood to their national church, so long as it really was the national church. Monastic wealth, monastic power, the monastic system in general – these things had to go, extinguished by the royal supremacy. With the individual monk, so long as he acquiesced, the Crown had no quarrel. Even abbots had often preserved their security and comfort by a voluntary surrender.

But Richard Whiting had not surrendered. It was time to make an end of him. In the next few days the commissioners gathered such evidence as they could, taking down statements about the Abbot's treasonable opinions from local informers. On 2nd October they sent the results to Cromwell. The document has vanished, but Pollard obviously thought it would give satisfaction, since he applied almost immediately to have a friend of his made auditor of the Abbey lands. When he returned to London he further established the logical necessity of finding the Abbot guilty by handing over the valuables carried off in anticipation of such a verdict: 71 ounces of gold and jewels, 7214 ounces of gilt plate, and 6387 ounces of silver.

Whiting's case should in theory have been tried by Parliament. The meeting fixed for 1st November was postponed till the arrival of Anne of Cleves, Henry's fourth wife, and it was supposed that the Abbot would remain in the Tower till then. Cromwell, however, had already reached his decision. In a memorandum written before the end of October he summed it up: 'Item, the Abbot of Glaston to be tried at Glaston and also executed there with his complices.' The note tells the whole story. Cromwell, as prosecuting counsel, had stated the Crown's case; Cromwell, as jury, had delivered the verdict; Cromwell, as judge, had passed sentence. All that remained was to give the business an air of legality by a mock trial.

Pollard conveyed the Abbot back to Somerset. On the way he concealed the fate of the Abbey and left Whiting in doubt as to whether he himself was a guard or an escort. On 14th November the party reached Wells, where Lord Russell had empanelled a reliable jury. Whiting was hustled into the bishop's palace without time for rest or reflection, and the proceedings opened in the presence of a large crowd. Pollard conducted the indictment. The records of the trial are so casual that it is not even possible to ascertain what the charges were, or whether the jury was asked to return a verdict. Treason was presumably mentioned, but only as a matter already determined. The Crown probably introduced that incredible charge of robbing the church, since Whiting was lumped together with several ordinary felons accused of rape and burglary. Abbey tenants with grievances were brought forward to testify against him, no defence or cross-examination being permitted. Several Somerset gentlemen had been active in staging the affair, notably Thomas Horner and Nicholas FitzJames, the same who had written to Cromwell on the Abbot's behalf a few years earlier. These received their reward at the King's hands.

Next day Richard Whiting was taken to Glastonbury with two monks whom the court had condemned to death as his accomplices. The elder of the pair, John Thorne, was Abbey Treasurer and a skilful amateur craftsman responsible for some fine furniture; the name he had taken in religion was Arthur. His companion was Roger James, recently professed. Whiting himself was given the complete traitor's doom. At the outskirts of Glastonbury he was stretched on a hurdle and bound to it with ropes. A horse dragged him through the town, past the desolate Abbey, and up the Tor. On the summit beside the tower of St Michael the gallows were set up. All three monks asked forgiveness and 'took their death,' as a hostile witness observes, 'very patiently.' The executioners cut Whiting's body down, struck the head off, and placed it over the Abbey gate. Then they hacked the rest of the corpse into four pieces. One was exhibited at Wells, one at Bath, one at Ilchester, and one at Bridgwater, so as to put the fear of the King in as many hearts as possible.

This Glastonbury savagery was no mere terroristic routine. At the time it was exceptional and startling. The blacker phases of the English religious upheaval were to come later, during the reigns of Henry's three children. When their father ruled, the sustained exterminatory impulse had yet to be unleashed. Cromwell's malignancy, which partly explains the ghastly atmosphere surrounding this particular dissolution, may well have arisen from a streak of sincerity in his nature. He was quite unscrupulous, and his motives were generally so far from religious that it is easy to set him down as a hypocrite. But he genuinely believed in his master's theory of the Anglican Church, and the trouble with Glastonbury was that it did not fit. According to Henry you could be a National Catholic or a Roman Catholic, but you could not be both. On the whole nothing encountered by the English reformers upset this view. Most of the King's subjects, including all the bishops but one and all the leading political men but one, drifted into the status of National Catholics. When a few religious communities did resist, the handful of martyrs could be condemned as Romanists. But Glastonbury was a challenge, and, indeed, a refutation. If Glastonbury was not national, then nothing was. It traced its origin to a first-century foundation by a saint only nebulously connected with Peter. It was the shrine of the majestic Arthurian monarchy. Almost within living memory it had been the mainstay of the English Church's claim to high dignity. Yet in spite of all it had been Roman. It stood for that synthesis of the local and universal which Henry denied. Therefore it had to be effaced; more than effaced, obliterated.

Such considerations account partly for what was done in the Isle of Avalon. But only partly. To recollect these things at the top of the Tor is to shudder, not so much at the martyrdom itself, as at the mentality of the men who arranged it. One senses a hateful darkness, a memory of witchcraft or druidical rites. For the task which they undertook was so needlessly burdensome. Look down the slope and imagine driving a horse up it, in the mud of late autumn, with a human body on a hurdle trailing behind; or carrying up the heavy timbers required for the gallows; or performing the work of execution on the tiny platform of level ground by the tower, with a perpetual wind blowing. If the object was to strike terror, the place to do it was in the town, or at any rate within sight of the town. The ascent of the Tor was the act of madmen or mystics. It would not have been difficult, on that day of inexplicable effort and preternaturally arduous crime, to believe that the old gods of the underworld had returned hungrily to their dedicated mountain.

And it would not have been possible to remain unaware (or suppose that the perpetrators remained unaware) of the monstrous irony which the Reformation had reared above Somerset: a gibbet on a hill.

6

The epilogue is brief. There was no attempt to preserve the Abbey for the King. Pillage was the sole aim. Gangs of workmen assailed the roof, tore off the lead, and melted it by burning the carved woodwork. Stained glass was smashed, bells were broken up, vestments were auctioned, books were sold – sometimes merely for what the parchment would fetch. A man named Goals wrecked and rifled St Joseph's Chapel while the boy William Good looked on. Out of this ruin Cromwell managed to save most of what the King wanted. One of those macabre memoranda of his contains a list of the spoils. 'The plate of Glastonbury, 11,000 ounces and over, besides golden. The furniture of the house of Glaston. In ready money from Glaston, £1100 and over. The rich copes from Glaston. The whole year's revenue of Glaston. The debts of Glaston' (he means debts owed *to* the Abbey) '£2000 and above.' In view of the financial trials revealed by the accounts, Glastonbury's wealth at its downfall speaks highly for Whiting's administration.

The King did not keep the property. He needed cash, not estates. Within a few weeks Abbey lands were being knocked down to those who had helped in the business. The Horners did especially well. One of them, John, was turned loose on a pile of title-deeds and emerged as lord of a manor, obtaining a sweeter and saner immortality than he deserved . . .

> Little Jack Horner sat in a corner
>   Eating his Christmas pie;
> He put in his thumb and pulled out a plum,
>   And said, 'What a good boy am I.'

The old West Country rhyme is the final and perfect epigram on these fellow-travellers of the dissolution. Poor Robert Burgess, left high and dry with his expensive buildings and Whiting's promise to pay for them, tried to assert his claim in the general scramble. It was useless. Four years later he was still struggling, and carpenters and stonemasons were trooping sullenly to a court in Wells to give inconclusive testimony.

Glastonbury's villagers paid homage to Whiting's memory. Like that other Henrician martyr St Thomas More, he was remembered as a friend to the common man. Traditions about the good Abbot lingered on into the eighteenth century and later. On 13th May, 1896, Pope Leo XIII accorded him the honour of formal beatification, together with John Thorne and Roger James. Eventually he may be revered as a saint. With Thomas Cromwell the case was otherwise. Soon after his Glastonbury coup the new Queen he had found for Henry landed in England. Henry disliked her and blamed his minister. On 28th July, 1540, Cromwell went to the block.

Chapter Ten

DESOLATION

King Henry's dream of becoming the greatest landlord in Christendom had long since evaporated. He sold most of his monastic loot for whatever he could get, and he was in no position to hold out for advantageous terms. Solvency eluded him. Towards the close of his reign he was debasing the coinage. But the more astute of his subjects were becoming perceptibly wealthier, and among these was Edward Seymour. When the death of Henry's diseased body transferred the crown to his frail son Edward VI, Seymour became Regent or Lord Protector. Created Duke of Somerset, he obtained possession of Glastonbury Abbey, with the remainder of its lands.

He stood firmly for the parvenu clique which had enriched itself by enclosing commons and by acquiring Church property from the Crown at bargain rates. These people mostly favoured Protestantism and private enterprise: the Protector encouraged both. As a result he had to face two rebellions, a religious one in Cornwall, an economic one in East Anglia. Both were extinguished. The Government, perhaps not fully trusting its English troops, took the detested course of importing foreigners – German mercenaries who massacred and looted abominably, but at least accomplished what they were paid to do. Somerset had the wisdom to note that the continental Protestant populations might equally be used in a more constructive way. In 1551 he did something that epitomised his whole programme. He turned Glastonbury Abbey into an industrial settlement of Calvinist Flemish weavers.

The idea was that these 'outlandish, learned, and godly men' should work in the Abbey and be assigned land in Worrall Park. Each family (here Somerset anticipated and bettered a later statesman) was to have four acres and two cows. The Protector appointed an overseer named Cornish to take charge of the immigration, and lent him £484 14s. for the construction and conversion of houses. Very soon afterwards he himself was attainted and fell from power. Thirty-four families and six widows had already arrived. The over-seer Cornish, unsupervised, proved 'deceitful and false,' and disappeared from the scene. The inhabitants resented the strangers. At length a new superintendent, Vallerand Pollan, drew King Edward's attention to the situation. Only six houses were ready; twenty-two, at a price, could be made habitable, but still had no roofs or doors or windows; ten more families had descended on the Land of Promise while inquiries were proceeding. The Flemings, in fact, were more or less camping out. They owed £131 locally and had neither premises nor equipment to ply their trade. The land allotted to them in Worrall Park would not support enough cows. They had never even been unequivocally authorised to make use of the Abbey buildings.

A royal commission reported that the stranded Calvinists were 'very godly, honest, poor folk, of quiet and sober conversation, and showing themselves ever willing and ready to instruct and teach young children and others their craft and occupations.' The plan, therefore, was pushed ahead. Cottages that fell vacant were requisitioned. Two dye-houses were set up in the Abbey. The King made Pollan a grant of forty pounds, and lent the Flemings three hundred.

This, they protested, was quite inadequate. They needed a thousand: three hundred for buying wool, five hundred for other materials, two hundred for labour. Six Englishmen of substance would act as guarantors, and the loan would be repaid in ten years. But they attached conditions. They wanted a monopoly; they wanted the right to import their materials duty free; they wanted to do their own marketing; they wanted to practise their religion in their own way; they wanted to elect their own warden and officials. The King's council, appropriately impressed by these hard-bargaining men, granted all their demands, but retained Pollan in a position of general authority. For a short while the weavers flourished, making a part-silken cloth called 'saye' and a cheaper type called 'sayette.' They were thus the pioneer silk-workers in England. But the sickly Edward died, Mary succeeded him, and the Flemings, foreseeing persecution, packed up and escaped to Frankfurt. All the trouble had gone for nothing. The only relics of their adventure which survived into modern times were a brass alms-dish presented to St John's Church and a derelict furnace among the ruins.

Somerset's attempt to transform Glastonbury had failed.

Its author, rightly or wrongly, had gone the way of traitors. The Abbey reverted to Crown ownership and desolation. There was talk of a restoration under Mary. Four of the former monks petitioned her in pathetic language. 'We ask nothing in gift to the foundation, but only the house and site, the residue for the accustomed rent, so that with our labour and husbandry we may live there a few of us in our religious habits, till the charity of good people may suffice a greater number; and the country there being so affected to our religion, we believe that we should find much help among them.' It is surprising that Mary did not respond. A few of the ex-monks found their way into the monasteries she did restore – Westminster, for example – and in 1557 the Rector of Hinton St George hopefully left £2 in his will towards 'edifying the abbey of Glastonbury.' (What happened to the money? Is there a vast sum, accumulated at compound interest, waiting to be spent?)

The Elizabethan poet Drayton had melancholy words to say about Glastonbury in his topographical cycle *Polyolbion*.

O who thy ruin sees, whom wonder doth not fill
With our great fathers' pomp, devotion, and their skill?
Thou more than mortal power (this judgment rightly
      weighed)
Then present to assist, at that foundation laid,
On whom for this sad waste should justice lay the crime?
Is there a power in fate, or doth it yield to time?
Or was their error such, that thou couldst not protect
Those buildings which thy hand did, with their zeal, erect?
To whom didst thou commit that monument to keep,
That suffereth, with their dead, their memory to sleep,
When not great Arthur's tomb, nor holy Joseph's grave,
From sacrilege had power their sacred bones to save;
He, who that God in Man to his sepulchre brought,
Or he which for the Faith twelve holy battles fought –
What? Did so many kings do honour to that place,
For Avarice at last so vilely to deface?

By Drayton's time there was evidently no more doubt that the past was past.

A few dying rays of the Abbey's glory remain to be commemorated. Seven of the ex-monks found a haven in Wales, at Strata Florida, and the last of them presented the Powells of Nanteos with a mysterious cup. Was it the Holy Grail? Whatever it was, the Powells kept it, and it exists to this day. Then again there was Austin Ringwode . . . but more of him in due course. The final glimpse of Catholic Glastonbury is in the autobiography of William Weston, a Jesuit who braved the Elizabethan régime for twenty years and lived to tell the tale in exile. His story is a strange one, showing how the rustic Christians combined a sort of devotional automatism with ancient folk-memories of Annwn and Avalon.

In 1586, Weston relates . . .

After I had visited several other places, I sought hospitality once at the house of a certain Catholic. He was a very old man, his hair completely white. He was at least an octogenarian. Before Henry VIII destroyed and did away with the monasteries, he had been in the employment of the abbey of Glastonbury. . . . In addition to other things which the old man was able to seize and save, as it were, from the conflagration was a certain cross, venerable and hallowed not so much for its material interest – though it was worked with gold and valuable gems – as because it encased the remains of revered saints. Its principal relic was one of the nails with which our Saviour Christ was fastened to the Cross, and an almost immemorial tradition held that it had been brought to England by St Joseph of Arimathea and his companions. . . . The old man's house was three or four miles from the ancient monastery, but barely a mile from the place which, according to tradition, St Joseph of Arimathea and his companions had chosen for their dwelling.[1] This was on a high hill, and its old foundations and broken fragments of masonry can be seen there to-day. He told me how occasionally he would visit it out of piety and devotion, climbing up, not on his feet, but on his knees; and how he would take with him the cross and the reliquary containing the nail – 'my protection,' he called it, 'against the molestation of spirits.' Indeed it was possible to hear there the groanings, sighs and wailing voices of people in distress, so that he thought it must be a kind of approach or vestibule for souls passing into the pains of Purgatory. As a constant religious ceremony he kept a lamp suspended and always burning in a

[1] Somebody has made a mistake about the distances.

part of the house which looked towards the hill.

2

Glastonbury had ceased to be Catholic. Yet for a while the Catholic mythos lingered. It even grew, like hair on a murdered man. Last, or next to last, of the legends was the tale of the Holy Thorn.

The Thorn was known in the Middle Ages: the doggerel *Joseph of Armathia* mentions it. There is no sign that it was specially venerated, or that anything in particular was asserted about its origin. Abbot Bere's fostering of the cult of Joseph, however, revived interest in the Abbey's beginnings on the very eve of its ending. Popular fancy seems to have adopted the Thorn just before the dissolution, and never to have let it go. There stood the tree on Wearyall Hill, a tall tree with a double trunk, faithfully blossoming at Christmas. Botanists and curiosity-seekers speculated from time to time: William Turner in 1562, Camden in 1594, Gerard in 1597; and meanwhile the country folk revered it. To the rising Puritan faction such archaic superstition was monstrous. When Elizabeth was still queen, one zealot scaled the hill with a hatchet and assaulted the larger of the two trunks. He cut it through, all but a sliver, and it crashed to the ground. Then he began to hack at the smaller trunk. But he aimed clumsily. The axe rebounded and hurt his leg; a chip flew up into his eye, so that he never had perfect sight again. He abandoned the undertaking. It is uncertain whether he represented himself afterwards as a penitent, or as a martyr in the cause of truth.

The not-quite-separated trunk lay on the earth, and apparently continued to bear blossoms for several years. By doing so it attracted still more attention. People thronged to visit the tree from every quarter. They carved their names on the bark of the standing portion. They broke off twigs as souvenirs. Bristol merchants carried the leaves and blossoms on continental voyages and sold them abroad. James I paid an exorbitant amount for a cutting. His queen, Anne, was delighted to receive blossoms of the original as a Christmas gift from the Bishop of Bath and Wells. Eventually the trunk on the ground was chopped off altogether and carted away. The rest of the tree flourished until the Civil War. Cattle took shelter under its boughs and wore the soil bare all round it. A second and more dexterous Puritan felled it at last. The halo faded from the hill.

Only in this late phase had any serious writer taken note of the Thorn as more than a botanical freak. In 1645 a clergyman, John Eachard, cited it as proof that Jesus was born on 25th December.

> I knowe that England doe keep the right day that Christ was borne on, above all the Nations of Christendome, because we have a miracle hath often been seene in England upon that day, for we have a tree in England, called the Holy Thorne, by Glassenbury Abbey, nigh the Bathe, which on the 25 day of December, which is our Christmasse day, hath constantly blossomed; which the people of that place have received from antiquitie, that it was that kind of thorne, wherewith Christ was crowned.

Even here, the story about St Joseph's staff has not yet made its way into print.

Trees grown from transplanted cuttings kept the marvel alive. Dr Plot, in 1677, referred to the Thorn and added a little more:

> Some take it for a miraculous remembrance of the birth of Christ, first planted by Joseph of Arimathea.

But the definitive version with the wonderful staff in it dates only from 1716, as a bit of local lore retailed by an innkeeper to the Catholic antiquarian Charles Eyston. Its oral form is probably not much older. It is no part of the authentic tradition.

In 1752-3, after England's adoption of the Gregorian calendar had shifted the date of Christmas eleven days, crowds gathered at Glastonbury to see what the trees would do. Those who hoped for a miracle of adaptation were disappointed. The blossoms came out on the fifth of January. At this period the stump of the parent Thorn was still to be seen. By the end of the century somebody had removed it, and a certain John Clark put a monumental slab on the spot, four feet eight by two feet eight, with the inscription 'J. A. Anno D. XXXI.' The absurd date, A.D. 31, shows that Clark – in common with several of the later dreamers – favoured an account of St Joseph's mission based on a mis-reading of the Abbey's inscription, not on *De Antiquitate*. His monument had the air of a gravestone, writing 'finis' to the whole matter. In 1929, however, royal interest awoke again. King George V accepted a gift of winter blossoms, and the gift has been repeated to his successors.

The Reverend Mr Eachard, incidentally, was not alone in his attempted theological exploitation of Glastonbury. A few Anglicans, not among the wiser sort, had already tried to launch an anticipatory Oxford Movement based on the theory of a branch Church established alongside the Roman Church and co-equal in dignity. The Grail motif had returned on a lower level. Instead of Grail Christianity, these Elizabethans and Jacobeans experimented with Thorn Christianity. Their master was Archbishop Parker, whose treatise *On the Antiquity of the British Church* (the title sounds like a deliberate Malmesburian echo) appeared in 1572 as a counterblast to the papal denunciation of the Queen. A controversy raged between the Anglican John Hastings and the Jesuit Robert Persons. Persons retorted to the Anglican claim with a pamphlet entitled *The Three Conversions of England,* giving the legends a Roman interpretation. He himself had a curious link with Glastonbury. A convert, he was received into the Catholic Church by Father William Good, the author of that illuminating account of the Abbey in Whiting's day. Father Good's reminiscences of the spoliation would have been enough to convince Persons that the Church of England had no right to exploit the shrine which its founder had ruined. Another Catholic, Richard Broughton, cited a late legend about a visit to Britain by St Peter, and maintained that it proved the Petrine origin of the British Church. He conceded St Joseph, but said the Arimathean was only a 'contemplative.' At about this point responsible Anglicans retired from the useless argument. Usher gave an account of the Glastonbury legends, but attached little importance to them, and Stillingfleet rejected them altogether. Nevertheless, Parker's notion has never entirely perished. A Victorian book called *St Paul in Britain,* by R. W. Morgan, gave it a new form and has recently been reprinted.

On 22nd June, 1685, the citizens of Glastonbury watched the arrival of a remarkable person. He did not arrive alone; he came at the head of a military force. It was feebly armed, however, and in poor order. The leader himself was its most noticeable member. He had just begun styling himself King James the Second, in rivalry with the other James the Second in London. To the public at large he could never be anything but the Duke of Monmouth, son of the late King Charles by Lucy Walter. Had Charles secretly married her? He always denied it, and refused to recognise the Duke as his heir.

Monmouth was the hope of the extreme Whigs and uncompromising Protestants. He was popular, but not popular enough in the right quarters. While the parliamentary magnates had no love for the Catholic absolutist who sat on the throne, few of them were prepared to back Monmouth against him. The Duke's depressed army tramped to Glastonbury through pouring rain and camped in the Abbey, lighting fires to dry themselves.

One of the buildings, the Abbot's Kitchen, was still intact and actually used. It had become, of all things, a Quaker meeting-house. Monmouth hoped for much from the Quakers. Their local leader, Thomas Pheere, in a spirit far removed from the later pacifism of his religious society, had offered to collect a force in the Polden area. They would come armed only with clubs, but at least they would come. The Duke dated a dispatch from 'our camp at Glastonbury, 23rd June, 1685, the first year of our reign,' authorising the club-men to 'disarm, seize, take, prosecute, and kill all manner of persons that shall appear in arms for the Duke of York' – viz. James II. He then headed for Bristol, but shied away on the advance of the royalist army. The second of July saw him at Glastonbury again. Here he expected to recruit a thousand club-men, but the too sanguine Quaker only brought him a hundred and sixty. They, together with the rest of the rebel force, were swept away at the Battle of Sedgemoor.

The work of suppression and retribution was placed in

the hands of Judge Jeffreys. He was not a Catholic, but in his brutal pacification of the West Country he was the approved agent of a Catholic master, to whom, indeed, he remained loyal when few other important persons did. As a result the two became linked in the public hatred as Popery in Practice, and the Protestantism of Somerset was firmly established for many years.

The huge Gothic wreck at Glastonbury slid into deeper dereliction, signifying nothing, and cared for by nobody. Enmity during this period was sometimes active. The marks of Guy Fawkes bonfires, deliberately heaped up against the Lady Chapel, are visible yet, and in 1714 the zealot who had acquired possession blew up part of the same chapel with a bomb. Stukely describes the situation just afterwards: 'As yet there are magnificent ruins, but within a lustrum of years a Presbyterian tenant has made more barbarous havoc there than had been since the dissolution; for every week a pillar or buttress, a window jamb or an angle of fine hewn stone is sold to the best bidder. Whilst I was there they were excoriating St Joseph's Chapel for that purpose, and the squared stones were laid up by lots in the Abbot's Kitchen; the rest goes to paving yards and stalls for cattle, or to the highway.'

Though the ruin was too big to slip out of men's consciousness altogether, it survived under the Hanoverian sovereigns as an enormous curiosity, a rather bewildering local asset, not to be thought of in its half-forgotten institutional capacity. When we encounter Glastonbury in the news of the period, or in the non-historical literature, we encounter anything rather than an abbey.

By an odd irony, it was a papist who first re-directed attention to it. Charles Eyston, a Berkshire Jacobite squire, visited Glastonbury in 1716 and compiled a quite pleasant little 'Monument.' This was used by later antiquarians such as Hearn, and by Richard Warner, a clergyman who published a chaotic but valuable *History of the Abbey of Glaston* in 1826 (prefixed with page upon page of arguments against Catholic emancipation). From Eyston's time forward, indeed, Glastonbury was safely on the map for the more educated part of the public; but not usually as a home of monks.

Near the bottom of the pathway that leads up the Tor, they still exhibit a spring of water and a well called Chalice Well. Some stonework has prompted queer conjectures. Sir Flinders Petrie had a theory about an Egyptian trading post. The spring and the well, at any rate, were there in the eighteenth century, and a slight iron impregnation was supposed to give the water an exceptional character. In 1750 a Mr Matthew Chancellor deposed in a sworn statement that he had suffered from asthma for thirty years; that he had dreamt he would be cured by drinking the water; that, accordingly, he had taken a quarter of a pint each Sunday morning for seven consecutive Sundays; and that his asthma was gone. The rumour spread through all England. In May ten thousand visitors came to drink or bathe, and a pump room was put up. It should be remarked that there was no explicit suggestion of a miracle of the Christian type, no anticipation of Lourdes. Mr Chancellor had created a new spa, in a newsworthy spot, which happened to coincide with an old shrine. That was all. Doctors analysed the water and ridiculed the whole excitement. It soon blew over.

Pre-Romantic poetry of the school exemplified by Gray might have been expected to glance at Glastonbury, and so it did. The above-average Laureate Dr Warton composed *Arthur's Grave*, a bit of metrical history based directly or indirectly on Giraldus Cambrensis. It tells how Henry II was entertained in Wales by the bards. A bard rises to sing the passing of Arthur:

> When he fell, an elfin queen,
> All in secret, and unseen,
> O'er the fainting hero threw
> Her mantle of ambrosial blue;
> And bade her spirits bear him far,
> In Merlin's agate-axled car,
> To her green isle's enamelled steep,
> Far in the navel of the deep. . . .
> There, renewed the vital spring,
> Again he reigns a mighty king. . . .
> Thence to Britain shall return,
> (If right prophetic rolls I learn,)
> Borne on Victory's spreading plume,
> His ancient sceptre to resume.

Another bard rises and contradicts the first.

> When Arthur bowed his haughty crest,
> No princess, veiled in azure vest,
> Snatched him by Merlin's potent spell,

In groves of golden bliss to dwell. . . .
But when he fell, with wingèd speed,
His champions, on a milk-white steed,
From the battle's hurricane,
Bore him to Joseph's tower'd fane,
In the fair isle of Avalon;
There, with chanted orison,
And the long blaze of tapers clear,
The stolèd fathers met the bier. . . .
The faded tomb, with honour due,
'Tis thine, O Henry, to renew.

Whatever its literary merits, this is an excellent statement of the case. Warton delineates the rival stories with a sure touch.

Blake's poem *And did those feet in ancient time* (a true alternative National Anthem) is doubtless the finest piece of writing which Glastonbury has so far inspired. Characteristically, Blake uses one of the strangest fancies of all. No medieval Benedictine would have dared affirm such a thing: it was left to the Age of Reason to devise it. This fancy, of course, is the supposition that Christ himself came to Glastonbury as a youth, with Joseph of Arimathea. It is presumably based on two passages in the early historians – the reference in the *Life of Dunstan* to a church 'not built by art of man, but prepared by God himself,' and the vision of St David in William of Malmesbury, where Christ declares that he has already dedicated the Old Church to his mother. From these texts taken together it is possible to extract the notion that the Incarnate God visited Britain and built the church, before beginning his public ministry.

Where did this fable come from? I do not know. There are said to be some wild scraps of Cornish and Mendip folk-lore with a bearing on it, and there is certainly a connection with eighteenth-century academic extravaganzas about the druids. By embedding it in his verse, Blake ensured that he would be misunderstood; most people who read or sing his lines take them in a not very lucid metaphorical sense, because the literal sense is too far-fetched to occur to them. Yet Blake's instinct was sound. Glastonbury is England's only real national shrine, and a Glastonbury legend, however unlikely, is one of the few adequate themes for a national hymn.

After Blake, Tennyson. It is through his *Idylls of the King*, directly or indirectly, that most modern readers have become aware of the Holy Grail. Early in his career he seems to have meditated an Arthurian épic. But he gave it up. The Victorians had less reason than we have to believe in Arthur, and Tennyson was too conscientious to fake his history. The *Idylls,* when they appeared, were loosely-connected episodes founded on Malory, and in his epilogue addressed to the Queen the author declared them to be allegorical. The good British legend was a tale

> New-old, and shadowing Sense at War with Soul,
> Ideal manhood closed in real man,
> Rather than that grey king . . .

Such a view was in keeping with the antecedents of Grail romance, and in keeping, also, with Tennyson's own philosophy. He himself belonged to the Gnostic-Manichee tradition. He saw the soul as a pre-existing entity entrapped in the prison of the body, which (as Darwin and others pointed out) was a base thing full of the brutish promptings of an animal ancestry. In his *In Memoriam* phase Tennyson had called upon Man to 'move upward, working out the beast, and let the ape and tiger die.' Later he became more doubtful as to whether this movement could be executed, even by the 'crowning race' to which, as a liberal, he looked forward. The theme is central to the *Idylls.*

Arthur's realm, created by the extermination of heathens and wild beasts, is the earthly City of God or Christian society in so far as this can ever be realised. The code of chivalry inspires it. The Round Table is a quasi-religious order. Tennyson, with some skill, brings the conception to a focus in his sole major innovation – the stress on Christian marriage, which is conspicuously lacking in all earlier treatments. The sacrament of matrimony is the Church's supreme effort to spiritualise and discipline the unruly flesh. It is the basic institution of the Arthurian order.

The King reigns; and the City of God is tested; and it fails. For two reasons. The Queen commits adultery with Sir Lancelot, the most splendid of all the knights. Their fatal example undoes the chastity of the Table and brings the ideal of marriage into contempt. Moral unity is sapped from below. The beast returns. But at the same time, the aspirations of the spirit render it impatient of matter. Forsaking Camelot, many of the knights ride out in quest of the

Grail, and the best and holiest never come back. Moral unity is shattered above also. Precisely in so far as the spirit is pure, it deserts its post. Only the King's prestige holds the realm together for a while longer. But his own legitimacy is doubtful (in other words no earthly voice can speak with a sufficiently sure authority), and his power at last disintegrates. Thus the *Idylls* conclude in something like Gnostic pessimism. The way of salvation – Galahad's way – is simply to escape from an irredeemable world.

The *Holy Grail* idyll itself has fine passages, but is rather cryptic and baffling. Tennyson unifies the legends, indeed, with a concise charm unapproached by previous writers. He introduces one of the former Grail-seekers as a monk, retired from the court. A brother asks him about the Grail.

> 'What is it?
> The phantom of a cup that comes and goes?'
> 'Nay, monk! What phantom?' answer'd Percivale.
> 'The cup, the cup itself, from which Our Lord
> Drank at the last sad supper with his own.
> This, from the blessed land of Aromat –
> After the day of darkness, when the dead
> Went wandering o'er Moriah – the good saint
> Arimathaean Joseph, journeying brought
> To Glastonbury, where the winter thorn
> Blossoms at Christmas, mindful of the Lord.
> And there awhile it bode; and if a man
> Could touch or see it, he was heal'd at once,
> By faith, of all his ills. But then the times
> Grew to such evil that the holy cup
> Was caught away to Heaven, and disappeared.'
> To whom the monk: 'From our old books I know
> That Joseph came of old to Glastonbury,
> And there the heathen prince, Arviragus,
> Gave him an isle of marsh whereon to build;
> And there he built with wattles from the marsh
> A little lonely church.'

This is straightforward. The Grail is simply a superlative holy relic. But in its apparition before the Table it has become transfigured:

> All at once, as there we sat, we heard
> A cracking and a riving of the roofs,

And rending, and a blast, and overhead
Thunder, and in the thunder was a cry,
And in the blast there smote along the hall
A beam of light seven times more clear than day;
And down the long beam stole the Holy Grail,
All cover'd over with a luminous cloud,
And none might see who bore it, and it past.

The catastrophic adventures that ensue are plainly meant to
be symbolic. The symbolism, however, is none too clear.
What is perfectly clear is the King's summing-up, in a
decaying Camelot.

'Was I too dark a prophet when I said
To those who went upon the Holy Quest,
That most of them would follow wandering fires,
Lost in a quagmire? – lost to me and gone,
And left me gazing at a barren board,
And a lean Order – scarce return'd a tithe –
And out of those to whom the vision came
My greatest hardly will believe he saw;
Another hath beheld it afar off,
And leaving human wrongs to right themselves,
Cares but to pass into the silent life.
And one hath had the vision face to face,
And now his chair desires him here in vain,
However they may crown him otherwhere.'

There is no bridging the gulf between Earth and Heaven. It
is a mournful moral, mournfully reinforced by Tennyson's
ill-informed undervaluation of the 'silent life.'

Our sketch of this non-monastic or anti-monastic literature would be inadequate without an allusion to *A Glastonbury Romance,* by John Cowper Powys. It is a colossal and
frankly pagan novel in which the author draws upon everything (and a good deal more than everything) that is known
about the pre-Christian Grail.

4

The Abbey site passed through several changes of ownership. In 1559 Queen Elizabeth granted it to Sir Peter Carew. On Carew's death it went to the Earl of Sussex; his brother sold it to William Stone; Stone sold it in 1596 to the Earl of Devonshire. The Devonshire family was the only one which kept it for long. In 1733 Thomas Bladen acquired it. During the eighteenth century the monastic lands were further split up, and at the beginning of the twentieth the Abbey itself belonged to a Mr Stanley Austin.

By this time the scanty ruins were in a tumbledown and dangerous state. The two remaining piers of the central tower were threatening to fall. The Lady Chapel was crumbling. Debris and creepers had gained ground at every point. To Austin his extraordinary property was a white elephant. Early in 1907 he announced that he was offering it for auction. On 6th June, amid rumours of a transplanting to America, the ruins were knocked down (if the metaphor is permissible) to Ernest Jardine of Nottingham for £30,000. Jardine was wealthy enough to complete the purchase, but he did not actually want the property. His bid was a subterfuge. Very shortly afterwards Dr Kennion, the Bishop of Bath and Wells, announced that he had a private arrangement with Jardine for re-sale to the Church of England.

Dr Kennion had not yet found the money. Having presented his *fait accompli* – or *presqu' accompli* – he launched a fund. King Edward VII, Queen Alexandra, and the Prince of Wales (later George V) subscribed. In October 1908 the Church of England took possession. The following June, in the presence of the Prince of Wales, the deeds were ceremoniously handed over to the Archbishop of Canterbury. Ownership was vested henceforth in the Bath and Wells Diocesan Trust. The board of trustees proceeded quickly to carry out emergency jobs of repairing and shoring-up. Rubbish and climbing plants were removed. The ground was levelled. The entrance on the High Street was blocked, and a new one was made adjacent to the almshouses of St Mary Magdalene: here, at a price, it is still possible to push through the turnstile into the spacious grounds, and pick up books and pictures from a variously-stocked souvenir booth.

While the trustees themselves had no plan for excavations, they acceded promptly to a proposal on the subject from the Somerset Archæological Society. Work began before the close of 1908 under the direction of Frederick Bligh Bond, a Bristol architect. His first move was to settle a doubt about the eastern end of the great church. Several antiquarians had questioned the existence of Abbot Bere's Edgar Chapel. Bond, however, soon uncovered a massive end wall four feet six inches thick, and side walls six feet six inches thick, with stalwart buttresses obviously designed to support an imposing superstructure. There were bits of a vaulted roof with panelled fanwork and moulded ribs, recalling the Henry VII Chapel at Westminster. These finds bore out the statements of early writers giving the total length of the church, including the Lady Chapel, as about 580 feet. A chapel of St John to the west made up the full length of 594 feet.

During the digging an ancient trench was discovered, filled with bones and broken pottery. Arthur Bulleid and H. St. George Gray, the archæologists who had resurrected the Lake Village, were asked for their opinions. Gray described the pottery as 'a rude, brittle, hard-baked quality of earthenware containing a large percentage of small grains of quartz, and typical of late Norman or medieval times.' Apparently Bere had built on top of a refuse dump.

Surprises like this were to prove characteristic of the whole project. Near the western end of the great church, as work proceeded, the excavators unearthed a red terra-cotta medallion. On one side it bore a cross and the sacred monogram IHS, badly battered. On the other it bore the date 1105 in Roman numerals, 'MCV,' with stars over the M and the V, and above them a hand held out in an attitude of blessing with two fingers extended. In the centre of the hand was a little round indentation probably meant to hold a jewel. The natural explanation of the medallion was that it was made to commemorate the founding of Herlewin's church. But why the indentation? Was it an allusion to the legend about St David and the wounding of his hand by Christ? If so, it was oddly cryptic.

Evidence of burials were found everywhere; to this day you can pick up bones from almost any hole or trench in the Abbey grounds. By the south-western extremity of the nave, hard up against the wall, an astonishing skeleton was revealed lying on its back in the clay. It belonged to a tall elderly man, about six feet three inches in height, with a finely developed head. His right wrist had been broken and set clumsily, and his lower teeth were missing. What was most curious about the interment was that the skull was carefully framed in a sort of stone horseshoe. The horseshoe's arms curved in to the lower jaw. With the flesh still on, the fit must have been very snug indeed. No one had any convincing reason to offer, and the likeliest date – thirteenth or fourteenth century – seemed to rule out any primitive ritual. The finding of somewhat similar Roman interments at Bath prompted a conjecture that the burial was much older than the pioneer investigators imagined. But it remained mysterious.

Once these things had begun to happen, all manner of local rumours revived. Most of them concerned underground passages and hidden treasure. There were three principal stories, or groups of stories, about the subterranean feats of the monks. The boldest legend averred flatly that they had burrowed all the way to the top of the Tor. Nobody knew why they should have done so, and this particular legend remained a legend, never checked because it never struck anyone as worth checking.

Other tales asserted (of course with an insinuation about monastic morals) that a passage led from inside the Abbey to the cellars of the Pilgrims' Inn, or to some house outside the walls. The cellar version was the most circumstantial, and traces of a small orifice appeared to confirm it. In June 1911 Bligh Bond found the clue he was looking for, in a back number of a magazine describing the Inn's role as a resort of pilgrims during the fifteenth century. A search was made, with the landlord's co-operation, and the searchers detected the outline of a low archway in the cellar wall. Removal of stones at this point revealed an empty space behind, and a tunnel going south-west toward the Abbey. A workman groped along it for twenty feet, but a brick wall blocked his progress, and the destination had to be left in doubt.

Another passage was discovered leading out of the basement of a house nearby. An antiquated lamp lay on the floor. The owner, however, had the entry sealed up and forbade further exploration.

Finally, there were strangely precise reports about a tunnel running south from the well by St Joseph's Chapel. As with the supposed Tor passage, its purpose was obscure, and opinions differed as to the terminal point. The well itself, with the small passage-way leading to it, had been rediscovered in Warner's time, giving rise to speculations which he records. But a notion existed that the passage went farther. The curator of the museum told in picturesque detail about a long tunnel leading to underground rooms used as a treasury.

The secret, he avowed, had never been simultaneously entrusted to more than three monks, and after the dissolution it was entirely lost, except as a rumour. Down in that Aladdin's cave you might still chance upon the lost golden gates of the sanctuary in the great church.

Senior citizens of the town stepped forward to corroborate the curator's words. A venerable lady remembered how, as a girl, she had tended sheep in the Abbey grounds, and ventured into a high stone corridor with iron brackets in the walls to hold candles. Her contemporaries added that those sheep of hers were the clue to the mystery: the entrance had disappeared because lambs used to wander underground, and so the owner had walled it up.

The excavators dug a trench ten feet deep immediately south of the chapel wall. They saw no sign of stonework. A change in the soil implied the bare possibility that a tunnel had been filled in, but that was all. Their impression was that the ex-shepherdess and her friends had simply remembered the passage-way leading to the well, which had once been more narrowly enclosed and mysterious-looking. However, a workman's account of the filling in of a short underground corridor near the choir – more or less confirmed – showed that the rival theory could not be absolutely dismissed.

As for the minor 'buried treasure' stories, the root of these was the fact that Abbot Whiting and his monks undoubtedly did try to hide money and plate from the royal commissioners. Glastonbury had always believed that the lay owners never found it all. But every quest proved a wild goose chase. That was not to be wondered at. Almost everything in the Abbey had been broken and rifled. The coffins had been carried away and turned into cisterns; the bones had been scattered. The only recorded instance of treasure trove had occurred much earlier than Bligh Bond's activities, in the eighteenth century. A man had tried to sell an old mantelpiece taken from the porter's lodge of the Abbey. The prospective purchaser offered three shillings, the owner held out for three and fourpence. After the mantelpiece had been lying in the road for years, the owner's daughter got a workman to saw it up for stairs, and inside they found a hundred gold coins from the reigns of Edward III and Richard II! Modern searchers failed to equal this haul.

In general, the attempts to utilise folk-memory as a means

to discoveries bore no fruit worth mentioning. Bligh Bond, however, had already resorted to memory of another kind. He revealed that he had directed his programme by spiritual-istic methods, using automatic writing to draw on the dis-embodied reminiscences of various monks at the Abbey. By 1922 the archæological project was sliding fast toward a serio-comic disrepute. Accordingly the Dean of the Wells, Joseph Armitage Robinson, intervened. We have met this Dean already. His books are the foundation of all serious recent writing about Glastonbury. Anxious for the good name of a place very dear to him, he dismissed Bond and called a halt to the excavations. Trenches were filled in and land-marks removed. Six years were to elapse before another ex-ploratory spade entered the Abbey's soil.

Speculation and spiritualism continued to browse in the Avalonian pasture. Jessie Weston's anthropological study of the Grail, poetically applied in Eliot's *Waste Land,* helped to foster interest even though Miss Weston refused to allow Glastonbury's importance. Verses generated by the automatic writing of other agents professed to give the early history of the Abbey. Mrs K. Maltwood charted her Temple of the Stars.[1]

5

If this book has seemed to neglect Glastonbury town, that is only because the annals of towns belong to a different kind of history. Glastonbury to-day is a village that has grown without fatally defacing itself. It has its beauties and its blots like any other old English town. There are housing developments, not very extensive, and one or two well-run factories.

The significance of the legends and history for the present inhabitants is hard to assess. Most certainly there is no risk of oblivion. Agreeable eccentrics and serious collectors of infor-mation dot the whole neighbourhood. Renewed programmes of excavation, some of them American-subsidised, have con-tinued to attract public attention and inspire articles in the local paper. Spectacles like the Avalon Constitutional Club, the Avalon Basket Works, and the Avalon Housing Estate,

[1] See further Appendix B.

may provoke a smile; they show that the traditions are not forgotten. St Dunstan's Garage appropriately recalls the mind to practical historic realities. Rooms in the George and Pilgrims Inn have monastic names. There are museums, stalls and shops, where genuine relics may be inspected and highly imaginative books may be bought. The National Trust owns the Tor.

Since the turn of the century Glastonbury has recovered some shreds of importance as a Christian centre. The Church of England keeps the ruins in tidy condition. Pilgrimages have been resumed. To Anglicans, however, the place is ambiguous. They do not attempt to defend the dissolution, but the fact of the dissolution is inescapable. Nothing can make Glastonbury a Protestant shrine. The commendable course often followed is to stress the legends, the earlier days, and the national aspect.

Catholicism has returned too. A small church facing the ruins serves a parish of about three hundred. Beside it is the convent of a teaching order. A pilgrimage in July is a major fixture in the Clifton diocesan calendar. Among its principal organisers was an architect who served his articles in the office of Bligh Bond. Largely through his initiative a beginning has been made on a restored shrine of Our Lady of Glastonbury, with a gentle-eyed, ethereal statue imitated from the rose-bearing figure in the Abbey seal. The main emphasis of the pilgrimage has frequently lain on the Tudor martyrdoms. As long as this is so, Glastonbury's unique character will be least appreciated by that portion of the practising Christian community which has the most reason for interest.

Last of the Glastonbury monks, it is said, was Austin Ringwode. He lived in a cottage near the Abbey till 1587, in prayer and fasting and vigil. People believed that he was endowed with a gift of prophecy. On his deathbed he uttered his parting word to the world: *The Abbey will one day be repaired and rebuilt for the like worship which has ceased; and then peace and plenty will for a long time abound.*

Appendix A

THE GRAIL AND 'BARTHOLOMEW'

By universal consent Grail romance owes a debt to the New Testament apocrypha: specifically, to the *Acts of Pilate*. The same body of literature includes a scrappy production entitled *The Questions of Bartholomew*. St Jerome, in the fourth century, condemns as spurious a Gospel attributed to the same apostle, and a later papal decree condemns it again. In the *Questions* we probably have a mangled version of part of it. The manuscripts, in Greek, Latin and Slavonic, are widely scattered. They all cover a brief period after the Resurrection, when the risen Christ is instructing Bartholomew and others at a place called Chairoudec or Cherubim or Cheltoura (readings vary), 'the place of truth.' Here are some extracts from the second chapter.

1. Now the apostles were in the place with Mary.

2. And Bartholomew came and said unto Peter and Andrew and John: Let us ask her that is highly favoured how she conceived the incomprehensible, or how she bare him that cannot be carried, or how she brought forth so much greatness. But they doubted to ask her.

3. Bartholomew therefore said' unto Peter: Thou that art the chief, and my teacher, draw near and ask her. But Peter said to John: Thou art a virgin and undefiled, and thou must ask her.

4. And as they all doubted and disputed, Bartholomew came near unto her with a cheerful countenance and said to her: Thou that art highly favoured, the tabernacle of the Most High, unblemished, we, even all the apostles, ask thee to tell us how thou didst conceive the incomprehensible, or how thou didst bear him that cannot be carried, or how thou didst bring forth so much greatness.

5. But Mary said unto them: Ask me not concerning this mystery. If I should begin to tell you, fire will issue forth

out of my mouth and consume the world.

6. But they continued yet the more to ask her. And she, for she could not refuse to hear the apostles, said: Let us stand up in prayer.

They disagree as to precedence. Mary asks Peter to pray, but the apostles insist that she must do it herself.

13. Then Mary stood up before them and spread out her hands toward the heavens and began to speak thus:

Elphuë Zarethra Charboum Nemioth Melitho Thra-
boutha
Mephnounos Chemiath Aroura Maridōn Elisōn
Marmiadōn Seption Hesaboutha Ennouna Saktinos
Athoōr Belelam Opheōth Abō Chrasar.

(Or, according to the Latin text:
Helfoith Alaritha arbar Neniotho Melitho Tarasunt
Chanabonos Umia Theirura Marada Seliso   19½
Heliphomar Mabon Saruth Gefutha Enunnas Sacinos
Thatis Etelelam Tetheo abocia Rusar.)

Which is in the Greek tongue, O God the exceeding great and all-wise . . .

(a long invocation, then –)

Son of the Father, thou whom the seven heavens hardly contained, but who wast well-pleased to be contained without pain in me, thou that art thyself the full word of the Father in whom all things came to be: give glory to thine exceeding great name, and bid me to speak before thy holy apostles.

No importance attaches to the alleged translation; it is a mere flourish. Mary now bids them sit on the ground. There is a grotesque passage in which she asks them to sit close in case the revelation should cause her to fly asunder.

15. And when they had so done she began to say: When I abode in the temple of God and received my food from an angel, on a certain day there appeared unto me one in the

297

likeness of an angel, but his face was incomprehensible . . ,

16. And straightway the veil of the temple was rent and there was a very great earthquake, and I fell upon the earth, for I was not able to endure the sight of him.

17. But he put his hand beneath me and raised me up, and I looked up into heaven and there came a cloud of dew and sprinkled me from the head to the feet, and he wiped me with his robe:

18. And said unto me: Hail, thou that art highly favoured, the chosen vessel, grace inexhaustible. And he smote his garment upon the right hand and there came a very great piece of bread, and he set it upon the altar of the temple and did eat of it first himself, and gave unto me also.

19. And again he smote his garment upon the left hand and there came a very great cup full of wine: and he set it upon the altar of the temple and did drink of it first himself, and gave also unto me. And I beheld and saw the bread and the cup whole as they were.

20. And he said unto me: Yet three years, and I will send my word unto thee and thou shalt conceive a son, and through him shall the whole creation be saved. Peace be unto thee, my beloved, and my peace shall be with thee continually.

21. And when he had so said he vanished away from mine eyes, and the temple was restored as it had been before.

22. And as she was saying this, fire issued out of her mouth; and the world was at the point to come to an end: but Jesus appeared quickly and said to Mary: Utter not this mystery, or this day my whole creation will come to an end. And the apostles were taken with fear lest haply the Lord should be wroth with them.

'Bartholomew' is almost impossible to square with St Luke, and some of his minor touches are merely extravagant. Yet surely he brings us close to the Holy Grail. What the apostles seek is, precisely, the truth about the Incarnation as known to Mary. St John, whom Peter deputes to extract the secret, is held to qualify by virtue of his virginity – like Galahad. Mary demurs, but yields, and utters twenty-one or twenty-two mysterious words.[1] Then she begins to tell a story closely connecting the Incarnation with the Eucharist. She mentions two angels; or rather, one angel, and One in the likeness of an angel. (Gawain saw two angels in the Grail.) She introduces a divine cup. There is a sudden blaze, as in some of the Grail manifestations. Christ suppresses the climax. The unfathomable act of the Holy Spirit which determined the event must remain undivulged.

Supposing that a twelfth-century author took this book seriously, at least for symbolic or poetical purposes. A student of Celtic matters might well have done so, for the 'Dionysian' treatises, which an Irishman translated, bestow on pseudo-Bartholomew a pseudo-apostolic endorsement. What would such an author have made of this Annunciation? There is not much room for doubt. The essential concept – and it really is an arresting concept, far above the usual level of apocryphal fancy – is that the Son of God entered the world and the Virgin's womb by an anticipation of the sacrament. His eucharistic presence was prior in time to his ordinary human presence. He came as bread and wine consecrated in heaven by the power of his eternal priesthood; and Mary, eating and drinking, conceived, or was materially prepared to do so.

More is involved than a simple anticipation of the Eucharist. To state the distinction in crude terms, holy communion does not, under normal conditions, induce pregnancy. What explanation would occur to a mind imaginative enough to adopt the story, yet sharp enough to probe it? Catholic dogma seems to rule out any idea that Christ could have

[1] Probably twenty-two. It is more likely that the Greek copyist dropped a word than that the Latin copyist added one. The number is remarkable, since the Tarot fortune-telling pack, in which the Grail hallows are the four suits, has a series of precisely twenty-two extraneous trumps. Occultists have maintained that these cards correspond to the twenty-two letters of the Hebrew alphabet, and symbolise a Great Secret. Charles Williams exploited the belief in one of his supernatural thrillers, *The Greater Trumps*. The same cards make an appearance in Eliot's *Waste Land*.

At the close of the *Divine Comedy* (see page 226), why exactly does Dante allude to circle-squaring? His lacking 'principle' is the value of *pi*, the ratio of circumference to diameter. The impossibility of working this out was not demonstrated till 1882. For practical purposes the standard approximation is 22/7. In other words, if the diameter is given by the holy number 7, the circumference is 22.

been more fully present in the elements given to Mary than he is in those normally consecrated at Mass. He is always there in his entirety under the appearances of bread and wine. The added property could only have been a power of physical operation, superimposed in the consecratory act. Through this power came results perceptible to the senses. The sacramental Christ turned into an actual human organism.

The substratum of Christian Grail romance, I would suggest, is a real or fictitious cult derived from 'Bartholomew' or from a common source. The Grail is the heaven-descended vessel itself, faithfully preserved by the Holy Family and used by Jesus at the Last Supper. The Secret Words are the twenty-two in the apocryphal text. The Great Sacrament is that which was administered to Mary. It will be recalled that the Waste Land of the romances can only revive if the knight asks a crucial question: 'Whom does the Grail serve?' Or more accurately: 'Who is served from the Grail?' This query seems to be a legacy of the pagan myth, and no one has managed to guess the answer. If 'Bartholomew' is once admitted the question becomes what it obviously should be, the solvent of the mystery. For the Grail is the communion-cup of one special person. The answer 'Mary' reveals the hidden key which is hinted at but never expressed. The Grail can now be expounded, and once Our Lady is discovered, the spiritual Waste Land bursts into life. Quite apart from any mystical meaning, the last fact would have struck any observer of twelfth-century European culture as evident. The three damsels who attend the Grail, and can never be accurately counted, may well typify the earthly trinity of Marys (the Virgin herself, the Magdalene, and the mother of James) whom early apocryphal and heretical writers connect and confuse very curiously – notably in another fragment of 'Bartholomew.' *Matthew* xxvii. 55-61 associates two of them with St Joseph and the tomb.

A fact which conceivably has a bearing on Grail romance is that the Syriac and Armenian texts of Eusebius's *Church History* preserve an eastern tradition that the man chosen to fill the place of Judas (*Acts* i. 23-6) was called Bartholomew. Matthias is his scriptural name. It would be possible, if implausible, to take the second Bartholomew as the protagonist of the *Questions*; Christian literature has known much worse confusions. If this identity were part of the legend, it would explain why the Grail-keeper, the inheritor of the Bartholomaean mystery, has to sit in Judas's chair at the table.

BIBLIOGRAPHICAL NOTE

The standard modern works are those of Joseph Armitage Robinson: *Somerset Historical Essays, The Times of St Dunstan,* and *Two Glastonbury Legends*. I personally feel bound to dissent from the conclusions of the last-named, but all serious study of Glastonbury must base itself on these books.

The history of the medieval Abbey has never been adequately treated, because too many documents have remained in manuscript. Dom Aelred Watkin's three-volume transcript *The Great Chartulary of Glastonbury Abbey* (1947-56) goes far toward supplying the need, but it is doubtful whether a satisfactory history can be compiled without a good deal of further research.

Of the various articles cited in the main bibliography, those of Clark H. Slover in *Speculum* deserve special praise.

Much of the recent Glastonbury literature has unfortunately a crankish flavour. Bligh Bond's *Architectural Handbook* is fairly sound; his excursions into the occult (*The Gate of Remembrance, The Company of Avalon, etc.*) have little more than psychological interest. A caveat must also be entered against the Reverend L. S. Lewis, Vicar of Glastonbury in the 1920s and 30s. He perpetrated two volumes of fable and conjecture which ran to several editions. Ardent, painstaking, and more nearly right in spirit than many a wiser author, he spoiled both books by an utter inability or unwillingness to criticise evidence. He refused to concede that William of Malmesbury had been interpolated, preferring – it is a literary libel – to ascribe the weak, verbose additions to William himself. He assembled all the fancies about Caractacus's family and tried to combine these with *De Antiquitate* and the incompatible Vatican manuscript to get a complete history of the early missions. He even extorted evidence from a Roman drainpipe. When the guesswork has been discounted, Lewis's books have a certain value in suggesting lines of research. But anybody who follows these up will be distressed to find that Lewis's authorities are largely outmoded, and that he is capable of quoting a document with name, date and an air of scholarship, but with no hint whatever that all scholars regard the document as a forgery.

It is interesting to note that Mr Christopher Hollis's first book was a collection of essays entitled *Glastonbury and England*. Violently argumentative in tone (the author had not yet ceased from mental fight with his teachers at Oxford) it none the less embodied a good deal of intelligent study, and it is still worth reading.

To explore the literature covering the post-Reformation era is to discover a whole series of curious episodes, each deserving an essay in itself. Some have been glanced at in the text. The most accessible introduction is *Sedgemoor and Avalon*, by Desmond Hawkins, an excellent guide-book with plenty of historical matter.

BIBLIOGRAPHY

(*Proceedings* of Somersetshire Archaeological and Natural History Society abbreviated as *Proc. Som. Arch.*)

ADAM OF DOMERHAM, *Chronicle*, ed. T. Hearne. 1727
ADDISON, C. G., *History of the Knights Templars*. 1842.
ALCOCK, Leslie, *Arthur's Britain*. 1971.
——'*By South Cadbury is that Camelot . . .*' 1972.
ANDERSON, Flavia, *The Ancient Secret*. 1953.
Anglo-Saxon Chronicle, ed. G. N. Garmonsway. 1953.
ANON, *The History and Antiquities of Glastonbury*. 1794.
ANON, *The Lyfe of Joseph of Armathia*. 1520.
ANON, see also Maltwood.
ASHE, Geoffrey, *Camelot and the Vision of Albion*. 1971.
——*From Caesar to Arthur*. 1960.
——(ed.), *The Quest for Arthur's Britain*. 1968.

BARING-GOULD, S., and FISHER, John, *Lives of the British Saints*. 1911.
BASKERVILLE, Geoffrey, *English Monks and the Suppression of the Monasteries*. 1937.
BATTEN, E. Chisholm, 'The Holy Thorn of Glastonbury.' *Proc. Som. Arch.*, Vol. 26 (1880).
BAYNES, W. E. C., *St Joseph of Arimathea*. 1929.
BEDE, *History of the English Church and People*, ed. and trans. Leo Sherley-Price. 1955.
BETT, Henry, *Joachim of Flora*. 1931.
BOND, F. Bligh, *The Gate of Remembrance*. 1933.
——*Architectural Handbook of Glastonbury Abbey*. 1920.
BREWER, J. I., and GAIRDNER, James, *Letters and Papers of the Reign of Henry VIII*. 1920-32.
BROMWICH, Rachel, *Trioedd Ynys Prydein* (i.e. the Welsh Triads, with translation and notes). 1961.
BULLEID, A., and GRAY, H., *The Glastonbury Lake Village*. 1911-19.

CARADOC OF LLANCARFAN, *Life of Gildas*. See Baring-Gould.
CARAMAN, Philip, *The Autobiography of William Weston*. 1955.
Catholic Encyclopedia, arts. 'Glastonbury,' 'Grail'.
CHADWICK, Nora K., *The Age of the Saints in the Early Celtic Church*. 1961.

——*Studies in Early British History*. 1954.

Chambers's Encyclopedia, art. 'Grail.'

CHAMBERS, E. K., *Arthur of Britain*. 1927.

COBURN, K. (ed.), *The Philosophical Lectures of Samuel Taylor Coleridge*. 1949.

COLLINGWOOD, R. G., and MYRES, J., *Roman Britain and the English Settlements*. 1936.

COMFORT, W. W. (ed. and trans.), *The Quest of the Holy Grail*. 1926.

DENOMY, Alexander J., *The Heresy of Courtly Love*. 1947.

Dictionary of National Biography.

D'OYLEY, Elizabeth, *James, Duke of Monmouth*. 1938.

DUCKETT, Eleanor Shipley, *Anglo-Saxon Saints and Scholars*. 1947.

DUGGAN, Alfred, *Thomas Becket of Canterbury*. 1952.

Encyclopedia of Religion and Ethics, arts. 'Druids,' 'Grail.'

ESCHENBACH, Wolfram von, *Parzival*. Translated by Jessie L. Weston. 1894.

EVANS, Sebastian (ed. and trans.), *The High History of the Holy Graal* (i.e. *Perlesvaus*). 1910.

——*In Quest of the Holy Graal*. 1898.

FISHER, L. A., *The Mystic Vision in the Grail Legend and in the Divine Comedy*. 1917.

FRASER, Maxwell, *Wales*. 1952.

FRAZER, James, *The Golden Bough*. 1936.

FREEMAN, E. A., 'King Ine.' *Proc. Som. Arch.*, Vol. 20 (1874).

——Presidential Address. *Proc. Som. Arch.*, Vol. 26 (1880).

FRERE, Sheppard, *Britannia*. 1967.

GASQUET, F. A., *The Last Abbot of Glastonbury*. 1895.

GEOFFREY OF MONMOUTH, *History of the Kings of Britain*, ed. and trans. Lewis Thorpe. 1966.

——*Life of Merlin*. See Parry.

GEROULD, G. H., "King Arthur and Politics." *Speculum*, January 1927.

GIBBON, Edward, *The Decline and Fall of the Roman Empire*, ed. O. Smeaton. 1910.

GILDAS. See Giles and Hugh Williams.

GILES, J. A., *History of the Ancient Britons*. 1847.

——*Six Old English Chronicles*. 1878.

GIRALDUS CAMBRENSIS, *De Principis Instructione*. Rolls Series. 1891.

——*Speculum Ecclesiæ*. Rolls Series. 1873.

GOUGAUD, Louis, *Christianity in Celtic Lands*. 1932.

GRAVES, Robert, *The White Goddess*. 1952.

GRAY, L. H., 'The Origin of the Name of Glastonbury.' *Speculum*, January 1935.

GREEN, Emanuel, 'On some Flemish weavers settled at Glastonbury.' *Proc. Som. Arch.*, Vol. 26 (1880).

GREEN, J. R., 'Dunstan at Glastonbury.' *Proc. Som. Arch.*, Vol. 11 (1861-2).

——'Giso and Savaric.' *Proc. Som. Arch.* Vol. 12 (1863-4).

GRESWELL, William H. P., *Chapters on the Early History of Glastonbury Abbey*. 1909.

HERVEY, John, *The Plantagenets*. 1948.

HAWKES, Jacquetta, *A Guide to the Prehistoric and Roman Monuments in England and Wales*. 1951.

HAWKINS, Desmond, *Sedgemoor and Avalon*. 1954.

HODGKIN, R. H., *A History of the Anglo-Saxons*. 1935.

HOLLIS, Christopher, *Glastonbury and England*. 1927.

HOLMES, Edmond, *The Albigensian or Catharist Heresy*. 1925.

HORNE, Aethelbert, *Guide to Glastonbury Abbey*. N.d.

HOWGRAVE-GRAHAM, R. P., *Peter Lightfoot*. 1922.

HUGHES, Pennethorne, *Witchcraft*. 1952.

HULL, E., 'The Development of Hades in Celtic Literature.' *Folk-Lore*, 1907.

HUYSMAN, J. K., *Là-bas*. 1891.

JACKSON, Kenneth H., *A Celtic Miscellany*. 1951.

JAFFRAY, Robert, *King Arthur and the Holy Grail*. 1928.

JAMES, M. R., *The Apocryphal New Testament*. 1953.

JANELLE, Pierre, *The Catholic Reformation*. 1949.

JERROLD, Douglas, *An Introduction to the History of England*. 1949.

JOHN OF GLASTONBURY, *Chronicle*, ed. T. Hearne. 1726.

JONES, W. A., 'On the reputed discovery of King Arthur's remains at Glastonbury.' *Proc. Som. Arch.*, Vol. 9 (1859).

JONES, W. Lewis, *King Arthur in History and Legend*. 1911.

KELLY, Amy, *Eleanor of Aquitaine*. 1950.

KENDRICK, T. D., *British Antiquity*. 1950.

KNOWLES, David, *The Monastic Order in England*. 1950.

KRAPPE, Alexander H., *The Science of Folk-Lore*. 1930.

LELAND, John, *Itinerary*, ed. Lucy Toulmin Smith. 1964.

LEWIS, L. S., *Glastonbury the Mother of Saints*. 1927.
——*St Joseph of Arimathea at Glastonbury*. 1937.
LLOYD, John Edward, *A History of Wales*. 1911.
LOOMIS, R. S., *Celtic Myth and Arthurian Romance*. 1927.
——(ed.), *Arthurian Literature in the Middle Ages*. 1959.
LOT, Ferdinand, 'Glastonbury et Avalon.' *Romania* (Paris), Vol. 27.

MALORY, Sir Thomas, *Works*, ed. E. Vinaver. 1948.
MALTWOOD, K. E., *A Guide to Glastonbury's Temple of the Stars*. Published anonymously, 1935.
MANTLE, George E., *Glastonbury Abbey: recent discoveries*. 1913.
MAP, Walter, *De Nugis Curialium*, ed. E. S. Hartland. 1923.
MARSON, C. L., *Glastonbury or the English Jerusalem*. 1909.
MORGAN, R. W., *St Paul in Britain*. 1861.
MURRAY, Gilbert, *Five Stages of Greek Religion*. 1925.
MURRAY, Margaret, *The Divine King in England*. 1954.
——*The God of the Witches*. 1933.

NASH, D. W., *Taliesin*. 1858.
NENNIUS. See Giles and Wade-Evans.
NESTLE, E., 'Matthias equals Bartholomew.' *Expository Times*. 1898.
NITZE, William A., *Le Haut Livre du Graal, Perlesvaus*. 1932-7.
——'On the Chronology of the Grail Romances.' *Modern Philology*, Vol. 17 (1919-20).
NUTT, Alfred, *Studies on the Legend of the Holy Grail*. 1888.

PARIS, A. Paulin, *Les Romans de la Table Ronde*. 1868-77.
PARKER, James, 'Glastonbury: the Abbey Ruins.' *Proc. Som. Arch.*, Vol. 26 (1880).
PARRY, J. J. (ed. and trans.), *The Vita Merlini of Geoffrey of Monmouth*. 1925.
Perlesvaus. See Evans.
PROBERT, William, *The Ancient Laws of Cambria*. 1823.

Queste. See Comfort.

RADFORD, C. A. Ralegh, *The Excavations at Glastonbury Abbey*. Various dates.
RHYS, John, *Celtic Folklore*. 1901.
——*Studies in the Arthurian Legend*. 1891.
ROBINSON, Joseph Armitage, *Somerset Historical Essays*. 1921.
——*The Times of St Dunstan*. 1923.
——*Two Glastonbury Legends*. 1926.

RUNCIMAN, Stephen, *The Medieval Manichee*. 1947.

S. T., *The Legend of the Holy Thorn of Glastonbury*. 1880.
SHELDON, Gilbert, *The Transition from Roman Britain to Christian England, A.D. 368-664*. 1932.
SKENE, William F., *The Four Ancient Books of Wales*. 1868.
SLOVER, Clark H., 'Glastonbury Abbey and the Fusing of English Literary Culture.' *Speculum*, April 1935.
——'William of Malmesbury and the Irish.' *Speculum*, July 1927.
SPENCE, Lewis, *The Magic Arts in Celtic Britain*. 1945.
——*The Minor Traditions of British Mythology*. 1948.
——*British Fairy Origins*. 1946.
STENTON, F. M., *Anglo-Saxon England*. 1943.
STOKES, Whitley, *The Tripartite Life of St Patrick*. 1887.
STRADLING, W., 'The Turbaries between Glaston and the Sea.' *Proc. Som. Arch.*, Vol. 1 (1849-50).

THOMAS, N. W., *Crystal Gazing*. 1905.

THURSTON, Herbert, 'The English Legend of St Joseph of Arimathea.' *The Month*, July 1931.
TREHARNE, R. F., *The Glastonbury Legends*. 1967.
TUNISON, J. S., *The Graal Problem*. 1904.

USHER, James, *Glastonbury Traditions concerning Joseph of Arimathea*. Translated by H. Kendra Baker from *Britannicarum Ecclesiarum Antiquitates*, chapter 2. 1930.

Victoria History of Somerset. 1906-11.

WADE-EVANS, A. W., *Nennius's History of the Britons* (with *Annales Cambriae* etc.). 1938.
WAITE, A. E., *The Hidden Church of the Holy Graal*. 1909.
WARNER, Richard, *History of the Abbey of Glaston*. 1826.
WARRE, F., 'Glastonbury Abbey.' *Proc. Som. Arch.*, Vol. 1 (1849-50).
WATKIN, Aelred, 'Glastonbury 1538-9.' *Downside Review*, Autumn 1949.
——*The Great Chartulary of Glastonbury Abbey*. 1947-56.
——'Last Glimpses of Glastonbury.' *Downside Review*, Winter 1948-49.
WESTON, Jessie L., *From Ritual to Romance*. 1920.
——*The Legend of Sir Lancelot du Lac*. 1901.
WHITE, Jon Manchip, 'Tristan and Isolt.' *History Today*, April 1953.

WILLIAM OF MALMESBURY, *The Acts of the Kings of England.*
   Translated by J. Sharpe. 1854.
——*De Antiquitate Glastoniensis Ecclesiæ.* Translated by Frank
   Lomax as *The Antiquities of Glastonbury.* 1908.
WILLIAMS, Charles, *Arthurian Torso.* 1948.
——*Witchcraft.* 1941.
WILLIAMS, Hugh, *Gildas* (i.e. Works and Lives). 1901.
WILLIAMSON, Hugh Ross, *The Arrow and the Sword.* 1947.

INDEX

310

Fontana Modern Novels

The Tin Men   Michael Frayn   *35p*
'One knew, sourly, that this book was going to be funny; one did not see how it could be so continuously funny . . . The fun of *The Tin Men* is outrageous because it is so serious.'
Guardian

Ordinary Families   E. Arnot Robertson   *35p*
'The loves and jealousies, miseries and raptures of adolescence, woven with a very dexterous hand.' *Observer*. 'A splendid book . . . It is one of the few books to yield treasures on a second reading.' *Evening Standard*. 'A wise, witty and brilliant book.' *Sunday Times*

The Once and Future King   T. H. White   *75p*
'T. H. White is much more than a spinner of good plots; his prose gives as much pleasure as his matter. There are witty and learned asides on every subject under the sun. He can draw living people; he can describe a landscape; and he can enter into the inmost minds of birds and beasts. This ambitious work will long remain a memorial to an author who is at once civilised, learned, witty and humane.'
Times Literary Supplement

Fontana History

Fontana History includes the well-known History of Europe, edited by J. H. Plumb and the Fontana Economic History of Europe, edited by Carlo Cipolla. Other books available include:

Lectures on Modern History   Lord Acton

The Conservative Party from Peel to Churchill
Robert Blake

A Short History of the Second World War
Basil Collier

American Presidents and the Presidency
Marcus Cunliffe

The English Reformation   A. G. Dickens

The Norman Achievement   David C. Douglas

The Practice of History   G. R. Elton

Politics and the Nation, 1450-1660   D. M. Loades

Ireland Since the Famine   F. S. L. Lyons

Britain and the Second World War   Henry Pelling

Foundations of American Independence   J. R. Pole

A History of the Scottish People   T. C. Smout

The Ancien Regime and the French Revolution
Tocqueville

The King's Peace 1637-1641   C. V. Wedgwood

The King's War 1641-1647   C. V. Wedgwood

The British Monarchy

This series describes the evolution of the British monarchy from the Saxon and Norman kings to George V—their personalities and lives, their influence on their ages. Six volumes, each with twelve pages of illustrations.

The Saxon and Norman Kings Christopher Brooke
'An illuminating and imaginative reconstruction of what it really meant to be a king in Saxon and Norman times. The essential merits of this book are its lightness of touch and its firm grounding in scholarship.' *The Economist*

The Plantagenets John Harvey
'A portrait gallery of medieval English sovereigns, illustrated with many splendid photographs. Learned, informative and entertaining.' *Daily Mail*

The Tudors Christopher Morris
'Brilliant . . . Mr. Morris's flair for the apt point or quotation is remarkable.' *History*

The Stuarts J. P. Kenyon
'A sardonic, witty, yet scholarly book, written with splendid gusto.' *Sunday Times*

The First Four Georges J. H. Plumb
'The vitality and frankness of a literary Hogarth. He is never dull or merely derivative.' *The Economist*

Hanover to Windsor Roger Fulford
'As accurate as it is amusing, and conspicuously fair in its judgments.' *The Times Literary Supplement*

The Fontana History of Europe

Praised by academics, teachers and general readers alike, this series aims to provide an account, based on the latest research, that combines narrative and explanation. Each volume has been specially commissioned from a leading English, American or European scholar, and is complete in itself. The general editor of the series is J. H. Plumb, lately Professor of Modern History at Cambridge University, and Fellow of Christ's College, Cambridge.

Fontana Books

Fontana is best known as one of the leading paperback publishers of popular fiction and non-fiction. It also includes an outstanding, and expanding, section of books on history, natural history, religion and social sciences.

Most of the fiction authors need no introduction. They include Agatha Christie, Hammond Innes, Alistair MacLean, Catherine Gaskin, Victoria Holt and Lucy Walker. Desmond Bagley and Maureen Peters are among the relative newcomers.

The non-fiction list features a superb collection of animal books by such favourites as Gerald Durrell and Joy Adamson.

All Fontana books are available at your bookshop or newsagent; or can be ordered direct. Just fill in the form below and list the titles you want.

_ _

FONTANA BOOKS, Cash Sales Department, P.O. Box 4, Godalming, Surrey, GU7 1JY. Please send purchase price plus 7p postage per book by cheque, postal or money order. No currency.

NAME (Block letters)

ADDRESS

While every effort is made to keep prices low, it is sometimes necessary to increase prices at short notice. Fontana Books reserve the right to show new retail prices on covers which may differ from those previously advertised in the text or elsewhere.